MARRIAGE ENHANCEMENT GUIDE

A Do-It-Yourself Marriage Counseling Manual

James M. Hassenger

with

Thomas R. Hassenger

The Center for Marriage Enhancement
Sioux City, Iowa

Published by: Loess Hills Publishing Co.
Box 214
Sioux City, Iowa 51102

For: The Center for Marriage Enhancement
520 Buckwalter Drive
Sioux City, Iowa 51104

ALL RIGHTS RESERVED.

Copyright © 2001 by James M. Hassenger

Printed in the United States of America.

Publishers Cataloging-in-Publication
(Provided by Quality Books Inc.)

Hassenger, James M.

Marriage enhancement guide: a do-it-yourself marriage counseling manual / James M. Hassenger with Thomas R. Hassenger – 1st ed.

p. cm.
Includes bibliographical references and index.
ISBN: 0-9675865-4-2

1. Marriage. 2. Marriage counseling—Popular Works. 3. Marital conflict. I. Hassenger, Thomas R. II. Title.

HQ734.H37 2000 646.7'8
QBI00-370

ACKNOWLEDGMENTS

The authors gratefully acknowledge all of the psychologists/authors whose names appear in the bibliography, for without their knowledge, effort and expertise, the essence of this work would not have been possible.

The authors gratefully acknowledge permission to reprint the poem "The Rose," by Steve Kowit, appearing in *The Men Of Our times, An Anthology of Male Poetry in Contemporary America*, edited by Fred Moramarco and Al Zolynas, The University of Georgia Press, Athens, GA and London, 1992.

Special thanks also go out to Mr. Paul Lippman of the PRO-EDIT company for his very patient and knowledgeable help in getting through the early editing process.

CONTENTS

Acknowledgments iii
Introduction vii

THE CHALLENGE

ONE—Mirror, Mirror on the Wall 1
TWO—The Wages of Divorce 13
THREE—A Brief History 27
FOUR—The Components of Marriage 31
FIVE—Definitions and Explanations 35
SIX—The Quiz 47
SEVEN—The Game of Life, and of Marriage 53

SOME POSSIBLE SOLUTIONS AND INTERVENTIONS

Introduction 63
  M   Stands for Money 65
  A   Stands for Anger 83
  R   Stands for Relatives 93
  R   Stands for Reversals 103
  I   Stands for Integrity 111
  A   Stands for Abuse 117
  G   Stands for General Codependence 125
  E   Stands for Energy 143

  R   Stands for Respect 151
  E   Stands for Expectations 159
  L   Stands for Living 165
  A   Stands for Addiction 179
  T   Stands for Time 193
  I   Stands for Intrusions 203
  O   Stands for Outsiders 209
  N   Stands for Negotiation 221
  S   Stands for Sex 233
  H   Stands for Honesty 243
  I   Stands for Intimacy 253
  P   Stands for Priorities 259

Conclusion 267
Bibliography 271
Index 279

INTRODUCTION

This book can make your marriage relationship better.

In fact, if your marriage seems on shaky ground, or if you are having what appears to you to be more than your share of marital strife, please pay close attention to the substance of this book and, in the privacy of your own home, you can even save your own marriage.

Perhaps now you are using a wait-and-see strategy with your situation. But this is a dangerous game you are playing, and it involves the very existence of your marriage and family. Most articles and books published on the subject of divorce are designed to help people get over the tragic after-effects of divorce. Many of these works attempt to address the trauma suffered by the children. Other articles tell of the struggle by grandparents to be able to visit their grandchildren, and, as well, we all have experienced the pain of a divorce by relatives, friends and co-workers.

Certainly these above-mentioned works are valuable because everyone knows the divorce situation as it exists at this time in our country is completely out of whack. But, rather than tell people how to get over the trauma of divorce, doesn't it make better sense to show folks how to avoid falling into the divorce trap in the first place?

Look at the facts: Personal experience, media information and abundant statistical evidence tell us the divorce rate in the United States for first-time marriages has hovered in the 50% fatality rate for the past few decades. Even staid old Iowa, in the heart of the Bible belt, reported a 46% divorce rate in the last year for which statistics are available. Worse news: Many studies show that second and third-time marriages suffer even higher divorce rates than the 50% cited for first-time marriages.

Love and marriage are not necessarily better the second time around as the dreamy song lyric claims.

Sociologists and ethics specialists warn that something must be done to reduce the rate of divorce in our United States, or society as we know it may well come crashing down upon us in a thunderous collapse of social disorder, loss of values, financial ruin, disease and personal anguish. Even as we speak, there is evidence of such disintegration in some segments of our American population.

But never forget this: The real casualties of divorce are the children who are caught in the middle. They will suffer lasting traumatic impact, no matter what their ages are at the time of their parents' divorce. Grown siblings are as negatively affected as young children. In Chapter Two, The Wages of Divorce, studies are cited which clearly show that a divorce which marks the death of an offspring's nuclear (original) family almost always results in deep-seated, long-lasting and dire psychological and behavioral consequences to the child or children, for the rest of their lives.

Getting a divorce is almost always a disaster, and don't let anyone tell you otherwise. Present-day liberal thinking, as well as advice from the walking wounded—those who have already fallen into the divorce trap—loudly proclaim that getting a divorce is the way to go. They say that divorcing is the modern, liberated, free-thinking way of life in our present day slick, sophisticated society. Some of the many catch-phrases you'll hear from the divorce proponents include: "Just for me," "On my own," "By myself," and so on. Not to forget the old saying: "Misery loves company."

It is true, however, there are actually some specific instances where divorce is the only reasonable and prudent course for an embattled couple. The conditions for those instances will be addressed here directly. But absent the exceptions, divorce is an unrecoverable mistake, a terrible error in judgement, an act of ultimate selfishness, a waste of time, money, assets, effort and affection (love).

More bad news: A divorce frequently results in the deterioration of family relationships in unforeseen and unexpected ways. But wait! I am not saying that a couple should live in, and endure, an unhappy relationship. Rather, I say and believe that a troubled couple, apparently mired in a marriage gone sour, should sit down with this marriage counseling guide and endeavor to identify what their real problems are.

Resolving conflicts to a level of acceptability for both partners takes negotiation, adjustments in thinking, a desire to reconcile, the intelligence to compromise, and loving patience. Only then can you go forward together in your marriage relationship with renewed vigor and understanding. Keep your word. Be honest with yourself and your partner. Keep your promises. Work to be happy. Keep in mind that people have total responsibility for their own bodies, their own actions and their own lives. Nobody "makes" anyone do something he/she doesn't want to do unless the person gives in or gives up.

So many times a divorcing couple, when asked if their marriage could or should be saved, will respond negatively. No way, they say, foolishly thinking that if they can't solve their own problems themselves, they cannot be solved at all. Not so here, because with this manual, an embattled couple does have the tools and the information needed to resolve a serious conflict. Too many couples just grit their teeth, put their heads down and set out to endure a married life grimly filled with anger, dispute, disagreement and perhaps even hatred. How sad, and what a horrific waste! No longer. This guide will show you how to solve almost any problem in a marriage. Think positively, not negatively, about your marriage relationship.

Okay, here's how to use this manual: The best course of action is to initially read the first seven chapters, in order to get a grasp on the whole general concept. Following those chapters, you will find the "Solutions" section, which addresses each one of the twenty categories of concern in the Marriage Relationship concept. Please don't hesitate to move directly to your area of greatest concern. For example, if you have "relative" trouble at this time, read that section first.

It is true that if you skip ahead to the solutions section before you read the first seven chapters, you might actually solve your current dispute. However, unless you gain some measure of understanding of the reason for the disagreement, that problem may well return because you will not have learned to recognize and avoid the circumstance which generated the trouble in the first place.

Learning to understand your marriage relationship and how to cope with the inevitable differences of opinion and arguments as they surface is the entire crux of this discourse. Finally, as a footnote to this introduction, I want to mention another book I have written which might help you understand your mate and yourself as well.

The gist of this book, *Some of the Reasons We Behave the Way We Do*, has to do with the many influences that affect and shape our behaviors, such as:

- the "right brain/left brain" concept

- the importance and impact of a person's birth order

- the effect and importance of the three elements of everyone's personality, which is the behavioral component; temperament, which is a person's emotional make-up; and character, which deals with the ability of an individual to conform to what is thought of as 'normal' or typical social behavior

Also included are an extensive explanation of the impact of general codependence and an outline of the predictable physical and mental changes we all go through in the aging process.

Your familiarity with these important concepts will not only help you see yourself more clearly, but also will enable you recognize and comprehend some of what may seem to be weird behavioral patterns displayed by your mate. Through this increased knowledge and understanding, you can make your own marriage relationship more enjoyable, stable and rewarding. And so we begin.

THE CHALLENGE

ONE

Mirror, Mirror, on the Wall . . . Will We Divorce After All?

One of the more unfortunate of human tendencies: When people get into trouble, they think for some reason or the other they are the only ones in the world with problems, and worse, no one else ever before has been in the same mess. Of course, both trains of thought are completely off base.

Face facts: The divorce rate in the United States is running at about 50% for first-time marriages and even higher for re-marriages, so why would anyone foolishly think that all the other 50% of the non-divorced first-time marriages are happy? Every marriage endures hard times and disagreements and, as you will see, one of the main keys to maintaining a happy marriage, getting to that state called "marital satisfaction," is the ability of the partners to resolve their inevitable conflicts. Note the word "inevitable." Obviously, it's one thing to find out what the problems are with your new marriage relationship, and quite something else to be able to resolve the disagreements as they come up in a win/win manner.

St. Jerome once wrote: "He who lives without argument is a bachelor."

Since the late 1970s, a great deal of study has been done with regard to the issue of "marital satisfaction," which is defined as " . . . the extent to which needs, expectations and desires have been met in the marriage relationship." It is my aim in this chapter to point out and try to put into focus some of the huge body of psychological research that has been accomplished in recent years, by investigating this wondrously elusive thing known as "marital satisfaction." Hopefully, from all this data, you should be able to see how your own marriage is doing, and what problems or areas of concern confront you, and need attention.

Many "tests" or "inventories" exist which set out to measure the level of satisfaction in the marriage. The issue of tests is covered in the section under "addiction," but to state what is known about tests, the result of any test, quiz, scale, inventory, survey, poll or attempt to measure satisfaction, dissatisfaction or any other response, gives just a clue, only one clue to any possible conclusion that might come out of that study. Never is **one** test, or even a "battery" (aka a series) of tests, final conclusive proof-positive of any existing condition or behavior.

The possibility exists that a married couple could take one, or even several, "marital satisfaction" tests or inventories or scales, and find out from the results they are perfectly suited for each other. Yet deep-down, that same couple might sense that their own personal levels of marital satisfaction are very low.

Therefore, you will not find any tests, adjustment scales, quizzes or so-called marital satisfaction inventories included in this text. In the event readers wish to take such a test, or engage in a series of tests or measurement scales to try to see how their own level or levels of marital satisfaction stack up, a listing of many of the various scales or inventories can be found within the text of the journal articles mentioned in the bibliography under the author's name. Many people have learned the hard way, that no matter how hot and steamy a relationship is at first, the passion fades and there better be something else to take its place.

Attributions

Noted psychologists Frank Fincham and Thomas Bradbury completed a study in 1993 which examined what they call the "attributions" or causes of a lack of marital satisfaction. For example, they asked the question, "On what particular factor(s) do you attribute (blame) the lack of satisfaction in your marriage relationship?"

The result of their efforts came to the conclusion that two separate factors: one, depression, and two, a lack of personal self-esteem on the part of one of the marriage partners were the culprits in many of the instances of marital dissatisfaction.

Their study came to a circular conclusion which asked the question: "Does a negative attribution (condition) such as a state of depression cause marital dissatisfaction, or do low levels of marital satisfaction cause depression?" It's clearly the same old chicken and egg thing, and the answer to both questions is probably an emphatic yes! But the fact remains that the disposition and attitude of each of the marriage partners individually will have a direct influence on the level of marital satisfaction of both marriage partners.

Negative Thinking

The very next year, 1994, the same two psychologists, along with two others, Benjamin Karney and Keran Sullivan, expanded on the earlier study, and more closely examined the effect of what they call "negative affectivity" (that is negative attitude and thinking) on marital satisfaction. The term "affectivity" in this instance has to do with feelings, emotions and reactions. "Negative affectivity," therefore, asks how much impact a (sour-puss) badly dispositioned, fault-finding, negative-attitude person would have on a marriage relationship. Some folks are so negative; they go out of their way to find fault with everyone and everything. Nothing is right, nor will it ever be, and things, all things, are terrible.

In addition to reaffirming the conclusions from the earlier study mentioned above, the four psychologists came to another conclusion which states that what they call the "coldness" of a person can have a tremendously negative effect on a marriage relationship. When we get to "G," which stands for General Codependence, you will learn that the original family atmosphere has a tremendous influence on the later behavior of children born into that family. For example, if youngsters are taught as children that showing any emotion is bad form, then later on in life when they get to the adult stage where they need this wondrous thing called "intimacy," and can't find it, you have a sure-fire recipe for a heap of trouble.

The obvious answer, of course, is for the marriage partners to work harder to develop a higher level of happy or pleasant emotional awareness and response. Achieving the goal of diminishing deeply imbedded negative attitudes may require a lot of personal effort. Easier said than done. But possible.

Stress and Sex

Two psychologists, Patricia Morokoff and Ruth Gilliland, completed a study in 1993 which examined the relationship between stress, sexual functioning and marital satisfaction. No surprises here. They found that not only do happy couples enjoy more sexual activity than unhappy couples, but also there is a direct link in both directions between sexual and marital satisfaction. More happy sex equals a happier marriage, and a happy marital relationship equals more sexual activity.

For the same reasons which we explore in the section titled "Sex," the authors found that the attitude and the influence of the female partner in marriage has predominant importance. Psychologists Morokoff and Gilliland cite that if, for example, the female sees sexual activity as dirty or evil or dysfunctional, then she will tend to react sexually in a negative manner, and the above cited wheel will turn in reverse, which means that: Less sex equals an unhappier marriage, and an unhappy marriage will provide for less sexual activity.

The bias or attitude of the female marriage partner towards the issue of sex is therefore of critical importance, according to the authors. But, as mentioned in the preceding paragraph, the sexual inclination of the female marriage partner is the attitude she received as a little girl, and was taught in her original family. General codependence again. Happy news: A brief stint of psychotherapy can usually correct, to a large degree, an existing "hang-up" of coldness, or what is sometimes called "frigidity," if that condition or state exists in either or both marriage partners.

Type A vs. Type B

In 1993, psychologists Karyl MacEwen and Julian Barling, who are educators and researchers at Queens University in Kingston, Ontario, Canada, did a study which examined the effect of "Type A" behavior on marital satisfaction. A "Type A" person is someone who typically exhibits very active, nervous, perhaps overly competitive, angry, impatient and often irritable behavior. "Type B" people, on the other hand, are just the opposite, and are typically more easy-going, laid-back, relaxed, patient, non-competitive and fun.

What their study showed is that a Type A individual can be bad news in a marriage relationship. Worse news is the case where the Type A marriage partner is the female. What happens if a Type A female has the bad luck to be married to a Type B male, (the old "opposites attract" thing) is that she will go absolutely nuts trying to get her laid-back male partner to do whatever it is she wants done "**right now.**" Since he does not, nor ever has he ever done anything RIGHT NOW, she can even eventually come to the incorrect conclusion that the reason he doesn't do her bidding immediately is that he doesn't love her any more. So she divorces him.

On the other hand, the psychologists found, quite surprisingly, that two Type A people who are personally highly achievement and goal-oriented make fine marriage partners because they spend so much of their time working on their own projects. As a result of their personal concentration they really do not have time, or care all that much about what the spouse does or doesn't do. Two Type B people married to each other would get along famously. Like, who cares if anything is cleaned up? Relax! When's dinner? It's party time!

Self-disclosure

In 1996, psychologists Ruth Bograd and Bernard Spilka of the University of Denver completed an interesting paper concerning how the amount of self-disclosure figures into the question of marital satisfaction. They were particularly interested in the correlation between the amount of self-disclosure and marital satisfaction in re-marriages which occurred in mid-life (ages 30-45) and late life (ages 60-75).

This material is mentioned later in the "communication" section found under "general codependence." The importance of their study warrants a close look at this thing called self-disclosure, because their findings can be very applicable at any time and in every marriage relationship.

Bograd and Spilka found that self-disclosure—that is, the ability and inclination of one marriage partner to share innermost thoughts, feelings and lives with the other marriage partner—can and will change the direction and intensity of a marriage relationship in a circular manner. By "circular manner," they mean the more honest, sincere and timely self-disclosure discussion that occurs, the happier the marriage will be, and the happier the marriage is, the more self-disclosure the marriage partners feel they can safely make without being criticized or ridiculed.

The doctors Bograd and Spilka found, too, that, " . . . in long-lasting successful marriage relationships, inter-personal communications are likely to grow in depth, and sensitivity; self-disclosure will increase as the marriage-time lengthens. The more self-disclosure there is, the more progress will be made in the marriage, which will result in a better quality of the relationship."

However, they hasten to add, care must be taken to assure that the self-disclosure is constructive and well-intentioned. For example, and as we mentioned earlier, marriage partners who disclose events in their past life, which they know, or ought to know, will hurt the feelings or cause the other partner distress, are not examples of wholesome self-disclosure and must be avoided.

The Ups and Downs of Marital Satisfaction

A forty-year study, completed in 1993 by Caroline and George Vaillant of the Dartmouth Medical School, de-bunked earlier theories which held that newly-marrieds were happiest when their marriage was new, but that their contentment plummeted when the first child arrived, and began to recover when that last "chick" left the nest. The old theory held; at the point when the last kid left home marital satisfaction began to build again, and, in due course, (a few years) the couple regained the earlier levels of happiness, and even stood the chance of exceeding the satisfaction of their early-days together when the marriage was new. So much for hallowed old theories.

The marriages the Vaillants followed over this forty-year span did not seem to go to the depths upon the arrival of the first child, as earlier thought, although the Vaillants did note some modest decline in marital satisfaction in those early can-be-tough child-rearing days.

However, two interesting points did emerge from their study. One was that, as the marriage went on through the years, the divorce rate declined sharply as the marriage partners grew older. The other salient notion which appeared was, that for women, the most difficult time in their marriage was in the 16th to the 20th years! The authors did not find or cite any reason or reasons why females find this to be a particularly trying period, or why women are more negatively affected and reportedly unhappy in that five-year time span than their male counterpart. Logic and consideration of the female development schema could point to possible hormonal changes to explain this phenomenon.

Section Summary

There is so much information concerning the issue of "marital satisfaction" in the few preceding paragraphs, a brief summary of findings seems to be appropriate.

1) We looked into the reasons people thought their marriage relationship was in trouble—the "attributions" or causes.
2) The effect "negative affectivity" has on a marriage.
3) Sexual "coldness" or "frigidity" was examined, and found to have roots in the area of "general codependence."
4) The effect of stress on sexual activity.
5) Original family attitudes towards sex were overviewed.
6) "Type A + Type B" marriages, and what if two Type A's marry?
7) The value and dangers of "self-disclosure" in marital satisfaction.
8) Marital satisfaction as it matures through the years.

The value in all this material is in answer to the question which asks, are YOU headed for divorce? Obviously, if one or more of the above symptoms exist in your marriage, be smart and do something about what ails you before it's too late. But, here's the payoff; what if someone could actually tell you whether or not your marriage will last? Read on.

Will Your Marriage Last?

In 1994, John Gottman, PhD., a research psychologist who resides in the

Seattle area, wrote an extremely interesting book titled *Why Marriages Succeed or Fail*. His book, listed in the bibliography, is relatively short, easy to read and crammed full of good tips for making marriage work. It could be worth far more to you than the few dollars it costs to purchase. What happened is that Dr. Gottman completed a body of work; then in retrospect he realized that if he knew at the time he began the research what he knew when he was through with the project, he could have predicted which couples would ultimately divorce to within a 94% degree of accuracy. Just imagine that, 94% accuracy!

Without engaging in an extensive review of his book, a brief synopsis of some of the more important points is in order. To begin with, Dr. Gottman suggests that the key to marital happiness and satisfaction is simply how the daily battles and wars which occur in every marriage are handled by the partners. The ability to successfully resolve the inevitable conflicts in an amicable and fair manner resulted in a better and a longer-lasting marriage relationship.

A low level of marital conflict does not indicate or mean the marriage is a happy one. If you run into a couple who says, " . . . we never fight," you have encountered some folks who are seriously out of balance, in that one of the marriage partners has total control and power over the other one, and trouble surely looms on the horizon for that marriage relationship.

Doctor Gottman identified three different types of marriage relationships and he defines the categories with their corresponding behavior patterns in this manner: Validating, Volatile, Avoidant. Here are the symptoms of each of these three types. Won't it be interesting to see if you can identify your own type of marriage relationship?

Patterns of a 'Validating' Marriage Relationship

The marriage partners validate, (accept, acknowledge) the right of the other person to have and hold their own points of view.

The marriage partners carefully pick the issue, substance and the time and place of their battles in order to minimize peripheral damage. That is, to avoid upsetting and causing stress to the children, or other relatives or relationships.

They do not allow the discussion to descend into screaming destructive exchanges which could leave scars and residual anger.

The marriage partners listen to each other. They know how to mirror or repeat the statements that are directed to them so each person is absolutely sure they understand the full meaning of what was said. Most importantly, they know how to make win/win deals.

The marriage partners see each other as equals.

Patterns of a 'Volatile' Marriage Relationship

Lots and lots of arguments with many interruptions. Nothing is ever settled. The partners express more emotions than substance.

The marriage partners may use "teasing" to make a point, but often end up hurting the other person's feelings.

Patterns of an 'Avoidant' Marriage Relationship

These people just don't argue very much. They think their marriage bond is strong, so they simply overlook minor disagreements.

Lead pleasant lives. Don't "test" their marriage relationship. Avoidant couples tend to live in a "his marriage," "her marriage," "their marriage" state, and not in "our marriage."

As a result of the separation within the marriage they may end up feeling all alone and feel their marriage partner doesn't know, care about or understand them. Of course this latter symptom is a serious disadvantage.

It should be an easy and quick thing for you to scan the list of symptoms and see just which type of relationship you have. But, of course, the "validating" marriage would be the most desirable one of the three types, and if you aren't there at this time, pitch in and work for it.

One of Dr. Gottman's excellent suggestions for a happier marriage is for each negative incident that happens, or comment made, there should be at least five positive incidents or comments to offset the one negative event. This conclusion emanates from his finding that what people want most of all in their lives and marriages is love and respect.

He found that destructive comments or interactions make people feel they are being criticized, and/or that they are being held in contempt. This set of conclusions brings him to what he calls the **"Four Horsemen of divorce,"** a play on title from the last book of the New Testament, "The Four Horsemen of the Apocalypse," which is interpreted as a prophetic revelation of the end of the world. In this case, Gottman's "Four Horsemen" would be predicting divorce. A disaster is a disaster, any way you look at it.

Here are the "Four Horsemen" of divorce:

Criticism by one marriage partner of the other, which eventually makes the critical partner feel **Contempt** because the criticism isn't working, which causes the one being criticized to become **Defensive**, and since he is losing all the battles, he **Withdraws**, and ultimately the whole mess ends up in court.

Here it is again:

> Criticism Leads to Contempt to Defensiveness to Withdrawal and ultimately to Divorce.

Obviously the "stonewalling" or withdrawal of one of the marriage partners from the marriage relationship because they feel they are being overly criticized or held in contempt by the marriage partner will almost always bring about a divorce. As we all know, when males feel they are being criticized, they are notorious stonewallers. When a lady is criticized she will usually either get mad, cry or retreat into silence. Have you ever heard a male say "whatever" as the sign-off to an argument or disagreement? The "whatever" equals withdrawal—the "Fourth Horseman." Adios.

The answer is obvious, isn't it? Don't start the first of the "Four Horsemen," known as "criticism," down the rocky path to a divorce. Gottman also differentiates between a complaint which is a statement that begins with "I . . . feel, hope etc.," and critical statements which begin with "You.always . . . ," or, "You never . . . " etc. We will go through this routine several times later on.

Here is how marriages start to get into trouble: First come the complaints; then, when no satisfactory results show up, next begins criticism, and trouble. Again: Don't criticize your spouse! Complain fairly if you feel you must, but don't fall into the habit of being constantly critical. Face the facts: They may not be perfect and do your every bidding, but neither are you perfect.

But, here is the astounding discovery that John Gottman made which would have allowed him to retrospectively achieve his 94% accuracy in predicting the divorce of a married couple: "Nothing foretells the future of a marriage relationship as accurately as how the couple retells their past marital history."

What happened is that, in the course of the study, part of the inquiry or "work up" involved having the married couple tell him the story of the early days of their marriage. Doctor Gottman found that in retrospect, the married couple who retells the history of their marriage relationship in a negative manner, recalling only the slights and disappointments, was doomed to divorce. The difference Dr. Gottman ascertained is that the reality—please get that: THE REALITY—of those first days of the marriage is not as important as the PERCEPTION of what actually happened, as told at that later time. Maybe in reality their situation wasn't all that bad, but in the telling of their story, it sounded like a trainwreck.

What Gottman discovered is perhaps in reality the couple did not have too difficult a time, but, as they later looked back on the early days of their marriage with a negative view, Dr. Gottman found he could have predicted they would divorce, and he would have been accurate to that 94% level. That concept is so important it warrants restatement:

"Negative recasting, or retelling, and/or recollections of the early days of a marriage relationship by the partners is an accurate warning of big problems ahead!"

So, if someone asked you to tell the story of your early days of marriage, how would you fare?

Doctor Gottman then sets out five different styles of retelling which may predict a negative future of the marriage relationship. These include if the couples look back:

- with feelings that their early marriage days were chaotic and out of control;

- indicating disappointment in their marriage relationship, as opposed to feeling that while the early days were indeed difficult, as a couple they had overcome their problems and their marriage at the present time is a success;

- not talking in terms of "we-ness," using too many "I" . . . "I this" . . . and "I that . . . "

- talking as if the marriage partners were leading separate lives;

- with a lack of expansiveness—that is, not talking in terms which indicate that the two marriage partners really like each other and take pride in each other's accomplishments and persona.

With relation to the possibility of divorce, Dr. Gottman cites the four stages that a marriage relationship typically goes through on the way to divorce:

Stage 1. A negative perception of the marriage relationship by the partners—if one of the marriage partners sees nothing but trouble ahead in their marriage, then that is indeed what they will have . . . trouble.

Stage 2. The marriage partners get so they can't talk problems over without getting into a fight, and a feeling of hopelessness overcomes one or both partners. "What's the use?"

Stage 3. The marriage partners start leading parallel lives. They may live together under the same roof, but they are not together. Separate hobbies. Separate vacations. Separate bank accounts. Separate bedrooms. Separate lives. And worst of all, separate attorneys.

Stage 4. Loneliness sets in. The marriage partners begin to feel there is no difference between their present married state and being single. Which is what they will likely be, soon.

Doctor John Gottman's book is crammed with good advice and sound reasoning, and anyone who is married should read his book.

We leave Dr. Gottman with mention of one of his best and final items: the subject, the issue of housework! According to Dr. Gottman, in his research he found that women view the issue of housework as a major concern in their lives, and in a direct ratio: The more help she receives with the housework, the more sexually responsive she will be. Men, how big a brick wall do you need to fall on you?

Here is what Gottman found is the problem, with regard to how women look at the issue of housework: Gals feel that if their man won't help with the housekeeping, he is demeaning and putting her down. The trouble with the subject of housework (as with money management) is that far too often, neither before nor in the early days of the marriage, is there ever any meaningful discussion between the partners about sharing the household chores. Gottman found out in his study that men admitted that they spent about an average of four minutes a day on housework. Four minutes?

Furthermore, using the word "help" is not fair either. Women do not like the word "help" when it comes to talking about housework because when a man says he "helps out" around the house, she feels that statement denotes that she has somehow unfairly inherited total responsibility for taking care of the home. It is her thought that the effort involved in keeping the residence clean and comfortable should be shared by both marriage partners. After all, both of them live there, so they should share and share alike the effort of maintaining the premises.

These feelings are especially deep and acute when both wife and husband work outside the home. What she hates, really hates with a passion, is to work all day at a job to help keep the family finances on an even keel, then have to come home and "go to work" again. Alone!

Predicting Divorce

Psychologists Paul Giblin and Judy Chan authored an article in the April 1995 issue of the *Family Journal* which overviewed other studies which set out to predict those couples who would be likely candidates for divorce from three points of view: family structure, background characteristics, and religious factors.

From the results found in these many studies you can quite easily apply the discovered symptoms of divorce, and see if your own marriage relationship could be in some jeopardy by simply comparing the after-the-fact "predictors" to your own situation, across these three dimensions:

Family Structure

Giblin and Chan reported on a 1962 study done by Walter Toman that the original, nuclear family structure of divorcing couples seemed to be a consistent factor. From his survey work Toman found the following similarities in divorcing couples:

- If the marriage partners were in the same sibling position, he found more incidence of divorce. For example, if an oldest child in a family married someone who was the oldest child in their family, or a youngest married a youngest, trouble could ensue.

- If one of the marriage partners came from an all-same-sex original family, for example all girls, or all boys, such a coincidence was found to be a symptom of eventual marital difficulty. Obviously, the advantage of growing up with someone of the opposite sex in the family gave insight about the differences between the sexes.

Along the same line, marrying an "only-child" can also be a rather dangerous situation, for not only has that only-child not had any experience with brothers and sisters, but worse, so often only-children are denied their childhood by the doting parents, who consider and treat the child as a little adult.

- The early loss of a parent, either through death or divorce. Especially divorce. Parental divorce was a common thread of occurrence in the failed marriages. This unfortunate circumstance is mentioned in chapter two, The Wages of Divorce.

Background Characteristics

Giblin and Chan cited a "highly detailed longitudinal" (five-year) 1993 study of 286 couples by L. Kurdek, which examined the backgrounds of the marriage partners to see what commonly negative **premarital** situations and conditions appeared over and over in the lives of these now-divorced people.

At the end of five years, Kurdek reported that 222 of the 286 couples in the study were still married. Here are some of the common areas of difficulty which he found repeated themselves in the four major categories or sources of conflict and disagreement which occurred to the 64 couples who divorced.

To quote the article: " . . . it was found that couples were more likely to end up in divorce court if, at the beginning of the marriage, some of the following conditions or situations existed:

- The husband had low levels of education and personal income.
- The husband was a stepfather to his new wife's children).
- The wife had low levels of education and personal income.
- The couple had a history of earlier divorces.
- The couple did not pool their finances.
- The couple had known each other only a few months before marriage.
- The husband or the wife, or both, held dysfunctional (incorrect) beliefs about how a marriage relationship should be. In other words, they had incorrect prior 'expectations' of marriage.
- The wife was low on conscientiousness.
- The wife was dissatisfied with her new husband's income level and she felt all alone.
- The husband had many external (selfish) reasons for getting married in the first place.
- The wife had few (core, real) reasons for getting married.
- The couple had large discrepancies on autonomy, or just exactly who was 'in charge.'
- One or both of the parties got married for the wrong reasons. For example, sometimes a young person will get married just to escape a dysfunctional family situation.

Religious Factors

A series of studies revealed some of the religious factors which might be predictive of marital dissatisfaction or divorce. A 1990 study done by Heaton and Pratt used data from a 1988 national survey of 13,000 Protestant American households to examine the relationship between marital satisfaction and three areas of religious activity, namely:

- which denomination did the couples belong to;
- stated frequency of attendance at church;
- the level of common belief by the marriage partners that the Bible provides solutions for contemporary problems.

The results of this massive study found:

1) The most critical factor is that both marriage partners belong to the same denomination.
2) The frequency of attendance at church of the marriage partners was found to contribute somewhat to the success of their marriage.
3) Similar beliefs about the Bible did not have a significant association with either marital satisfaction, or the stability of the relationship.

An earlier study done in 1985 by the same Paul Giblen and another psychologist named Kilgariff compared a random sample of 200 divorce cases from the records of a Roman Catholic marriage tribunal.

It was found, as in the study of Protestants mentioned above, divergent or differing religious practices **AFTER** marriage were a more accurate prediction of an impending divorce than the fact that before they got married the partners may have come from differing religious groups or affiliations.

Said another way, it was found that the marriage of persons from differing denominations wasn't as important as the fact that **AFTER** they got married both partners were members of, and attended the same church together.

From a self-help point of view, the value of all the above research would seem to apply mainly to two areas of concern:

First, anyone who is planning marriage needs to pay close attention to the factors which seem to contribute to divorce, and take care of them before the ceremony occurs. Work out what you are going to do about each category of concern, and then stick to your decisions.

Secondly, if you read the above summary of research and identify some of those troublespots in your own marriage relationship, watch out! Those predictors of divorce are definitely in the no-fooling class, and you would be well served to do something about any apparent conflict(s) before things get out of hand, and you end up in divorce court. Some conditions or situations you can do something about, while other situations or conditions marriage partners can only admit, learn to accept and then live with them.

But, as I said earlier, every marriage relationship has its ups and downs, its conflicts, fights, angry difficulties and disappointments, as well as all the good times. The trick is to not let the difficulties spoil the relationship, and to keep working on solutions to insure a long and happy (happier) marriage. Keep focused on the good side of your marriage and don't dwell only on the bad stuff. Keep faith in yourself and in each other, and always have hope for the better days which lie ahead.

And keep this manual handy for future reference.

Now that you know some of the contributing factors which either lead or predict an impending divorce and about which you can do something, let's take a look at the fall-out of divorce.

Modern liberal thought notwithstanding, a divorce deeply affects not only the children at any age, but other family members, friends and co-workers as well.

We call this next chapter the "wages" of divorce.

TWO

The Wages of Divorce

The Marriage Relationship concept, as presented, is intended to be a positive and up-beat guide designed to provide an understanding of the basic elements of a marriage relationship. In the "Solutions" section, I set out to show and explain some of the many possible ways to solve marital problems. But first, it's time to counter the modern liberal deluge of information about how wonderful and exciting it is to be a single-parent, or live the single life, by revealing some of the results of the huge number of studies which have explored the traumatic end-results of divorce.

Let us begin with a blanket statement: Divorce is almost always a disaster. Of course the size and scope of the calamity depends upon the specific set of circumstances which surround the divorce. But one thing you can count on for sure is that, if you divorce, anger, grief, remorse, regrets, dissension and all the other bad feelings that we humans can feel, will be in your life. Further, if you are the person pursuing the legal action, once you get "your decree," your own life will forever be profoundly impacted in so many different ways. Needless to say, "your divorce" process will deeply affect the person from whom you are being divorced for the rest of his/her life as well.

In addition, serious and often long-lasting adverse impact will be delivered to all the other members of both sides of your families, including your parents, grand-parents, in-laws, and, as well, others, including friends and relatives who share a portion or a place in your life. Not infrequently is a person's job or career also adversely affected. But worst of all, in addition to the horrendous impact of divorce on the two marriage partners and their parents, the real and tragic casualties of divorce are the offspring of the marriage.

Add to that casualty list the possible effect on one's credit standing, a dramatic change in social status for both parties, and the frequent descent of the divorced female partner into poverty. Friends who were once close can turn out to be not very friendly, and relatives who once were close can end up being decidedly distant.

One of the modern-day politically-correct directions taken in the various media sources is an attempt to lessen and even scoff at the mental and physical trauma caused to the offspring of divorce, no matter what their age might be at the time of their parents' divorce. "They'll get over it," they say. Many articles, books and TV programs devote time and space to the issue of healing the wounds of the offspring of divorce. Better the point ought to be: Don't get a divorce! All you really have to do is pitch in, resolve whatever issues might be troublesome or difficult in your marriage relationship and go forward in time, together.

A complete listing of all the troubles that a divorce can cause is too long to record within this text. But, as you will see on the following pages, just a sampling of the consequences of a divorce ought to be enough evidence to dissuade any thinking person from strolling down divorce lane unless one of the three valid reasons for a divorce does in fact exist.

If divorce is such a bad deal, you might ask, then where did all this madness come from? Why are people destroying their own families at the staggering 50+% rate cited in numerous studies and verified with ample statistics?

Several obvious reasons exist for the present-day divorce epidemic now in full swing in the United States. A 50% rate of occurrence of any illness or behavioral malfunction would be a full-blown epidemic in anybody's league, wouldn't it?

For one thing, with all our attempts to educate young people, we as a society simply do not teach or respect the basic principles of marriage. Nor, for that matter, is it even taught that marriage and family, as a way of life, is the most desirable living state to which an individual can aspire. Many schools teach sex education courses, but do not teach marriage education courses.

Indeed, in these wildly liberal times, the concept of the need for stability in marriage and the preservation of the family as the basic way of human life are not popular subjects in major spheres of influence in our country. Just take a quick look at these intrusions.

Media Influence

Can there be any question but that all the trash programming blithely pumped out on a daily basis, and which is too often aimed directly at millions of impressionable viewing children, has some effect on public value standards? Some groups attack the lyrics heard on the rock music stations listened to by the teenagers. Others complain of the lack of morality contained in television programming and movies. Violence, promiscuity and alternative lifestyles, once thought of as repugnant or at least dishonest, are held up and accepted as "politically correct" modern-day standards of behavior.

The age-old established principles of morality and family values are seen as old-fashioned and out of vogue, therefore to be ridiculed and held in contempt. Today's "thought police" are quick to tell us what words we can say, and what we must think.

Children are being taught by these "intrusions" that the family, the cornerstone of human existence, is something to make fun of, and is an ancient and out-moded institution. Children are being taught that personal integrity and adherence to any set of moral codes or conduct is of no value in these "modern" times.

Legal influence

Another reason for the divorce explosion in the USA since WW II is the passage of "no-fault" divorce laws in most states that make divorcing far too easy, and, in fact, pretty much of a rubber-stamp process. You can thank the greedy legal system, including the courts and especially the shyster lawyers who specialize in destroying families, for this sad state of affairs.

One can see now and again via a TV exposé and in some newspaper and magazine articles, the antics of greedy divorce lawyers who skin their clients alive, financially. They strip their clients of all their money and resources in a callous fashion to the extent that the one being stripped, usually the woman, has to seek recourse in the federal bankruptcy courts to solve her overwhelming financial problems.

Our local newspaper has carried articles with regard to addresses given to other legal groups by our resident legal "divorce expert" advising the other "Family Law" attorneys to prepare themselves to guide their divorce clients through bankruptcy, which of course increases their own "fee-ability."

Never mind that the reason they are bankrupt is that the attorney very frequently charged exorbitantly high legal fees for the divorce proceeding.

In all fairness, mention must be made that some states are in the process of realizing that our American society is falling apart, and are moving to repeal or at least modify the "no-fault" divorce laws so that divorcing will not be the easy process it now is. But of course the lawyers oppose this movement.

General Codependence

Another consideration for rampant present-day divorce could be the lack of "stick-to-it-ivity" now in existence in our society, which is fostered to a good extent by the example of divorcing parents. Like parents, like children, is the principle of general codependence. In these times, when things get just a little rough in a marriage relationship, as they are bound to, too frequently the very first course of action considered is a divorce. Divorce is seen as the ultimate solution to all life's problems. People just don't seem to persist, and hang in there any more, or work things out in their marriages like they once did.

Can anyone today imagine that folks in earlier times did not have conflict and struggle in their marriages? Of course they did. But when they got married they promised each other they would stay together in sickness and health, through good times and bad, and all the other myriad of marital states that come up in the course of every marriage. In days of yore, people held a firm commitment to their marriage vows. In days of now, there is little if any level of commitment, even though the persons getting married do in fact promise such an unending commitment to each other on the day they exchange marriage vows.

Peer Pressure

There is the familiar old saying: "Misery loves company." As a rule, when a marriage goes sour, one or both of the marriage partners will start talking and complaining to other people about the sad state of their marriage relationship.

This revelation seems to bring forth others who have been divorced and feel that they must somehow reinforce the resolve of the one whose marriage is in trouble by telling how wonderful it is to be single. Or maybe re-married. Of course, as "apostles," "pimps" and "hustlers" of divorce, they do not tell of the pain and anguish which their own divorce has caused, but talk only of their wonderful new freedom . . . etc. etc. Blah, blah, blah.

Some people do care about the children, and about the poor fools who are plunging into the quicksand of divorce, day after day, month after month. These good people, who are listed in the bibliography, develop studies and do surveys of the casualties of divorce and make this information available to anyone who cares to give a thought about the consequences of an unwise divorce. So we begin with some of the hard evidence of the indigestible fruits of divorce.

SEMINAR:
Counseling the Divorced and the Divorcing: The Effect of Divorce, as Seen by School Counselors

Let's take a look at what some folks have found out about the consequences of divorce, either by having been through the mill themselves, or as observers of divorce by functioning in their capacity as marriage and school counselors.

A recent seminar on "Counseling the Divorced and the Divorcing" was designed to do just that; to help those of us in the counseling profession learn about and understand the trauma experienced not only by those caught up as participants in the divorce trap, but also by their offspring and others as well.

The main thrust of the seminar was not to teach us how to function as marriage counselors and to learn how to repair damaged marriages, but as counselors, how we might better help divorced people try to cope with, and then hopefully overcome, the damage of their divorce disaster.

Keep in mind that a divorce involves two people: the one who wants and thereby sues for the divorce and who is known as the plaintiff, and the one who is left standing on the curb holding the bag, so to speak, aka, the defendant. Each principal, the defendant and the plaintiff, have, to an extent, a differing set of agonies to contend with.

The seminar, which was attended by 32 counselors, was given by the prominent Nebraska psychologist, Dr. Wes Wingett. The opening topic or exercise was to go around the room, person by person, and each attendee was to name a serious detrimental effect they had witnessed happening to either or both of the two people divorcing. As the counselors in turn added the various negative symptoms they had witnessed, Dr. Wingett wrote furiously in small print on the huge blackboard in the classroom, until he finally ran out of room and there was no more space to write even one more observed adverse symptom or result of divorce.

Here is a partial list of the bad things that happen to the **principals** (the adults) in a divorce, in the observed experience of the counselors who were present:

- restricted social activity
- confusion and uncertainty
- anger; pursuit to try to get revenge.
- total family concerns, alienation of in-laws and relatives
- grief, both short term and long term.
- Rejection of others because of being divorced
- Profound feelings of guilt by both parties
- Profound changes in everyday lifestyle
- Labels as a result of: e.g. "s/he's an/a _____. (e.g. being unfairly indicted as an alcoholic, abusive etc.)
- Emotional separation from mate, even though the one seeking the divorce thought they "had" to get a divorce
- Legal expenses. Lots and lots and lots of legal expenses.
- Pain of property division procedures.
- Agony of custody fights over children.
- Great stress and the real possibility of serious illness resulting from the trauma of the divorcing experience.
- Possible violence.
- Loss of identity, resulting in anonymity and isolation.
- Financial difficulties.
- Loneliness.
- Depression.
- Time problems, too much or too little.
- Loss of self-esteem.
- Problems with telling the whole truth, outright lying, evading issues, and engaging in self-enhancing exaggerations.
- Manipulation of children, parents, relatives, etc., in an attempt to "gain the upper hand" or emerge as the "good guy," or "good gal."
- Failure as individuals to accept responsibility for own actions.
- Public disapproval.
- Loss of control over own life.
- What to do with holidays, weekends, vacations?
- Isolation, and finally,
- causing confusion in children, which will be explained momentarily in a separate disclosure.

As mentioned, the above list is a condensation of the adverse or down-side results of a divorce. It is not the complete schedule of all the complaints, because while some of the many cited conditions or results seemed at the moment to be separate concerns, later examination indicated that some overlapping occurred with other already-stated symptoms. But the point remains; the entire blackboard was totally full of observed negative results of divorce, as they happened to the adults in the legal action.

The Effects of Divorce on Younger Children

The next thing Dr. Wingett did was to go around the room in the same manner and ask each counselor to list a symptom of a behavioral problem they had observed in the children of divorce.

Again, this is not the entire list, because, as above, some of the items, upon later scrutiny, had a measure of overlap or were more or less repeat circumstances with some small degree of variation.

Here is the composite list of negative and detrimental mental and behavioral symptoms observed to be suffered by the young children of divorce listed in alphabetical order:

aggressiveness
alcohol use/abuse
anger
bed wetting
behavioral problems
blame
cheating
crying
confusion
delinquency
denial
depression
destructiveness
discourteousness
disobedience
divided loyalties
drug use/abuse
eating problems
embarrassment
fear of abandonment
fear of intimacy
feeling rejected
fighting
guilt
hostility to others
hypermaturity (acts too old)
hypomaturity (acts too young)
immaturity
insecurity
irresponsibility
learning difficulties
low self-esteem
moodiness
nightmares
poor school grades
reconciliation fantasies
running away from home
regression (behavioral)
resentment
school truancy
self-abusiveness

self-centeredness
sexual identification problems
sexual misconduct
shame
sleep disorders
stealing
suicidal thoughts or attempts
temper tantrums
return to thumb sucking
withdrawal and worry

If that list isn't enough to give you pause about a divorce, then you must be like the famous "Tin Man" in the *Wizard of Oz;* heartless. How in the world could anyone capable of even a shred of compassion and possessed of some degree of right thinking deliberately expose their own children to even the most remote chance of having to endure such severe emotional and behavioral pressure and all those possibly severe reactions, just because someone thinks they have to get a divorce?

Such a conclusion brings us to the point wherein people will ask: "Are you saying that a couple should stay together for the sake of the children?"

And the answer: Yes, yes, and yes! A thousand times yes!

I am not saying that you must both be miserable and unhappy or that you have to offer up your life for your offspring. I am saying: Get your act together; and if it's broke, fix it! Fix what is the matter with your marriage relationship and stay together. Look forward to better times. Take control of your marriage and your lives, and look out for your children! Believe in preventive maintenance in your marriage!

Popular propaganda heard these days is that the children will "get over" the divorce, and that the death of their original family will not affect them in later years. Indeed, such is not the case, as you will see in the next section.

The Effect of Parental Divorce on Older Siblings

Until recently, most of the discussion about the effects of divorce has centered upon the young children who visibly suffer the trauma of divorce, and who are indeed the most pathetic victims of divorce.

However, in recent years, additional substantial investigative effort and extensive research has been expended by psychologists to examine the effect of a parental divorce on grown children. These studies show that adult children also endure great amounts of stress, confusion, uncertainty, loss of identity and grief when their parents divorce later in life.

Here is the problem: Adult children can't help but mourn for the now-broken family of their childhood, especially when both the parents are still alive. Not only do these adult children have all their childhood memories, which are now jumbled in the melee, but also when the parents divorce late in life these adult children are faced with a whole new set of feelings they never had before, or even knew existed.

To cite but one source for this work on the effect of parental divorce on adult children, two leading psychologists, Fintushel and Williard completed a study and have written a book about the adverse phenomenon and conditions in which adult children can and do find themselves when their parents divorce later in life. The exact title of the book is listed in the bibliography. While the two psychologists readily concede that up to this time not nearly enough research has been accomplished with regard to the fallout and effect of divorcing parents on older siblings, nonetheless, their work is notable, apparently valid, and certainly deserves the attention it is getting.

The statistical investigative process for their study involved the interviewing by the psychologists of 100 adult individuals whose parents had divorced after the children were grown, out of their teens and living their own lives as adults.

The conclusion of the authors is that the divorce of parents at any age is a terribly traumatic event in the lives of the offspring, no matter whether the descendants be young children, teens or even adults, some with families and children of their own, and others still single.

As a result of their survey work, here is an abbreviated list of detrimental effects that the authors found in these adult children of later-year parental divorce:

- Personal re-evaluation of values: Adult children find themselves with altered attitudes toward love and marriage, including holding a blanket suspicion of all the members of the opposite sex.

- Loss of faith in marriage: Even if their own marriage is sound at the time of the parental divorce, these adult children of divorced parents report a tendency to continually "test" their own mates, trying to see if their spouse exhibits some or any of the perceived negative traits or characteristics of the now-divorced parents.

- Great difficulty and pain in maintaining

what were once "normal" family relationships. After all, a lot of things happen in the course of a family's history, including, to name a few typical events, deaths, weddings, funerals, birthdays. And what about holidays? How do they talk to their children about their own divorced parents? Who talks to whom and when? Which of the divorced parents goes to what event? If the divorced parents are angry, as is so frequently the case, how do the adult children keep the divorced parents apart and yet try to maintain some sort of family continuity?

- Their findings report that the strain and grief of the parents late-life divorce can be so great, it can come to pass that these adult children will never talk to their own parent(s) again!

- Choosing sides: The parents' divorce can result in brothers and sisters having no contact with each other ever again.

That is a sampling of some of the conditions that can come to pass to young and older children after a family has been destroyed by a divorce.

But what about the situations and conditions which exist when one of the parents leaves their marriage to be with another person after the divorce? Watch.

Re-marriage Concerns

What about the selfish people who bring about a divorce, the plaintiffs, who think they must get a divorce because they "just can't stand it any more"; who think they have someone new to stroll off into the sunset with and, presto, make a bright new life for themselves, their children and their fresh love.

What are the divorcing parents, the perpetrators and the victims actually getting into? What are their chances of rebuilding their life with another partner in a new marriage, called a "re-marriage" situation?

A recent issue of *The Journal of Counseling & Development,* the official publication of the *American Counseling Association,* contains an article by Dr. William M. Walsh entitled "Twenty Major Issues in Re-marriage Families." "Re-marriage," in case you are unfamiliar with the term, is the marrying-again of divorced people into new family units. Many of those going into another marriage have their own children to take care of. In his study, Dr. Walsh sets out to summarize the results of his extensive survey, which points out the troublesome issues confronting those who divorce and then re-marry.

Doctor Walsh categorizes the problem areas into separate sets of concerns facing the couple to be remarried, and they are: initial issues, developing issues, feelings about self and others, and finally what he calls "adult issues." Time and space prohibit an extensive explanation of Dr. Walsh's work, but here is a brief summary of some real trouble spots he found in the world of re-marriage. The issues re-marriage couples encounter are presented here numerically, not in any order of importance;

Issue #1. By what name do you call the new parent? Dad #2? Mom #4? My "mother-by-marriage?" "Bruce" or "Phyllis," as the case may be. My mother's husband, or my father's wife? Or what?

Issue #2. How can a child manage to develop a level of affection for the new parent? What does the child or the children do about their normal inbred loyalty to the now-absent natural parent? Doctor Walsh says the issue of parental loyalty is a major stressor for children in newly formed re-marriages.

Issue #3. The loss of the natural parent through a divorce usually triggers a grief reaction in a child, just as if a death or a desertion had occurred. New family rituals, rites, customs and traditions, as well as managing the blending of newly acquired relatives must be accomplished. All while both sets of children in the newly blended family are frequently still mourning the loss of their natural parent.

Issue #4. Is instant love for the new family members possible, or ever in the cards? As one of the new parents, are you going to feel immediate affection for any new step-children? Will the new step-children suddenly be able to feel love and respect for you? Will "your kids" and "his kids" become real brothers and sisters overnight? Hardly! Studies show that, just because the two re-married adults think they are in love with each other and sincerely try to form a new blended family unit, there is little or no evidence that they will ever come to love, or, for that matter even like their new partner's children, or the new partner's relatives either.

Failure of the new blended-family parents to achieve new close relationships on almost an instant basis probably accounts to a great degree for the fact the second-time-around divorce rate is pegged at 10% higher than first-marriages, up to a staggering 60% level.

Issue #5. Continued fantasies and remembrances about the old family structure by the children of the newly formed, "blended" family. Some children, Dr. Walsh reports, seem to hold on very strongly to the parent that isn't there any more, and will even consciously, or subconsciously, try to cause trouble between their own parent and the new spouse, all the while hoping to spark a possible reconciliation between their birth-parents.

Issue #6. What about disciplining by the new parent? Doctor Walsh discovered that the issue of the disciplining of step-children is the top # 1 problem in the re-marriage jungle. It's a well known fact that discipline works only when the one being disciplined cares about the one doing the disciplining. "Who is this awful new person who is abusing me?" the child thinks. On top of that, perhaps because of what is seen as stern correcting efforts, the child may not ever see the newcomer-parent as a member of their family. Rather, a step-child may see the new parent as an ogre, an abuser, an enemy, and an all-around bad person.

Issue #7. Confusion in family roles. Women have more trouble with this issue than men do, according to Dr. Walsh, because women frequently don't feel that they have the authority to discipline "his kids." In addition, they are afraid of winding up becoming an "outsider," ultimately playing the role of a scapegoat, and eventually ending up back in divorce court.

Issue #8. Sibling conflicts. "Your kids are fighting with my kids, and what are you going to do about that?" can easily be asked. Especially when the anger of a child towards a new step-sister or brother is only a submerged and deep sign of the pain they feel over the parental divorce mess. Being children, they can quite mistakenly and unfairly place the blame for the divorce and for their own pain and sense of loss on the step-brother or sister who is perceived as a co-conspirator. The truth of the matter is that the new step-sisters and brothers are probably as upset about their own lost parent as the first child who initially lashed out.

Issue #9. Competition for time. This is a frequent problem because of what is called the "visitation rights" granted by the court to the now-absent parent. The child or children see one of their parents more than the other, which seems unfair to them, and frequently a child will fight back sometimes unknowingly on behalf of the absent parent. The children feel that they are unjustly being made to choose between the newly acquired step-parent whom they might not like at all, and their original now-missing parent, who is more and more likely to achieve sainthood in the eyes of the child. Sainthood by absence.

Issue #10. Extended kinship network. The children get another whole new set of relatives, in addition to the ones they formerly had and may have loved. The kids are up to their elbows in relatives, many of whom they don't know or care about anyhow.

Issue #11. Sexual conflicts can erupt. Because of a new aura of sexual intensity between the newlyweds, aka "in heat," there can be a loosening of sexual boundaries between the children. This sexually-charged state can entice children to "act out" in unusual ways. Unfortunately, daily publications and newscasts attest to the incidence of sexual abuse which seems to happen too frequently between a new male parent and the newly acquired female step-daughters. In addition, the prospects for highly undesirable sexual contact between the newly-blended step-children are greatly increased.

Issue #12. The time it will take for adjustments to take place which will put the new blended family in the same status as the nuclear or original family is an issue, Dr. Walsh reports. According to his study, it takes at least two years for the basic family reorganization to be completed, and for peace, acceptance and harmony to prevail in the newly-blended family. The dreamy "Brady Bunch" television show notwithstanding, fiction is fiction. Please recall that in the "Brady Bunch" story both of the missing parents had died. Absence by death is usually easier to cope with than absence by divorce. In some cases, Dr. Walsh found the familial reorganization process to take as long as twelve years for normalization to occur. In other cases such normalization never occurred at all. Ever.

Issue #13. The coming and going of the

children from their new home because of weekend visitation rights by the non-custodial parent greatly confuses the children. Don't think that they won't try to make the new step-mother or step-father pay for their discomfort. In addition, the seemingly endless transit by the kids has been documented by experts to frequently be the source of a child's having serious trouble in school, from scholastic as well as behavioral points of view. For a list of possible adverse effects on children, in case you've forgotten, go back to page 17 and see for yourself.

Issue #14. No matter how modern or sophisticated you think you are, the cold fact is that society's attitude toward the blended or re-married family is not as good or the same as society's opinion of the typical nuclear or original family. Never forget that all marriages have their share of troubles, but evidently 50% of the marriages have stuck it out through thick and thin; they have weathered the tough times and the conflicts, and have managed to preserve and maintain their relationships, and then look at those who quit on their marriages and divorce with a different (lower) level of acceptance or approval.

Issue #15. Familial self-concept is an issue, that is, what the children of divorce think of themselves as individuals and as a family. Doctor Walsh found that some children in a blended family think of themselves as losers because of their feelings of guilt and remorse, due to the failure of their original family. Long has it been known that the children of divorce tend to think that they themselves were somehow responsible for their parents' divorce and therefore for the collapse and failure of their own family.

Doctor Walsh further found that the lack of personal self-esteem felt in the blended family, especially by the children, comes about because of the unrealistic expectations of the newlyweds who dreamily thought, as they remarried, they had at last found the perfect mate and would forevermore have a perfect marriage and family. However, before long the children begin to observe that the remarried parents are right back into the same arguments and disagreements they witnessed between their parents in their original family unit. So where is the gain? Who won? Guess who lost?

Issue #16. Individual self-concepts of divorced people who re-marry can be very low. The same negative thoughts will occur in each of their attitudes as they existed in their earlier marriages, and both persons will likely become depressed and wary. Descent into these new and unexpected levels of despair and uncertainty can almost assuredly predict that this new remarriage, like its predecessor(s), will indeed likely fail. The newlyweds, since they already know how to get a divorce, will once again find themselves in the loser's column and in court.

Issue #17. Instant family problems will crop up because there has not been the chance for the normal family bonding processes to take place that occur in first-time marriages. Parenting in the remarriage situation becomes THE most critical issue! In the normal establishment of an original or nuclear family the initial bonding and adjusting of the parents to each other, and later to the children when they start to arrive, is accomplished over the normal spans of time and in the typical manner.

Human pregnancy term is typically nine months long, no matter when the marriage ceremony occurs, and in a first-time marriage situation this almost-a-year period gives the new couple time and a chance to settle in and become about as comfortable with each other as they can be. Once the first child appears on the scene, the parents normally then turn to, and devote, most of their time and energy to the new offspring. In a blended family setting both new parents must not only manage instant adjustment to each other, but also they must immediately begin coping and contending with the newly gained family members and the parenting difficulties pointed out above.

Issue #18. Financial concerns could be another very troublesome issue in a remarriage or blended family situation because if there is any component in the entire Marriage Enhancement format that consistently causes serious trouble between marriage partners, it is money. People married for the first time have enough trouble figuring out their newly created financial situation.

Just imagine the huge financial mess that second- or third-time marriages can encounter. For example, frequently in a re-marriage situation there are problems (fights) over previous debt obligations, child-support payments and alimony owed to a previous spouse. As set out in the "M is for money" explanation, just exactly how, by whom, and when the family monies are to be handled is always a critical and potentially dangerous consideration in any marriage relationship.

Issue #19. Continuing adult conflict is a problem discovered by Dr. Walsh. This rather unexpected area of concern has to do with the torn feelings, residual anger, psychic wounds and old conflicts left over from the earlier failed marriages that can be carried by the divorced persons into their new re-marriage situation. So typically in human fashion, these deep feelings and resentments are too often unfairly transferred to the new second- or third-marriage partner, and occasionally even to the new marriage partner's children.

Issue #20. Competition for the affection of the child or children by the non-custodial parent appearing as unwanted advice, criticism or demands made by the original natural parent—intrusions if you will—into the re-marriage situation are a major topic of concern and strife between the new husband and wife. Or, said another way, the original parent is not going to "let go" of, or abandon, what they perceive is their natural right to oversee and contribute to the development and well-being of their own child.

Another symptom of this competition would be the spending of unusual or excessive amounts of time and money by the non-custodial parent on and with the child or children in an effort to "buy" the affection and loyalty of the child(ren). Needless to say, some of this intrusionary effort is only an attempt to keep themselves as "weekend parents" from feeling totally abandoned. The excessive and surely welcome behavior by the non-custodial parent can greatly confuse the child(ren), who then wonder just who is this awful new person mommy or daddy is married to? And, why did they do this to me?

Such is the essence of that study by Dr. Walsh. The exact title and location of the study can be found in the bibliography section at the end of this book. But to inject a note of reality. If by any chance you are thinking about destroying your family for "someone else," please compare the modest cost of Dr. Walsh's book with what it will cost you to pay for a divorce! $30 vs. $3000, $30,000, or $300,000?

If all the foregoing information isn't enough bad news, here's a bit more. Doctor Judith Wallerstein, who wrote the best-selling book titled *The Good Marriage,* has recently published *The Unexpected Legacy of Divorce,* a 25-year study concerning how the children of divorce survived their affluent parents' divorce. In an article which appeared in the *Washington Post* on June 3, 1997, Mrs. Wallerstein is quoted as saying that her newest research provides more evidence that the impact of divorce on children is both long-lasting and cumulative. She reports: "The effect of the parents' high-conflict divorce is played and replayed all throughout the first several decades of the children's lives."

Doctor Wallerstein reports that half of the 131 young people in her study were involved later on as teens in serious drug and alcohol abuse problems. They were also likely to become sexually active as early adolescents, particularly the girls. One-third of the subjects, about 40 students, ended their education at high school level. Eventually 40% (about 52) graduated from college, with only six students having had their college expenses paid by their well-to-do parents. The rest worked their way through school. Remember, these are the offspring of well-to-do people.

When the subjects reached their twenties, "all without exception were very afraid they would repeat the failure they saw around them when they got into relationships." Roughly one-quarter (about 35) have married, and of those, two have divorced. Another quarter do not date, and the remaining one-half (about 65) are "in search of people with whom to be in totally uncommitted and casual relationships." Grade school math would bring out the conclusion that three-fourths, or about 95 of the study group of children of divorce, relive the trauma and terror of their parents divorce for the rest of their lives!

As if that isn't enough bad news, more is on the way by virtue of Dr. Wallerstein's conclusion that the amount of trauma and damage inflicted upon the offspring by the parental divorce is IN DIRECT PROPORTION TO THE AMOUNT OF CONFLICT DURING THE DIVORCE! More conflict equals more damage!

To some extent, a few courts are becoming aware of the correlation that more conflict equals more damage, and require the divorcing parents to attend brief seminars in which an attempt is made to explain the inevitable negative consequences of divorce to their children. This program is called "Kids First" in our community, and the course is taught by a lawyer.

Obviously the thrust of the effort was not to encourage the divorcing parents to recant, solve their problems and save their marriage relationship, but to try to provide some insight to the divorcing parents as to the depth of pain and lifelong hurt their divorcing will cause their children. And, but of course, keep the opposing attorneys in a position to be able to charge and collect their fees while the fight goes on.

Further evidence of the legal system's emerging awareness of the seriousness of the divorce situation is that a few judicial districts are now mandating that divorcing couples consult with a "mediator" and provide certification of that consultation before they may proceed with the divorce.

Almost everyone thinks they have to hire an attorney in order to get a divorce. This is not so. Individuals in most jurisdictions can process their own divorce WITHOUT LAWYERS in the manner known as "pro-se" (for yourself) (pronounced: pro-say).

Some folks are savvy enough to handle their divorce entirely on their own, and other folks can get through a LOW-CONFLICT divorce situation with the help of a divorce mediator. Much more will be said in the solutions section about mediation as an "alternative dispute resolution" (ADR) process.

One wonders just how much information would be enough to dissuade a couple from divorcing and pursuing their own personal and selfish purposes without regard to the consequences of their actions.

In view of these adverse and even disastrous effects of a divorce, not only on the principal combatants themselves, but also on their children and entire families, any thinking person will realize that divorce is dumb, really dumb. Is the divorce rate likely to lower in the foreseeable future? Many psychologists and sociologists seemingly agree that, with the way things are going in our country at this time in history, the high incidence of divorce in our society will only continue unabated in the foreseeable future.

THREE

A Brief History of the "Marriage Relationship" Concept

Now that I've shown you how to take a hard look at the status of your own marriage, and then told you of some of the awful things that happen to people who divorce, their families, relatives and friends, let me tell you how this all came about. It was no accident.

To clearly explain the genesis of this concept, it is necessary for the next couple of chapters to write in the subjective or personal "I" mode. So let's begin with my story. I went through a divorce, which my wife started in 1984. We finally wound up, 17 months later, after 14 bitter court appearances and legal fees well into six figures, with she getting the final decree in late 1985. So, as they say, 'been there, done that.'

But to say that our divorce started in 1984 overlooks 30 some years of struggle and strife, arguments and anger, which we both endured prior to her actually beginning the legal action. No matter that we were both very busy rearing our seven children; she was taking care of our home and I was busy making what they call "a living." The sad truth of the matter is, as I look back now, our marriage troubles began very shortly after we got through the "I do" part of the wedding ceremony on a November morning in 1951.

It seems to me now that we really never did get our act together. And isn't it interesting how much pain and anguish we human beings can stand until we "blow"?

Divorce is not a decision; rather, a divorce is the legal action which takes place as a result of a whole series of decisions that have been made along the way. Perhaps that is why it's called a divorce "action."

When the final gavel banged in October of 1985 and my wife was granted her decree of divorce, I began to see more and more clearly, in the days and weeks that followed, just how horrible and devastating this legal conclusion was going to be, in a lot of different ways for a lot of different people, including myself. With, of course, the ever-present yet-to-be-answered question: Why?

I confess that my most immediate concern was my own personal anguish and realization of loss. To say I fell into a deep depression would be a gross understatement.

I kept wondering how in the world it all happened. I'm not going to try to tell you that my wife and I were getting along very well, because we weren't. I'll take more than the lion's share of blame for the poor state of the relationship between us. But, what really was the matter? What event or events brought our 33 year marriage to this sorry state of affairs? How did we ever get into the position which catapulted my beautiful family into a state of almost total disintegration? What went wrong? Where did I screw up?

I pondered and contemplated, wondered and remembered, trying so hard to put the many, many events and issues that had occurred over the years into some sort of logical order. Thus, I began to isolate and identify the various parts and elements of our failed marriage. I realized (hoped) that once I identified the basic elements of a marriage relationship, I could then think about each single facet in a clearer manner; and perhaps figure out what had happened. Not that my figuring out what went wrong with my own relationship would in any way undo the damage of our divorce, but I am one of those people who believe it's important to know what actually happened.

At that time I had no thought of developing this exercise to the point at which it has arrived. And certainly no thought of ever sitting down and writing this information in a manner that could be understood by anybody who might find the concept useful.

The question which was driving me nuts was:

What Are the Pieces of the Puzzle? Or: What Are the Basic Elements of a Marriage Relationship?

Of course, by that time I **clearly** recognized the end-products of a failed marriage relationship: anger, sorrow, greed, dishonesty, dissension, lying, side-taking, disappointment, lawyers deliberately causing trouble to enhance their fees, financial concerns, and alienation within the entire family.

What I needed was some sort of organizational table which would list all of the parts of a marriage relationship on an item-by-item basis. I needed some way to be able to think about particular issues, one at a time. I found that if I tried to think about our marriage relationship as a big entity, without separating the various elements, each to their own level of meaning and understanding, I got confused. I took a notepad and pencil in hand, and jotted down every element I could think of . . . far too many elements to be workable, More confusion!

Then one night in the fall of 1986, about a year after the divorce was final, I was sitting on the couch eating popcorn watching the popular "Wheel of Fortune" game show, and whammo, it hit me! I got it! Just like that . . . the key to unraveling the mystery.

For anyone who may not be familiar with the "Wheel of Fortune" TV program, which is the most popular daily game show on television at this point in history, the format is a puzzle-solving contest between three contestants in which blank spaces are put up on the game board. The spaces, when properly filled in with the appropriate letters of the alphabet, will then provide the answer to the clue that's been previously given by the show host. The contestants, in turn, guess the various letters of the alphabet and eventually fill the blank spaces, so the answer to the puzzle is apparent, at least to them. Whichever contestant is able to solve the puzzle first, wins the prize.

Well, the Wheel of Fortune gave me the idea to identify the basic elements of a marriage relationship from the very letters of the term. All I had to do was let each letter stand for its own word/value, and then all these individually assigned meanings and ultimately their correlation to each other would provide the basis for solving the puzzle: What are the various components, the basic elements which form the essence of a marriage relationship?

I used this game concept to establish a framework which would help shed light on the elements of a marriage relationship. I know it's too late for me to pick up the pieces of my failed marriage. However, I am convinced that this discourse is valuable, so my goal is:

- to try to help people better understand their own marriage relationships and thereby find happier lives, have happier marriages

- to try to help insulate children from the awful damaging and permanent effects of a parental divorce

- to try to gain even a miniscule lowering of the divorce rate in our country and society, thereby slowing the disintegration of the family unit.

In the next chapter I am going to identify and explain the meaning of each of the components in the Marriage Relationship puzzle. But, I thought you might be interested to see how this all came about, and, perhaps along with me, realize how lucky I was to have been sitting there watching television on that cold fall evening in 1986.

FOUR

The Components of a Marriage Relationship

A marriage relationship is within itself a whole entity, a complete relationship made up of 20 inter-related components, all of which are clearly important in their own right, but many of which are, to some extent, inter-dependent on each other. Once I had finally grasped the idea—or perhaps better said, the idea grasped me—I began assigning a value or meaning to each letter in the words "Marriage Relationship." The meaning or value of each of the letters could be either a clear-cut and easily understood consideration like M stands for money, or the meaning could perhaps have a more obscure human behavioral or relationship connotation, like the E which stands for energy, the T which stands for time, and most importantly the G for general co-dependence, a concept almost no one understands.

The assignment of a meaning to each letter was by no means an easy task. The procedure involved not only going over my own life and marriage, but also engaging in extensive consultation with others, including friends, professionals and relatives as well. I must confess that, thanks to their help and input, more than one value was changed because the original definition I had assigned was incomplete, or somehow missed the mark.

After some time and contemplation, and thanks to the above-mentioned support, all the values were duly assigned, the concept was firmly in mind, and I thought I was ready to begin putting the elements of the concept on paper.

I began writing, and in a short period of time I started to realize that I simply did not know enough about the science of psychology to be able to adequately complete the formalization of my Marriage Relationship format.

The only thing to do was to return to school, which I did, and in 1992, at the age of 68, I earned a Master of Arts degree in "Educational Psychology and Counseling." The nearly four years I spent in that educational environment sopping up all of that information were worth far more than I ever could imagine.

Upon completion of my learning experience I had a good grasp of the basic psychological theories and protocols, and could begin writing an accurate documentation of the concept.

Mention might be made that several very interesting notions and valuable insights were gained from my educational experience. One is that at no time did I ever find any other theory published or idea advanced that either conflicted with or preceded my basic Marriage Relationship idea. In every instance, an earlier theory that had been developed by someone else, while perhaps moving in the general direction of the Marriage Relationship concept, always stopped short. Of course I was delighted and relieved with this knowledge. Wouldn't it be disappointing to re-invent the wheel?

Another thing I learned, and this fact really staggered me, is that the science of Psychology is very young. Only since the beginning of the 20th century, give or take a decade or three, have great amounts of experimentation, thought and study in the field of human psychology and development been accomplished. And only since the late 1970s or early 1980s has the huge explosion of research and theoretical innovation which we see happening now, come to pass.

By learning about all the existing theories and practicalities of the human mind, body and behaviors, I arrived at the sad conclusion that as far as a marriage relationship between a man and a woman is concerned, what really exists is that two people undertake to live together in what they call a marriage, which is probably the most complex relationship known to mankind. And, for openers, these two very well-intentioned individuals are completely different each from the other in so many ways. Worse, these basic fundamental differences between men and women, between husbands and wives and between individuals, have been either largely overlooked, not admitted and certainly not understood.

Never should one forget that we each have our own sets of behaviors, hopes, traits, family backgrounds, mindsets, beliefs, temperaments, personalities, characters, and very importantly, rights. These all come into play while trying to live together in a complicated relationship. Add the day-to-day routines—rearing children, paying the bills, mowing the lawn, doing the dishes, and all the rest—then try to be happy. Does that sound like a full agenda or what?

On top of that, if things aren't complicated enough, as we age, our minds and bodies change. Levels of energy and abilities diminish. Our thought processes shift and our life-priorities become adjusted to the age of the mind and body. To summarize these few paragraphs: It is necessary that we understand not only the Marriage Relationship concept with its many elements, but also these undeniable facts:

■ We are, for the most part, quite different from each other with regard to personalities, temperaments and characters.

■ We are each in our own continual process of personal change or flux, simply from the fact of our lifelong human developmental processes; it's called aging.

■ The impact of our early life experiences and certain genetic dispositions will affect individual behaviors and attitudes, which will inevitably be carried on into our later lives.

A companion book to this Marriage Relationship manual, titled *Some of the Reasons We Behave the Way We Do,* is of critical importance to anyone involved in some non-understandable marital strife. While a basic comprehension of the Marriage Relationship concept will prove to be of great value to the happy maintenance of any marriage contract, also of clear-cut importance is some level of understanding of the impact or each person's order of birth in their original family, a degree of tolerance for personal behavioral quirks, and a grasp of the inevitable changes that the aging process will bring into each of our lives and minds.

Here are the values that have been assigned to each letter in the words "Marriage Relationship" and which contain the basic and essential elements of every marriage relationship. As you see, the values are lined up to the right of the letters of the words "Marriage Relationship" which are positioned vertically. The values assigned to the letters in the first word, "Marriage," are:

M	stands for	MONEY
A	stands for	ANGER
R	stands for	RELATIVES
R	stands for	REVERSALS
I	stands for	INTEGRITY
A	stands for	ABUSE
G	stands for	GENERAL CODEPENDENCE
E	stands for	ENERGY

The values assigned for the second word, "Relationship," are:

R	stands for	RESPECT
E	stands for	EXPECTATIONS
L	stands for	LIVING
A	stands for	ADDICTION
T	stands for	TIME
I	stands for	INTRUSIONS
O	stands for	OUTSIDERS
N	stands for	NEGOTIATION
S	stands for	SEX
H	stands for	HONESTY
I	stands for	INTIMACY
P	stands for	PRIORITIES

Many of the values assigned to the various letters are well known to all of us. For example, we all know about difficulties that money problems can cause, but some other values as used within the Marriage Relationship concept have more contextual definitions that may not be immediately clear until an explanation of their meaning is given. You'll find this information in the next chapter. To recap briefly, when a couple gets married they THINK that just because they are married and in "love" that they have everything under control and they THINK that their Marriage Relationship puzzle is all filled out and looks like this:

<u>M A R R I A G E</u>
<u>R E L A T I O N S H I P</u>

But, actually, since the game has only begun, their marriage is brand new and untested, so this is what their new marriage relationship really looks like:

_ _ _ _ _ _ _ _
_ _ _ _ _ _ _ _ _ _ _ _

Nothing. Nada. Zip. The puzzle is blank.

As a rule when people get married, they haven't even started to build their own marriage relationship because they have not gotten down to the brass tacks of life. They've not had to work through the rough spots that are bound to show up in every marriage.

Unfortunately, as life goes on and the marriage earns a degree of longevity, what usually happens is that some issue, however slight in the offing, becomes contentious. Conflict erupts, and the relationship between the marriage partners begins to erode. Then, just as sure as anything, some other issue pops up, and of course here cometh another two or three issues or problems, also unresolved. Pretty soon that marriage relationship which seemed to be so promising and wonderful at its outset, finds itself in trouble.

So why do people get married?

The truth is that people get married for a whole lot of different reasons, and too often the goals and purposes of one individual won't be anywhere near those of the other partner. To make matters worse, far too often neither person knows the reasons or motives of the other intended marriage partner.

Some people get married because they can't stand to be alone. Remarriages occur because people get it in their heads that they can't stand to be with the one they are with, so they set out to find that new and "perfect" partner. Once in a while, even in these times, people get married because they feel they "have to"; this being prior to the impending arrival of an unplanned and unexpected offspring. Some pundit once wrote that kids in the back seat can cause accidents, and that an accident in the back seat can cause kids.

Sometimes people get married because it is the "thing to do," since all of her friends are married. We do live in a "couples" society. Other times, family pressure will precipitate a marriage. Considering the above, I think it's some sort of a miracle that the divorce rate isn't higher than 50%!

Next: definitions and explanations.

FIVE

Definitions and Explanations

To say that marriage as a social institution is a complicated and difficult relationship to maintain and sustain is a serious understatement. But why? Why is this relationship, which is and has been the basic cornerstone of human social existence, so very easy to get into, and evidently so terribly difficult to keep going on an even keel? Why does this relationship suffer such an appalling failure rate?

"When we got married, I thought everything would be so very wonderful, and then ____(he or she)____ etc., etc." said the distressed marriage partner. What went wrong? What happened?

Well, several things.

In the first place, as the point was made in the previous chapter, when people marry they really don't know this other person whom they have vowed to take as their life's companion " . . . for better or for worse . . . for the rest of their life." Nor do most of us know ourselves well enough either. Then add in the typically unrealistic thought pattern which says that, once married, one or both of the marriage partners foolishly thinks that he/she can bring about changes in the other partner so that they will be more to their liking, more like themselves.

In the second place, up to now no one has ever established what the basic components of a marriage relationship really are. It is the function of this chapter to clearly define each one of the twenty basic components of a marriage so at last people can know and understand what issues and factors make up their marriage relationship, starting with the first letter in the first word, "Marriage."

M stands for 'Money'

Money as a category, and as a potential source of interpersonal difficulty between marriage partners, is probably the biggest and most consistent troublemaker in any marriage relationship.

Obviously, the simple and direct way for a family to solve money troubles is for the two parties to sit down together and develop a mutually agreeable plan for handling their family money. That sounds easy, but here is what it takes:

- a reasonable and realistic plan of action, and
- the couple's ability and willingness to negotiate

In our 40-year financial business career, one of the things my brother and I enjoyed doing was working with families as their personal banker, helping them with the management of their budgets and finances. We know from firsthand experience that developing a workable and mutually agreeable family financial plan can be accomplished only if the two requirements listed above are met.

That's not to say that working out a family's financial mess and arriving at a mutually agreeable family budget is an easy task to accomplish. What I am saying is that, with good will, honesty, reasonableness, patience and a good proven model or financial plan, money problems in any marriage relationship can be resolved and brought under control. One thing I did learn in those years is that the family with money troubles also has family troubles.

Mention must be made, too, that in my experience only rarely did the first attempt to solve a family's money problems find total success. If the first stab at it fell short of the mark, a different approach or a complete re-start was needed. By tinkering with management procedures, making some adjustments as required, the desired happy result usually came forth, and the family's squabbles over money were reduced to a more manageable state. This process takes patience.

One of the thumb-rules I tried to get folks to grasp (with mixed results) is: when you find yourself in a hole, quit digging. The credit card fiasco in progress in our country is a great source of financial difficulty. Credit cards are too easy to get, carry too-high interest rates, and don't have realistic final payoff date goals because the public is virtually handed a blank check, month after month, year after year. Surely some responsibility, some culpability rests on the shoulders of those who mail "pre-approved" credit cards and encourage a family to go into perpetual debt.

In the solution section of this work, I've supplied a great deal of information about solving family money troubles. Included in that section, in addition to suggested plans for money handling and allocation, is the "family budget" that I developed. Thousands of families used it successfully, so I know it will work for you too.

A stands for 'Anger'

The consideration of anger referred to herein does not include the concept of someone being just "upset" or "miffed." Anger in the context of the marriage relationship deals with a deep-seated and abiding rage one marriage partner feels towards the other, without any relief. Whether the anger is rational or not is beside the point.

Anger is a terrible thing to feel, and if the anger somebody feels isn't somehow eased or coped with, awful things can and do happen. "Anger is a short madness," the Roman poet Horace wrote. The bad news is that there's really no way to work with anyone who is so angry that they're out of control. When that happens, all one can do is wait out the storm, then attempt to introduce reason and order.

In the "solution" section some suggestions are made which will enable a person to learn how to cope not only with his/her own anger, but also with another angry person as well.

R stands for 'Relatives'

How fortunate to get the second of the three biggest trouble-makers in a marriage relationship up for consideration so early in the game. Typically the "Big-3" trouble-makers in a marriage relationship are money, sex and relatives.

"Relatives" as an issue is a frequent source of trouble in a marriage relationship. Trouble, with a capital T. Before marriage, a person doesn't know the depth of loyalty to, or how much control an original family member or members have over the new spouse. Control of a spouse, exercised by a controlling relative, means that the relative(s) will also have a degree of control over you and your marriage relationship itself. Marriages can actually be destroyed by meddling relatives. The truth of the matter is that you can pick your spouse, but you can't pick the relatives.

Relatives, as used herein, can be a serious threat to even the most solid and well intentioned marriage relationship. If you are experiencing "relative trouble," rest assured that later on in the "solutions" section some suggestions are made for solving problems with relatives. Of course, a good batch of relatives would simply be a godsend, and, yes, there are good relatives, too.

R stands for 'Reversals'

A 'reversal', as the term is being used in our Marriage Relationship context, is defined as a rather sudden change of status or fortune in a couple's lives, either for good or for ill. A reversal can split a marriage relationship wide open. A death, an illness, a business failure, serious financial disaster, the loss of a job, a legal setback, can cause so much stress and strain in the relationship that the marriage will fail. The sudden loss of family balance from such a negative event can blow up even a long-standing marriage relationship. In like manner, a divorce will far too frequently occur when a family falls on good times and prospers beyond their wildest dreams.

The definitive point to remember is that a reversal is the occurrence of any dramatic or earth-shaking change in the family structures or fortunes, which happenstance completely upsets the family balance either way, plus or minus, good or bad.

One thing of which we can be certain is that almost inevitably some sort of reversal will occur in our lives. So forewarned is forearmed. Anticipation of the inevitable reversal, and having a basic plan for accommodating the reversal, will better insure the marriage partners' ability to persevere and move forward in their marriage relationship.

I stands for 'Integrity'

Generally speaking, people think that the word integrity means honesty and truthfulness. While this definition does fall within the context of the marriage relationship to some extent, you will see that we are using the word "integrity" in our concept with the main focus on and reference to the ability of the marriage partners to be in close agreement, to be of one accord, and to work together in unison on the important issues within their relationship. One issue which springs to mind is the obvious need for agreement between the marriage partners when it comes to disciplining children. By the same token, agreement on financial matters, and on moral issues, is important.

A stands for 'Abuse'

Within the scope of our definition, abuse is any detrimental activity within the family that is perpetrated upon family members and which cannot be curtailed by the victim(s). Abuse, as a category of concern, is one of the three valid reasons for divorce. Abuse, as the term is used in the Marriage Relationship concept, comes in three general categories.

Physical Abuse

Physical abuse is the act of hitting, striking or hurting someone else, causing physical pain to the one or ones being abused. The physical abuse rule, as used in our Marriage Relationship context, applies to the abuse being directed toward anyone in the family.

Sexual Abuse

Sexual abuse would include any unwanted, forced or illicit sexual contact of any type conducted in any manner under any pretext at any time by a "perpetrator" upon another person. It makes no difference whether the victim is a child or an adult. The sexual abuse of a child is an illegal activity and can frequently result in perpetrators (aka "perps") being jailed, which they richly deserve.

The sexual abuse of an adult, such as a rape, also is a criminal offense. Hopefully the need to explicitly define and describe instances of sexual abuse is unnecessary. In the event that any instance of sexual abuse is suspected or known to be occurring, refer immediately to the later *Solution* section under "abuse."

Mental Abuse

Mental abuse is that abuse which comes to pass when one individual, or perhaps a conspiracy of family members, steadily over a period of time and with determined persistence, directs a continuous stream of talk and/or actions toward others in the family with the intent to belittle, demean, degrade and humiliate the person or persons who are the target of the verbal invective or actions. The goal of such abuse is to destroy the self-esteem, self-confidence, or feelings of self-worth of the family members being abused. People who destroy others' self-esteem are usually personally bankrupt themselves when it comes to their own feelings of self-worth. Sometimes people who mentally abuse others aren't even aware of the harm they are doing. I know that might be a little hard to swallow, but 'tis true.

Not included in the definition of mental abuse are the normal levels of carping, bitching or complaining, which traits of human behavior are common to us all.

Everyone is entitled to a good whine once in a while, and sometimes someone voicing occasional displeasure with or disappointment over something to their marriage partner, when done in the correct "I" manner as a complaint, might simply be a form of communication, or perhaps even the beginning of a negotiation process.

Abuse, as defined above, is something that no one has to live with, and the abuse of someone in the family, be it yourself or another member of the family, must be stopped immediately! The *Solution and Intervention* section contains several effective methods to stop abuse.

G stands for 'General Codependence'

The concept of codependence is a tough idea to understand and is not that easy to explain. To begin with, the basic concept or idea of codependence came from the early alcoholism treatment programs. The pioneer addiction therapists discovered that if one person in a family was dependent upon or addicted to alcohol the lives of the other members of the family would be directly affected and perhaps even dominated by the addiction of the family member. The effect of the addiction on the other non-drinking and non-addicted members of the family makes them "codependent" to the existing family member's addiction. This is called "addictive codependence."

Other forms of addiction such as substance or drug abuse, gambling or sex also exist and fall under the general category of "addictive codependence." Addiction, as it relates to substance abuse, is one of the 20 categories of concern in the total Marriage Relationship idea and will be considered later under A for 'Addiction.'

In some cases the behavior of the family tolerating the excessive indulgence of the one who is addicted is called "enabling." Enabling, as such, can range from deliberately helping the addict continue his/her addiction to becoming an unintentional accomplice of the family member's addiction. Being an unwitting enabler can actually serve to prolong the addiction suffered by the addict.

Enabling as a concept, and corrective measures which might be pursued to stop the process of enabling are considered later in the *Solution* section.

From this original concept of addictive codependence, new research has uncovered another form of codependence which deals with the carrying forward into later life of some dysfunctional behaviors from a person's original or nuclear family life. It is this "behavioral codependence" that we are calling "general codependence" in order to provide separation from addictive codependence.

Here is a good definition of "general codependence" which might make sense to you:

> General codependence is a dysfunctional pattern of living and problem-solving nurtured (kept going) by an unwritten set of family rules.

If you live in a family setting which is or was deeply involved in a state of general codependency then you will likely know from your own experience the part about the "family rules." It generally holds true that the rules are unwritten and exist as family tradition or ritual. For example, a person brought up in a family which cannot communicate effectively, or is unable to show any emotional response or display affection, will very likely carry these deficiencies with him/her into the new marriage.

The new partner in life is almost surely still living under the influence of his/her own old original set of dysfunctional family rules and traditions, which is consciously or unconsciously brought forward into the new marriage relationship. The chances that one person's original family rules will prove to be the same and merge without hitch with the new spouse's family rules are twofold: slim and none.

Later, in the *Solution* section, extensive description and identification of a list of typical behaviors and symptoms will be given which will help you recognize the existence of general codependence in your own background, or perhaps even now in your own family. Codependence in itself is never a cause for divorce unless one of the manifestations of the codependence happens to be in the abuse category, as set out above. But, of all the issues that can come up unexpectedly in a marriage relationship to cause trouble and stress, this issue of general codependence is close to the top of the list.

E stands for 'Energy'

Putting forth the personal effort to make the marriage relationship work and a happy place wherein to abide constitutes the definition of the word "energy."

A lot of people get off on the wrong foot early on with regard to the amount of raw energy that they are willing or able to give to their new marriage relationship. A shortage or default of energy, as defined herein, can suddenly appear even for those who have been married for a long time.

Tips and hints are found in the next section, which not only focus attention on the need for energy in a relationship, but also includes some suggestions to energize your own marriage.

■

And so we have completed defining the values assigned to the eight letters in the word "Marriage." Now, we define the values assigned to the twelve letters in the word "Relationship."

R stands for 'Respect'

Respect, as an ingredient in a marriage relationship, encompasses several aspects of human relations:

■ All people needs to feel that they are personally respected for who and what they are as individuals.

■ Individuals deserve respect for their ideas and have the right to hold personal viewpoints and opinions without danger of being criticized or ridiculed because their opinion might be different than someone else's viewpoint.

Note: Respect for someone else's ideas does not carry the burden of mandatory agreement, but only the acknowledgement that the person is entitled to his or her own opinion(s).

■ In order to be happy and successful, the partners must have respect for and pride in their own marriage relationship, and for the basic principles of marriage. Later we shall consider the "Principle of Least Interest," which will be enlightening and perhaps even pertinent to your own marriage relationship.

E stands for 'Expectations'

This important issue in a marriage relationship has to do with assumptions or pre-determined mindsets a person might have regarding whatever events, circumstances or conditions that the person thinks, hopes, or assumes will in fact exist once they are married; in other words, what one **expects** to happen with regard to behaviors, customs, attitudes and events in their new relationship which might or might not come to pass. The subsequent failure of whatever variety of expected states, conditions or behaviors to actually materialize can cause great frustration and disappointment. Maybe even anger.

How many times do we hear someone say, "When we got married I thought . . . " This kind of statement is evidence of a failure of pre-marital expectations. Whether those expectations are realistic is beside the point.

A failure of expectations can occur at a later time in a marriage relationship when, or if, one of the marriage partners unexpectedly changes course. Conditions or attitudes that were once considered as cast in granite are found to have changed, causing concern in the mind of the person who believed that things, as they once stood, would continue forever. Of good importance in *Solutions* is the exploration of ways for a marriage partner to cope with possible shifts in attitudes and avoid, or at least minimize, the disappointments and frustration which can result from a failure of expectations.

L stands for 'Living'

"Living" as a component in the Marriage Relationship concept is a large category of concern and includes a varied list of considerations including, but not limited to, the following:

- Are you living where and as well as you want to live? Keep in mind that everything in this life is "penciled in" and changes always occur.

- Is there a problem with housekeeping, neatness, personal habits, cleanliness or the seemingly unnecessary exercise of rituals or habits which cause you concern or distress?

- Is your own life in good order and is your present lifestyle acceptable to your mate in most of its variances? As you will see, you might have to try to sense how he/she feels about your behavioral traits. You may even have to ask how they feel about something you do. Asking is okay.

Also included in our contemplation of "living" we address the issue of the health of each of the marriage partners from a physical as well as mental point of view. Each marriage partner has a responsibility to watch out, not only for his/her own health but also the well-being of the spouse.

Physical health concerns include not only the basic considerations of diet, exercise and a general state of physical and mental wellness, but also the need to work together as a team to help eliminate, or at least minimize, certain personal habits which are known to be unhealthy and therefore detrimental to the person's health, such as smoking, over-eating, drinking and such.

In the realm of mental health, pay attention to conditions or circumstances which cause undue stress to your marriage partner. Be watchful for sudden changes in behavior which might presage oncoming physical disorders. Learn about and accept the inevitable human developmental changes.

Also of **critical** importance in this issue of living is the need for the partners to be able to communicate effectively with each other, and to be able to negotiate solutions to problems as they may come up. Unfortunately, a person's ability or inability to communicate effectively is often linked to his/her early life experiences as set out in the General Codependence section. But, there is always hope. You can teach an old dog new tricks. Suggestions to remedy shortfalls in both communication skills and the ability to negotiate are found in the appropriate sections in *Solutions*.

A stands for 'Addiction'

A sad part of this world in which we live, and surely a curse on humanity, is the possibility of existence and sometimes the actual occurrence of what is known as an "addiction." An addiction comes about when someone loses his/her ability to control some facet or aspect of behavior. The range of activities in which one can become involved, and possibly become addicted to, is not endless but certainly lengthy. That list includes addictions to alcohol, food, sex, drugs, gambling and many other various activities and substances. Worse, addiction as a chronic and maladaptive behavior can sneak into anyone's life at almost any time, and therefore into the marriage relationship.

Having a marriage partner who is actually addicted to something is not in itself a reason for divorce, but such an addiction could possibly become a reason to divorce in case excessive levels of abuse exist.

Currently, an addiction is considered by most people involved in healthcare to be a disease, a sickness or a pathological disorder. Did you not promise the day you got married that you would remain together, " . . . in sickness and in health"? Later, consideration is given to the possible diagnosis of an addiction, an overview of treatment procedures, and very importantly, the way a marriage relationship can survive in the case of an apparent addiction problem.

T stands for 'Time'

At first glance one might think that this issue of time and the earlier described topic of energy to be one and the same. But they are not. Energy, as used in the marriage relationship concept, refers to the amount of EFFORT that is put into the marriage. Conversely, time as an issue involves just what it says: spending the necessary time with your marriage relationship to make it work. In *Solutions* we will give consideration to three types of time: "Quality," "gross" and "gone" time. Time as a category of concern is a very important consideration.

I stands for 'Intrusions'

An "intrusion" occurs when some outside factor or factors enter into the marriage relationship. An intrusion may be a new and consuming idea, or a new hobby or interest. The total range of ideas which may be classed as intrusions is very long indeed. For example, one of the marriage partners might get caught up in a religious fervor, the practice of which could upset the existing balance. Some alternative coping mechanisms that will enable a person to deal with an intrusion will be offered later. We will also cover this thing we call "balance," or "homeostasis," in a marriage relationship.

O stands for 'Outsiders'

Outsiders are people (other than relatives) who enter into someone's life and relationship and tend to cause discontent and disruption in the balance of that marriage.

One example of a type of outsider would be a neighborhood "kitchen attorney," who sits at the kitchen table and freely dispenses his/her pseudo-legal advice on almost any subject; unfortunately this usually includes the marriage relationship of the person with whom he/she is talking.

Kitchen attorneys will quickly tell you "what you ought to do is . . . " or, "If I were you I'd . . . " and with their deep well of knowledge on legal matters and general expertise (said facetiously) will offer detailed advice on all matters legal, marital, moral and ethical. Another variety of an outsider is the amateur psychologist who freely offers his/her patently unreliable advice on the complex psychological aspects of human behaviors and relationships.

The ultimate outsiders are the attorneys of the world, almost all of whom will do divorce work simply for the exorbitant fees they can collect. Worst of all are those attorneys who involve themselves in what they gratuitously call "Family Law."

"Anti-family law" is closer to the truth of the matter. The *Solutions* section to come along a bit later includes investigation of the role that outsiders play in our modern world. Also included are some suggested avenues that can be taken to elude and escape the destructive force of an outsider.

N stands for 'Negotiation'

The ability to negotiate, to work out suitable settlements or arrangements and thereby arrive at equitable solutions to problems is a critical facet not only to everyone's personal life, but especially to the well-being of a marriage relationship. Most people learn how to negotiate from the point of view of general codependence: The child-now-adult will probably negotiate marital problems in the same manner as their parents negotiated, or failed to negotiate their problems as the case may be, depending on a possible imbalance of power within the family structure. The *Solutions* section contains an extensive analysis of the three elements of any negotiation process, and a close tie-in with the suggested use of effective communication skills.

It is written: "In life we don't get what we deserve, we get what we negotiate."

S stands for 'Sex'

Sooner or later we had to get to that issue which is the cornerstone of the marriage relationship: sex. As a rule, in these liberal times, sex is not the problem before marriage that it can become once the marriage vows are spoken. As you recall, sex as an issue is one of the 'Big-3' troublemakers in marriages. To reiterate, the 'Big-3' trouble spots in marriage are money, sex and relatives. Problems over matters sexual sometimes come about when one of the marriage partners uses his/her sexual availability as a weapon in a negotiation process. If weapons are used in a negotiation, what you have is a battle or serious conflict, not a negotiation.

This overview of the 20 components of a marriage relationship is not a manual on sex, but later you will find some comments on the role sexual activity plays in marriage. I also offer some possible viewpoints or remedies designed to ease sexual tension.

H stands for 'Honesty'

Honesty, as a general topic, has several faces; however, I am going to confine discussion of honesty with a marriage to two areas of concern. Most of the time and space devoted to honesty deals primarily with the value and importance of the marriage partners' adherence to their marriage vows. This typically includes their promise to be sexually faithful to each other. Briefly stated, according to Atlanta psychiatrist Dr. Frank Pittman, who is considered the head guru of infidelity, those four varieties of infidelity include:
- accidental
- philandering
- marital arrangement
- romantic

The *Solutions* section explains and discusses those four types of marital infidelity or breach of faith that exist when one of the partners becomes sexually unfaithful. Also reviewed are some of the possible consequences of such unfaithfulness. The infidelity of one of the marriage partners which cannot be stopped or tolerated by the other person is one of the three valid reasons for divorce.

I stands for 'Intimacy'

One of the most valuable, and probably the most misunderstood component of the entire Marriage Relationship concept, is this interpersonal transaction between a husband and wife called "Intimacy."

Women know all about, need and in fact crave intimacy, while most males don't have the slightest clue what intimacy means, or how to go about being intimate. Most men think that being intimate or displaying intimacy means "making whoopee," and granting that "making whoopee" is indeed an intimate activity, it's not the type of intimacy that I am talking about here.

Intimacy, as defined in this context, is the transmission of feelings in one manner or the other to another person. Letting someone know that you care about them, either by gesture, a touch, a gentle caress, a verbal reassurance, being solicitous about someone's welfare and happiness is what intimacy is all about.

Further explanation of the phenomenon of intimacy, and how to go about it will be given later. The provision of a necessary amount of intimacy will help any set of marriage partners achieve a more even emotional balance in their marriage relationship.

P stands for 'Priorities'

How cruel it is that probably the most important component of any marriage relationship ends up here dead last.

Certainly, before marriage and **absolutely** afterwards, you need to think about what you personally want out of life, and the direction you want your marriage relationship to take. Later on, I will show you how to develop priority lists in a timely fashion, and how to go about defining and correlating your life and marriage priorities.

■

Thus I have identified and defined each of my 20 components of a marriage relationship. Every important concern that can occur within a marriage is included somewhere in my list of components. As I said earlier, some concerns will fall into more than just one category. You will also discover that some of the individual items have still more issues embedded within their general explanations. Example: The topic of general codependence not only enfolds the critical issues of communication, and the ability to display emotional response, but other personal concerns such as facing up to life's problems, "triangulation," stagnation, leadership and having the ability to live life in a full and meaningful fashion. In case some of those terms aren't clear at this point, stand by, and we'll get to the consideration of each one in due course.

Now before we move into the meat of the subject, there is one other facet of this concept that needs some explanation, namely the prevalence, if any, of competing ideas.

It seems that whenever someone says "These are the seven keys to happiness . . . " someone else will stand up and say, "No, there are 15 keys . . . " or " 256 keys" or some other number. That's all well and good because there are always other ways to look at any situation or concept. This idea is no different from any other new concept—there are bound to be other methods or models available now, or that will soon become available. Wonderful.

Most new psychological concepts are prepared and directed to the practicing psychological community for its use in the clinical setting. And while we dearly hope that the practicing family therapy and marriage counseling clinicians will eventually adopt and use our ideas, it is up to them. Meanwhile, it is our plan to market this concept directly to the public. We intend to talk directly to YOU !

The next thing we are going to do, now that you know the identity and definition of all the categories, is to help you find out what issues might be hurtful in your own marriage. Once you know what components are causing you trouble, the solutions are within your grasp.

This is what is known as "Marriage Counseling."

First isolate the sore spots, then apply corrective ideas and suggestions to solve the problems.

On to The Quiz.

SIX

The Quiz

In this chapter, you'll survey for yourself via the quiz just what issue or issues might be causing some problems. Problems, once revealed and admitted, are thereby vulnerable and can be solved. Before you get started, here are a few thoughts and suggestions about how you might best approach this questionnaire:

1. Don't get excited if it seems to you that you list too many "yes" answers to the questions. There is no grade or score on this quiz, and no pass/fail scenario. The results will appear as they do, and their appearance only indicates the possible presence of a problem area as far as YOU are concerned. For someone to think "I wrote down nine 'yes's, so that means I flunked, our marriage has failed, we should get a divorce," is absolutely not correct or fair. It doesn't make any difference if you answered **every** question with a "yes." If that happens, the result only means that you have a lot of straightening out to do in your marriage relationship.

2. Keep in mind that this is just your first time through this list of the 20 factors that make up your marriage relationship, and if you are smart it'll be just that, only the first time you will go through the quiz. Isn't it reasonable to think that the way to keep up with and take the pulse of your marriage relationship would be to go through the questions from time to time? People change and circumstances change, so keep this guide handy and every once in a while it wouldn't hurt a bit to do a quick review of the status of the 20 categories of concern. By the way, don't hesitate to make copies of the quiz for future use.

An occasional review of the quiz will achieve another valuable set of viewpoints for you. By periodically going through the questions, you will not only increase your understanding of the wide-ranging scope of the Marriage Relationship idea, but also you will gain added insight into the intrinsic value of the Marriage Relationship concept.

3. Don't mark your answers to the quiz questions directly on the quiz page.

I suggest that you either use one of the

copies you've made, or get another piece of paper and keep track of your "Yes" or "No" answers on that separate sheet. There are three reasons for this important suggestion. If you write your answers directly on the page, and someone else wants to run through the quiz, you lose the confidentiality of your own answers. Another consideration is that this is only paper, and over time there could be all kinds of erasing and over-writing which, in due course, would render the page unusable. But worst of all, if your answers appear directly on the page the chance always exists that your spouse could read and possibly challenge your "yes" answers before you are ready to negotiate solutions. As the old saying goes: "Gitcher ducks in line."

4. Keep in mind that you are answering each question just as you feel about that particular issue only at the moment that you are taking the quiz. The reason for emphasis on this point is that as time goes by, a problem which seemed so serious and hurty might fade away on its own. Do not have "carry-overs" on problems. Do not list a "yes" answer for an issue or problem which was troublesome a while ago, but which concern has since been pretty much resolved and is no longer a serious and earth-shaking bone of contention. At the same time, don't borrow trouble and start the old "what if" game, because who knows what the future holds and what might happen in reality? Within this Marriage Relationship concept, concern yourself just with today. Yesterday is gone, and tomorrow isn't here yet. All of us only have today.

5. Keep in mind that when your spouse eventually takes the quiz he/she may very likely respond differently to some of the questions than you did. Realize that spouses will, beyond the shadow of a doubt, see, feel and think differently about things because, not only are they of the "other sex," but also, even more importantly, their family background is as important to them as yours is to you. They are inclined to think and react now as they were taught to think and react as children. As do you. If you will recall in the earlier explanation of "general codependence," the familial history of your spouse is certain to differ from your family's history. You each have your own set of early-learned value systems and coping mechanisms.

6. You and your spouse should NOT initially take the quiz together at the same time and in the same place. The danger of such joint endeavor could well result in the hesitancy of one of the marriage partners to be completely honest in his/her answers in an attempt to avoid possible early conflict, which could arise from differing responses. Suggestions are offered later which hopefully will resolve and ease conflicts with communication between marriage partners as such problems might exist. Also examined extensively in the *Solutions* part is the crucial art of negotiation, without which skills the resolution of any dispute can be difficult indeed.

So, here is the quiz.

THE QUIZ

Here are the 20 questions and they are simple to answer:

1.	M	**Money.** Any troubles with? Management? Budgeting?	yes	no
2.	A	**Anger.** Any deep abiding disagreements? Arguing?	yes	no
3.	R	**Relatives.** Too close to? They influence too much?	yes	no
4.	R	**Reversals.** Job loss? Death? Disability? Illness?	yes	no
5.	I	**Integrity.** Family stick together? Supportive?	yes	no
6.	A	**Abuse.** Any physical, sexual, prolonged mental abuse?	yes	no
7.	G	**General codependence.** Unusual family behaviors?	yes	no
8.	E	**Energy.** Is everyone working hard at the marriage?	yes	no
9.	R	**Respect.** Do you each have enough for one another?	yes	no
10.	E	**Expectations.** Too high? Too low? Realistic?	yes	no
11.	L	**Living.** Standards and conditions okay? Personal?	yes	no
12.	A	**Addiction.** Real or perceived chemical, or other?	yes	no
13.	T	**Time.** Is enough Quality time being spent together?	yes	no
14.	I	**Intrusions.** New ideas, hobbies, interests intruding?	yes	no
15.	O	**Outsiders.** Meddling by neighbors or others?	yes	no
16.	N	**Negotiation.** Can you work things out when needed?	yes	no
17.	S	**Sex.** Problems with or over?	yes	no
18.	H	**Honesty.** Truthfulness, Unfaithfulness? Trust?	yes	no
19.	I	**Intimacy.** Do you show you care? Telling, feeling?	yes	no
20.	P	**Priorities.** Are yours the same as your mate's?	yes	no

Again, if you marked a whole bunch of yes answers don't get panicky. Keep cool. Hold things in perspective and keep matters to yourself for the time being. Continue on through the entire subject matter of the Marriage Relationship guide and in due course you will gain a better understanding of not only the various basic elements of the puzzle of a marriage relationship, but also you will begin to see how the various components of the marriage relationship concept are intertwined and possibly overlap in your particular instance.

Completion of the quiz brings your first challenge: in order to finish the game, try to get your mate to take the quiz too; otherwise, all you'll have is one-half of the pieces of the puzzle. In order to successfully accomplish the total overview of the status of your marriage relationship, you need to compare your answers with your spouse's responses to see what needs attention. Getting your mate to take the quiz may or may not be easy depending upon the amount of resistance shown, or the possible depth of denial he/she may be in. One defense mechanism that will be explained in detail later in the general codependence section is the old well-worn "don't rock the boat" syndrome, which holds that, no matter how bad things are, don't EVER change anything.

However, with persistence and gentle persuasion, you should eventually be able to overcome any defense mechanisms, and convince your spouse of the value of this Marriage Relationship guide. Eventually, if you hang in there, he/she will agree to look through the quiz. You will succeed.

Here's the problem: As a general rule, the one who invested in this Marriage Enhancement guide is the one who is most troubled about the status of their marriage. Concerned perhaps not only about the way the marriage seems to be going at this time, but also maybe worried about the direction in which their marriage relationship appears to be headed.

But please realize that just because you feel you are having some problems or distress at this time, that does not mean that your marriage partner is necessarily also unhappy to any extent. A very real possibility exists that your spouse might be quite delighted with the way his/her own life and marriage is going at this stage of the game, okay, maybe selfishly.

There is a real chance they may be quite unaware of your concern and unhappiness. This is what you are going to have to communicate to him/her in due course. In the correct manner. We'll get to that process.

Once both of you have taken the quiz, you can then match the two lists of answers and see just how different or alike they are. As mentioned earlier, there are almost always surprises in store when you begin comparing your list of responses with your spouse's and frequently some real eye-opening hidden or unrecognized areas of conflict can surface.

Another typical and usual advantage of taking the Marriage Relationship quiz is that, through the process of self-examination and the eventual comparison process of your two responses to the quiz, you will also both be able to see how very many positive things you have going for you as a couple.

Build on strengths.

Knowledge is power.

Now that you know what issues are bothering you, and you also know what issues are troubling your marriage partner, all you folks need now are some answers and an offering of some of the possible interventions or solutions to solve your problems.

Looking down the road a little, if you find yourselves to be at an impasse and decide to try some professional marriage counseling, you would already know which issue or issues are/were causing trouble because you have taken the Quiz. Actually the only reason a distressed couple would need some professional counseling help would be to assist them negotiate a solution to a problem or series of problems which the couple simply could not resolve by themselves. The counselor wouldn't have to go through the "What seems to be the matter?" routine, and have to spend his time and the client's money probing around trying to wade through all the typically frivolous "presenting" complaints.

Briefly explained, the process of "presenting" is a well-known defense mechanism people use to explain their reasoning or behavior, hoping or thinking that the prima facie excuse will be accepted as the whole truth.

For example, when asked why one seeks a divorce, the complainant replies "Oh, s/he's an alcoholic, you know." Or "S/he can't handle money." Or "S/he is too messy around the house." Or "I had to get a haircut" Or "My car isn't running very good." Or "I just didn't have a decent thing to wear." Or . . . or . . . or . . . , etc., etc., ad infinitum.

A complete list of the silly presenting complaints people offer as excuses would be far too long to include in this text, but you do get the idea don't you? And again, this is just an early brief explanation of the concept of presenting. A full and detailed explanation of the defense mechanism known as presenting will be given later in the N stands for 'Negotiation' section.

"Presenting" complaints, or excuses, are usually or even often true to some extent, but any competent counselor will never accept at face value in initially "presented" excuse as the real or total explanation for errant behavior or marital distress. A capable therapist will always continue with further questioning, trying to find out if other core problems exist which are, deep down, the real cause of the strife.

In the jargon of the counseling profession, the procedure of not accepting the initially presented complaint and pressing on is known as "peeling the onion." This process, often teary, consists of wading through all the presented material to at least see if there is not some serious underlying problem. Every once in a while the early "presented" complaints turn out to be the whole truth of the matter. Occasionally.

But that's what you could have to do, pass through any "presented" excuses or reasons for not addressing and solving a problem, and "peel your own onion." Stay with the conversation over time so that eventually the REAL reason for reluctance or perhaps even obstinacy can be discovered, and at that point a happy resolution of the problem can be in sight.

Your investment in and use of this Marriage Enhancement Guide will speed up the professional marriage counseling process should you decide to go that route, and your counseling efforts should be even more successful, and brief.

Before moving into the solution phase, here is a very important chapter, Chapter Seven, which will enable you to visually see just how your own game of life and marriage is going. In the event you don't recall how terribly important it is that you make your marriage live and work, go back and take a look at Chapter Two, which contains a brief outline of some of the terrible things that happen to people who fall into the divorce pool, and drown.

SEVEN

The Game of Life, and of Marriage

As mentioned earlier in this book, the inspiration for the Marriage Relationship program came like a bolt from the blue one evening while watching a television game show. That sudden revelational insight produced the idea, the realization that a marriage relationship is a contract between two people made up of a series of 20 different parts and considerations. Each of the 20 components maintains its own identity, but at the same time, many of the 20 separate categories of concern can be intertwined with each other.

As a result of your going through the quiz for the first time, you rather quickly identified which issues in your own mind seemed to be troublesome or of concern to you. Then when your spouse went through the quiz s/he too marked those issues or categories of concern which seemed troubling for him/her. Undoubtedly some of the answers were easy to record, while other questions made you pause and think a bit before circling the "yes" or "no." You did notice that there is no "perhaps" column or grading of the severity of a problem embodied in that simple first quiz. Each one of the 20 categories of concern is either a problem at this time or it is not a problem. Period.

However, realistically speaking, the severity or amount of mental distress caused by a particular problem is important. Some problems hurt so bad that they can't be tolerated, while others are in a more minor, or personally aggravating class. Thus, the simple yes or no answer is very important to identify exactly what concerns or problems may exist. Then comes the need to grade or measure the level of your personal upset or anguish over each particular issue on which you marked a "yes."

Following is what is known as a "Likert-scale" type review of the basic quiz which is designed to help you grade the amount of distress you feel on each question you marked "yes."

Please let me suggest that you take this book to a copy shop and also make several copies of this "Likert-style" quiz for your future use.

Obviously a problem which seems earth-shattering at this point in time could just go away or diminish in severity, perhaps through your using newly learned negotiation techniques. Sometimes problems just go away on their own. Often the aging or developmental process solves problems. Never forget that "Murphy's Law" is alive and well ("If anything can possibly go wrong it will."), and unfortunately, sometimes an issue, which was not of great concern a while ago, will, later on, become more serious and of more importance. So, realistically, you can work to solve the problems that exist now and succeed, only to find, in later days, another bone of contention has appeared and the new one is now of significant concern to you. That's life.

It is written somewhere that life is not full of problems, rather, life IS problems.

So, take the original quiz from page 49, review the answers you marked a "yes," and grade the severity of those problem areas. Locate the same question on this quiz, and note the amount of your stress, or distress in the four categories listed. Once again I suggest that this little quiz be done alone and in pencil, either on the copy shop duplicate or a separate piece of paper, so you can erase and/or change the answers as solutions resolve existing problems.

Once this quiz is finished you should have a pretty good idea not only what problems exist in your marriage relationship, but also which ones hurt the worst.

Generally speaking the pattern in psychotherapy is to resolve the least critical problem(s) first. The thinking is that you will undoubtedly succeed rather quickly in solving the pesky and rather minor areas of conflict. Then, since nothing succeeds like success, you will be better able to attack the major battles at a later time when you have more experience in problem-solving. But, if the "easiest issues first" system doesn't seem to want to work, tackle any problem you want, and begin to get some relief from your severe mental discomfort. The importance of gaining relief and some peace of mind cannot be understated.

Balance in life is everything. Therefore I suggest you memorize and recite the famous "Serenity Prayer" on a regular basis. Here it is:

> Lord Give Me The Serenity To
> Accept Things I Cannot Change,
> The Courage to Change
> The Things I Can,
> And The Wisdom To
> Know The Difference.

A word of caution: Do not focus too heavily on one or the other issues which are troubling you. Keep in mind that how you feel today or the day you ran through the quiz is only the way you feel today, or that day. Maybe you will feel differently about that particular issue or problem at a later date because changes have come to pass not only in your own way of thinking, but also because of the ever-changing conditions in which we live.

Another word of caution: Please remember, that in the Marriage Relationship puzzle, the various issues come in differing levels of importance. Some things in life are more important than others.

Obviously, as mentioned earlier, the

LIKERT-STYLE PROBLEM SEVERITY GRADING SCALE

The Problem With:	A Little Annoying	Quite Aggravating	Makes You Very Angry	Is Totally Intolerable
Money	_____	_____	_____	_____
Anger	_____	_____	_____	_____
Relatives	_____	_____	_____	_____
Reversals	_____	_____	_____	_____
Integrity	_____	_____	_____	_____
Abuse	_____	_____	_____	_____
Codependence	_____	_____	_____	_____
Energy	_____	_____	_____	_____
Respect	_____	_____	_____	_____
Expectations	_____	_____	_____	_____
Living	_____	_____	_____	_____
Addiction	_____	_____	_____	_____
Time	_____	_____	_____	_____
Intrusions	_____	_____	_____	_____
Outsiders	_____	_____	_____	_____
Negotiation	_____	_____	_____	_____
Sex	_____	_____	_____	_____
Honesty	_____	_____	_____	_____
Intimacy	_____	_____	_____	_____
Priorities	_____	_____	_____	_____

time will come for you and your marriage partner to sit down and go over each other's initial quiz results, (page 49) and the problem-gradation (Likert-scale) results too (page 55). When you do, prepare yourself for some surprises.

Plan, and firmly resolve not to be hurt or become angry when you find out what it is you should already have known about your mate but didn't, especially about the way s/he thinks.

Special note should be taken of those questions on which you both marked a "yes" as a answer, because those are very important areas of common concern and issues which need your early if not immediate joint attention.

Please, at this juncture, recall in the introduction that I freely admitted this is your typical male (Martian) problem-solving approach to a marriage relationship. For the obvious reason: I am a male, and we males tend to think we have to solve problems.

Many of the other self-help products now advertised in print and on television deal to a good extent with the communication and emotional aspects of marriage, viz. love and affection. Since most likely the two of you got married in the first place because you were in love, some attention needs to be given to the subject of love. In life, as in taking a test, your first guess was probably right, so when you picked _____ to be your life-partner and spouse, the chances are you were right when you picked him. Therefore, one could logically assume that if you can only get the darn problems solved in your marriage, the emotional love you felt so deeply for each other in the beginning will quickly return.

One famous psychotherapy technique that will get mentioned again is called "prescribing the symptom" in which at the end of a marriage counseling session the therapist gives the couple a "homework" assignment prescribing that they shall absolutely NOT have any sexual contact until the next session. However, they are to assume the same type of courtship-type lifestyle which they enjoyed in the early days of their relationship. The "salad" days.

The therapist, maintaining a straight face, suggests that the couple go out to dinner, go to shows, have quiet nights together, just the two of them, no kids, give each other back-rubs, front-rubs, whatever, and so on, but absolutely NO "hanky-panky." As you can guess, the couple comes back the next week and sheepishly admit they had broken the therapist's assignment, and they had engaged in some sexual activity. Drat. Oh, well . . . any port in a storm, I always say.

Here is a thoughtful contribution towards the issue of "love":

Love

Dr. Aaron Beck points out in his great book, titled *Love Is Never Enough,* that love as a normal human emotional response is a very wispish, elusive and wayward emotional response and, at best, depends upon each individual's thoughts and conditions. Love is, of course, the basic cornerstone of a marriage relationship. Without love, and except for considerations of companionship and conformity sought by some, why would anyone ever get married in the first place? Then answer this: How could anyone ever negotiate the issue of love? Two people can usually eventually agree or come to a compromise on a troublesome day-by-day problem, but how in the world could two people ever simply "agree" to be in love?

Love, as the concept pertains to a marriage relationship, is described as normally existing in two stages. The first stage is known as "romantic" love, which probably doesn't need much explanation. The other stage is known as "conjugal" love, which is the long-lasting respect and concern that a couple hopefully develops for each other later in their lives. Conjugal love is really the ultimate goal of any marriage, and is the sought-after love-state for which everyone is really striving whether they know it or not.

Of the several fine offerings of help or guidance available to couples at this time in history with regard to the emotional status known as "love," immediate reference must be made to Dr. John Gray's great and inspired book, *Men Are From Mars, Women Are From Venus*, which should be required reading for all married couples, and most definitely for any person planning marriage.

In the first few pages of his book Dr. Gray hits on what is perhaps the basic reason for conflict between males and females in a marriage relationship. It is his astute observation that much of the cause of marital misunderstanding and conflict centers on the differences between men and women with regard to how problems are handled, and the widely differing manners of communication, often faulty, between the partners.

Doctor Gray points out very quickly that males think they are put on earth to solve problems, everybody's problems. And to complicate matters, males do not want to and often will simply refuse to talk about problems. Especially their own.

Most males have been taught as little boys that big boys don't ever talk about their problems, or cry. Just wait a minute until you hear what males do about their problems—you won't believe it.

Females on the other hand want and need to talk about their problems, all their problems, and when they have them all talked out, extensively, they will arrive at their own decisions. That is why females talk to each other so much. Who else are they going to talk to? Their husbands? Forget it.

Trouble can easily erupt in a marriage relationship when the Lady Of The House tries to talk to her husband about a problem she has. This is normal behavior for her. But once she begins talking HE thinks he not only has to come up with a decision, but also, he has to come up with the right decision rather quickly or he will "lose face," and his status as the strong, omnipotent, always-correct, manly, all-knowing and virile male will be in serious jeopardy, and his precious male ego could be tarnished. Thou shalt not dally with the male ego.

More trouble comes up when the male has a problem, and since males don't talk about their problems with anyone, they will suddenly turn deaf and dumb and won't say a word. Women don't understand this turn of events at all since they always want and need to talk about their problems, so why doesn't he want to talk to her about his problems, and let her help him?

"You never talk to me," she says, which is both a correct observation and normal for males as far as problems are concerned. But then she tends to go a step further and thinks, perhaps even says, "(Since you won't talk to me about your problem,) "you don't love me any more."

Wait a minute!

"Love" has nothing to do with the way males think and react, and it is this default in the male psyche and behavioral manner that drives women absolutely out of their minds.

Doctor Gray further observes that when a male has a problem and turns deaf and dumb, he will "go into his cave," where he will remain until he has come to some sort of acceptable solution. Upon arriving at his solution he will emerge from his cave and will then, and only then, talk about the problem as if it were history, which it is.

Another big area of trouble in a marriage, according to Dr Gray is that a wife feels that it is her function in life and in her marriage relationship to help her man all she can, and therefore the Lady Of The House has an obligation to offer copious suggestions, lots of advice and supposedly constructive comments to her man. But the man takes the woman's suggestions and advice as criticism and as a direct attack on his ability to function as a typical highly intelligent, clever, all-knowing, gifted, macho, strong, problem-solving male; and of course there's hell to pay for that.

An amusing side-reference Dr. Gray points out is that:

Males think: "If it ain't broke, don't fix it."

Females think: "If it ain't broke, how wonderful, but let me help you, and together, we'll make it better."

Here's another problem that causes trouble in marriages, and again, it has to do with the way problems are approached.

Women are more concerned with emotions and feelings than men, and while they are talking and talking about a problem, what they are doing is probing and examining the possible emotional and relational outcome of a decision they may make. Then after they have delved into and examined all the possible eventual personal consequences, they will arrive at their practical solution.

Men, on the other hand, will tend to deal initially with the practicalities of life, and solve their problem before they can or will delve into any consideration of the emotional or relational outcome of their decision. Such is the stuff of marital conflict. This concept might not be completely clear, so here's a different way to say it:

Women first consider relational consequences, that is, how a possible decision will affect others, then come to what she feels is her best conclusion all things considered.

Men first find a solution, act on it, then after they've "made their move," figure (find) out how big a mess they have made and what the relational fallout of their decision might be. Or, how many people are mad at them.

Any way that's written it still sounds like trouble. Too much cannot be said about Dr.

Gray's wonderful book and as mentioned before, this author would strongly advise each and every married person or persons planning marriage to get and read *Men Are From Mars, Women Are From Venus*. Doctor Gray also has other books which are very appropriate to the establishment and nourishment of a marriage relationship.

Still other fine works are available at this time which can and will help in establishing a sound marriage relationship. To mention just a few, are the works of Barbara DeAngelis, Wayne Dyer, Gary Smalley and Robert Schuller.

We close this chapter with words of caution and encouragement: Don't think that just because you have identified what seems to be a lot of problems in your marriage relationship that a divorce is inevitable. Divorce is rarely the most viable solution to a condition of marital strife. We promised earlier to tell you what the three valid reasons to divorce are, and not necessarily in order of importance, they are:

1. Abuse. Any physical or sexual, and prolonged mental abuse.

2. Infidelity, that can't be stopped or tolerated.

3. Total incompatibility. They waited too long to get help.

Each of these three disastrous situations will be fully examined and explained later in the *Solutions* section.

The syndicated columnist L. M. Boyd authors a daily column of wit, trivia and wisdom which appears in many newspapers in the United States and this is an exact recitation of one of his recent quips:

> Item # 888C in our Love and War man's file on Divorce is the observation of Barbara Ehrenreich, the literary social activist: "For women, divorce can be the gateway to destitution. For men, it is more likely to be a golden parachute to freedom."

I might add that an article in *Time* magazine (April, 1996) authored by this same Ms. Ehrenreich was titled "In Defense of Splitting Up" clearly defending the present-day "Let's get a divorce" theme so prevalent.

But for now, in an effort to dispel any remaining thoughts that getting a divorce is a smart thing to do, and the only course of action to solve marital problems, please refer back again to Chapter Two, "The Wages of Divorce," which discusses in some detail some of the many downside results of a divorce.

SOME POSSIBLE SOLUTIONS AND INTERVENTIONS

A BRIEF INTRODUCTION TO SOLUTIONS AND INTERVENTIONS

Before launching into the solution phase of this endeavor, a little time and space should be inserted at this point to include some sort of common-sense disclaimer, and to add some thoughts about what some of the key personal requirements (elements) will be required for you to have success in enhancing, or in fact saving your marriage.

To begin with, all that realistically be accomplished in this section is to suggest or offer some or a few of the many possible remedies for the various sources of marital discord. By no means are these suggestions the ONLY answers available to solve problems.

Hopefully, the solutions we offer will solve the problem(s), but if they don't, or won't then our next hope is that the lesson will be learned and you will begin to think for yourself in a positive manner, and persist in your search for the remedies to problems. Don't give up. Keep thinking of alternative ways to solve the problem until you hit on the right one, and find the course of action that works.

Nobody in the entire world can positively tell someone else how to solve an interpersonal conflict. A solution that worked for one couple may not work in your situation. All you can do is try some possible remedies until you find the one that works . . . for you.

Remember this: Achieving the solution to a problem doesn't always mean getting your own way! Often, the most suitable solution found is a compromise.

Now, three other important behavioral considerations before we begin with the listing of possible solutions:

1. Be mentally flexible. No matter which of you has come down with a case of inflexibility, persist, don't give up.
2. Pay close attention to the later section, N Stands for 'Negotiation.'
3. Realize that it takes time to work out problems. Sometimes lots of time. So be patient.

So, here comes the *Solutions* section.

M

Stands for 'MONEY'

Of all the problems we have as couples, and as individuals, for that matter, the issue of money, both from an "amount-of" and management points of view, can be a huge concern. Trouble over money may well be the biggest root-cause of divorce in many marriage relationships. One doesn't run into very many people with too much money, but probably those few who have all the money they need or want still have troubles over financial matters. For purposes of our Marriage Relationship discussion and concerning the subject of money, we shall assume that if you have a financial problem it isn't either because you have too much, or have a firm lock on how to handle your family finances. Probably one or both of those defaults are in play. It is written somewhere: "Show me a happy person and I'll show you a person either with too much money or a screw loose."

As mentioned earlier in the "Definitions" section, how lucky we are that the subject of money comes up first, because I know from my many years as a family banker, helping families with their financial problems, that money problems are one of the easiest areas of family conflict to work with and to solve. Given, of course, the presence of the previously listed attributes, viz. mental flexibility, the ability to negotiate and compromise, and mutual possession of the basic intelligence and common sense it takes to understand and accept the fact that most change comes gradually. Unfortunately, there are some folks who simply cannot or will not yield an inch in their thought processes. Getting them to change their way of thinking about money matters is about the same as trying to nail Jello to the wall.

There are no studies which provide any statistical verification of this fact, but in my own experience of helping families with their finances for over 35 years, when a family came in for financial help and guidance, I automatically knew that some level of marital troubles followed hard on the heels of their money problems. Sometimes, it worked the other way around too. In any marriage, money is a lousy way to keep score.

Later experience lecturing in local high

school class rooms on the subject of family money management truly reinforced that conclusion. I would always begin the discussion by asking the students, "What do your parents argue about the most?" The answer was nearly always, money. Ah, the painful honesty of the young. My point, of course, being the information that was about to be imparted to them was of utmost importance to these young people whose lives lay before them.

The way our loan application process worked, and this situation might well apply to you, is that one of the marriage partners would realize more than the other that their family finances were not at all in good shape. After some family consultation, one of them would call, or the couple would come in together and seek our professional help with their money problems.

Occasionally, one marriage partner would strike out on his own in a search for answers. Often this unilateral action taken by one partner would initially upset the other person, but once the reluctant person found out that he wasn't under personal attack, or under any obligation, tempers which once flared became more calm. Chaotic financial conditions once accepted as being inevitably out of control were viewed in a more constructive fashion, and in need of some measure of adjustment and control, adjustment with regard to a fair allocation of funds, and control with regard to by whom and how the monies are spent.

At that point, once the marriage partners both got on the same page, as the saying goes, then typically both would join in the normal application and education process necessary to complete their transition to a reasonable and workable financial status.

We began the process of finding out, or trying to find out, how they got into financial troubles, by assuming that one of the two, or sometimes both of the following "rules" were in place and operational at the time they applied for the loan, to wit:

Rule #1. If there are family money problems, usually, but not always, the papa in the family is handling the money. For some reason yet to be determined, as a general rule the wife in the family will handle the money better than the husband, the "who" part of the money management puzzle.

Rule #2a. There is simply not enough money coming in, and/or

Rule #2b. If apparently there is enough money coming into the family coffers, according to our budget computations which will be covered directly, then comes the question, how or in what manner is the money being (mis)handled? The "how" part of the family's money management puzzle.

This chapter is going to proceed in the same manner as if you, the reader, came to our financial institution looking for guidance with regard to money management, or to make an application for funds to solve a money problem through debt restructuring. Bill consolidation, in other words. The basic principle which always existed when we set out to restructure a family's debts involved our concern about which of the money management mistake or mistakes listed above caused the trouble in the first place.

Unless care is taken to solve the management mistakes at the same time, simply restructuring the debt may only make an already poor situation worse. We used to say that unless we were careful, a debt consolidation loan could amount to taking a whole bunch of small unmanageable bills and lumping them into one big backbreaking monthly obligation. All well and good, but the reason(s) for the financial problems must also be addressed and corrected, and if they weren't or couldn't be solved, we wouldn't make the loan. We would complete their budgeting plan, and reluctantly send them on their way with our best wishes and the offer of further counseling.

The first step in the process, and the step which the client didn't seem to welcome, for obvious reasons, involved developing a comprehensive outline of their present debt and payment obligation levels by listing all of their bills and the amount of every payment due on each obligation.

The simple form for this initial process looked like this, and you can easily make your own form on a piece of paper:

Et cetera, on as long a piece of paper as needed.

Once the list of debts and obligations was complete, the next logical step in the loan application process involved inquiry to find out what the basic financial needs of the family happened to be, and then to find out the answer to the question: Is Rule 1 (who is handling the money) or Rule 2 (how is the money being handled) in full force and effect? We tried to accomplish this goal without appearing to be launching a personal attack on one of the marriage partners, but obviously, we were seriously trying to discover the causes of the family's financial woes.

The possibility certainly exists that money troubles and financial distress can come about through channels and in ways that are not of the person or family's choosing. Sometimes events happen in a family's life which bring about necessary but nonetheless disastrous expenses. Overwhelming medical bills, financial losses, or other family obligations, such as care of an aging parent, and God-only-knows what other variety of assorted personal disasters and conditions can be unwanted root causes of financial difficulty. But, as a general rule, as mentioned earlier, the applicant's money troubles were almost always caused either by a shortage of dollars to meet the family's

Creditor	Total Owed	Monthly Payment	Security
	Total	Total	

needs, or simple mismanagement of funds. We used to tell people that if they didn't think anybody cared about them, just skip a couple payments. Most already knew this.

Over the years, as we developed this procedure for helping families, the need for an understandable model of a family budget for people to live with became apparent, so we began to search for such a reasonable and workable budget form. Our search was to no avail, because all the budgets we examined were either far too complicated and complex, or too simple and inadequate. The only course was to develop our own budget plan, which was eventually accomplished from two sources; one was by using viable parts of existing budgets, the other was a trial and error process as we personally set up our own family finances.

The final budget which we ended up with is included in this text just a bit later, and this budget is the result of that research and subsequent personal use by my own family for over a decade. Therefore, I know that this budget works, but hasten to point out that the percentage figures, as presented in the form, are certainly arbitrary. Some families have different needs, priorities and obligations than others, so to say that "x" is the only percentage or amount of expenditure possible, or to be allowed for a specific category of expense is just not realistic. The "different strokes for different folks" rule is alive and well.

Family differences aside, however, when you look at the budget format you will see that the family expenses are divided into three categories and they are:

FIXED EXPENSES, which are expenses that must be paid every month, such as rent, (house payment) utilities, food and so on.

VARIABLE EXPENSES, are amounts that need to be spent and provided for, but which are purchases or expenditures that need not be made every month. For example, clothing is certainly a necessity, but typically the purchase of the attire can be delayed to a later and more convenient time.

FAMILY EXPENSES, which are items of expense that are completely discretionary and may not ever need to be spent at all, although they should be included, in order to have a well-rounded family life. There is more to life than working and paying bills.

As mentioned above, the first step in figuring out a family's budget is to ascertain where and how you are presently spending your family money. There is a place somewhere in the budget for every possible way for a family to spend the family money, so if the clear-cut category doesn't seem to jump out at you or you have an area of expense that isn't specifically named, simply use the "other" category listed at the end of the variety of expenses. For example, a monthly amount owed for the care of an aging parent in a nursing home is not specifically listed because such cost is not a typical "fixed" family expense, but rather an isolated burden for a particular family. Be sure that every expense that your family has is included somewhere and taken into consideration.

By the way, don't bother keeping track

of every penny, as the saying goes; just keep track of the dollars and round the figures one way, up or down, to the nearest dollar.

Mention must be made that this budget is based on a twelve month-per-year basis. If you get paid weekly, multiply the weekly pay x 52 and divide by 12. Multiplying your weekly pay amount x 4 is not quite close enough to arrive at a monthly figure since 4 x 12 = 48 and there are 52 weeks in a year which is almost a 10% time variation. Obviously, semi-monthly and monthly pay periods are easy to work with.

So now comes the first step on the road to financial stability, figuring out where your money is going at this time. Please note that the form on page 70 is a dual-use form and all you are trying to do at this point is to figure out and fill in the present monthly costs in each category. Later, when the new ideal dollar budgetary amounts have been computed you can go back and use the far right column titled "Proposed" monthly costs and fill in those projected amounts. You will then be working toward reaching your all-inclusive balanced family budget.

The easiest way to ascertain the amounts spent in each category is to either refer to the checkbook records, receipts, or perhaps inquire from the various vendors how much money you have spent with them in the past year or so. Most service facilities such as utility companies will know this amount. If you don't have any records, just take a good guess at the amount.

Between the two of you, it shouldn't be too hard to come up with fairly accurate estimates of your family expenses. Of course if you find in the coming months that your estimates are too far off the mark, then you can re-adjust the monthly budget amounts to come closer to the reality of your situation.

By the way, the form on the following page would also be a good one to take to the copy shop and get several copies made for future use.

Now the final piece of your present-day puzzle: What's your TOTAL PRESENT FAMILY NET TAKE-HOME (after taxes and deductions) income? $_____

(Combine your net incomes if you have more than one paycheck.)

A quick comparison of the difference between your net family income versus the net family expenditures from the form on page 70 will give you a comparison and appraisal of your family's present financial health. Too frequently I saw a situation wherein more money was spent or promised each month than was being earned, which then prompted overview and suggested changes of some of the amounts of expenditure.

If you wonder how anyone could spend more than they earn, don't forget the credit card debt now at all-time highs in this country. In these financially chaotic days, many ethics advocates seriously question the honesty and the good intentions of the banks and financial institutions who mail out unsolicited credit card applications by the millions. Please recall the earlier statement; money trouble equals family trouble almost every time. To encourage and facilitate people's going

MONTHLY EXPENDITURE SCHEDULE

	Present costs:	Proposed costs:
FIXED Family Overhead		
Shelter (rent)	$_____	$_____
Utilities	$_____	$_____
Food	$_____	$_____
Payments	$_____	$_____
Insurance	$_____	$_____
Other	$_____	$_____
Category Total	$_____	$_____
VARIABLE Family Overhead		
Clothing	$_____	$_____
Medical	$_____	$_____
Contributions	$_____	$_____
Savings	$_____	$_____
Other	$_____	$_____
Category Total	$_____	$_____
FAMILY EXPENSES		
Entertainment	$_____	$_____
House Repair, furnishings	$_____	$_____
Auto Expenses	$_____	$_____
Personal (his)	$_____	$_____
Personal (hers)	$_____	$_____
Other	$_____	$_____
Category Total	$_____	$_____
TOTAL OF ALL CATEGORIES	$_____	$_____

into debt, or to gamble funds that could and should be kept for family use, seems to many, including me, to be a morally bankrupt attitude, "presented" claims of free speech and enterprise notwithstanding. Baloney is baloney.

Did you know that it is now possible to gamble "on-line," and by giving them your credit card number you can (and will) quickly hit your maximum debt limit! Instant debt. Instant disaster. No wonder personal bankruptcies are also at an all-time high.

Money Management—Who

Too often at this point came barely shielded criticism by one of the marriage partners of the other partner, but to what avail? I would hasten to point out to the couple that this is a fresh start for them, a new beginning, a chance to restructure their finances and to work together toward a new agreement and to bring new levels of understanding between them for the reasonable and effective management of their family monies.

As mentioned before, usually if there's ample money in the family money pipeline the Daddy will be the manager and have control of the checkbook and manage fund disbursements. When things get a little tight and the money just won't spread itself thin enough, then the Mommy will suddenly get the job. The typical scenario and the reason for this change is because women, as a general rule, are better money managers than men. Sorry boys, but this is true. Not always, but generally.

If the family is in some financial distress and it is determined that the husband is handling the funds, then one obvious course of action is to effect a change in money management and let the wife have a try at managing the family finances for a while. Once the "who" is decided upon, then comes the question, how, or in what manner, is the family money to be handled? By cash? Checkbook? Credit cards? We shall get to the how of money management directly.

Here's a point to remember: Money equals power. A good deal of time and space are given to the issue of power in the negotiation (N) section, so I won't spend time here with regard to the issue, but the person who is presently handling the family money has some level or degree of power over the other marriage partner. For example, if he is handling the funds and she needs some money for groceries or family expenses, does she have to ask for help? How embarrassing and degrading that must be for her to have to beg for the money to keep the family going.

In the course of those many years I did see a sad thing happen from time to time: The wife would come in to see us with tears in her eyes. "George died," she would say. Husband George was the wise guy who insisted on keeping total control of his family's money. George's poor wife didn't have a clue about how to go forward in her life. "How do I write a check?" she would ask. "How do I make a payment?" Here is another reason for both of the marriage partners sharing management of the family monies. If both marriage partners have a handle on how to manage money, then neither spouse can get caught short when and if something awful happens.

Here's another point: In my long experience working with family money problems, I never saw a family who split up their funds be financially successful. By splitting up the funds I mean that she had "her money," and he had "his money." The very separation of funds indicates in itself an unhealthy split, and a division in the marriage relationship. If such division of funds is, in fact, occurring in your family, this separation of monies should be immediately abandoned. Most certainly, never should the splitting up of funds ever be begun in a brand new family money management plan.

It always was, and is to this day, my firm belief that all family money should be pooled into a joint account, or accounts, with both marriage partners being in agreement as to the allocation for the disbursement of funds. A sound, reasonable and fair plan for the sharing of responsibility, for the spending or disbursement of funds, should also be put in place.

From that point on, responsibility for the actual payment of funds owed and purchases is simply a matter of convenience and personal inclination. Or, who can more easily pay what bills, make needed purchases, and which marriage partner will accept and accomplish the responsibility for the payment of certain debts.

For example, who is to pay the utilities and how? Who makes the car payment(s) and how? Who makes the house payment or rent and how? A simple agreement can surely be made by both marriage partners and then embarked upon at least temporarily to see if the agreement works. If the agreed-upon disbursement plan doesn't seem to work for some reason or the other, then change the plan to that point where the payment of monies can most easily and reliably be accomplished.

Obviously what I am suggesting here is that a partnership be formed to take care of money issues, with both persons being involved as equally as possible, or as personally desired. Isn't it more important that your marriage relationship is a success than being silly and thinking that one person has more power over the other partner because he has control of the cash or the checkbook?

At the same time, changing your family money management process to a new system does not necessarily indicate that the person who was formerly handling the money is a failure. We each have our own strengths and weaknesses. All you are trying to do, when you get right down to it, is to bring about whatever adjustments it takes to gain control over your money problems. So much for the "who" issue. Work it out. Be reasonable.

Money Management—How

The number and combinations of methods for handling family money would be far too extensive to completely cover in the body of this text. The obvious answer to the question of how to handle the family money would be to handle it in the way that works best for your family. It didn't take a lot of brain power to say that, but, to be more constructive, here is a brief overview of several obvious alternatives and a conclusion:

Checkbook

Using only checks as a method of paying all the household bills and expenses simply does not work very well because the number of checks written for small piddley amounts results in a veritable blizzard of checks being written. In my own family I tried this "only check" system for a very brief while, and it was a train wreck. Even the dog was writing checks. But worse, there was no visible control on the amount of money spent on each specific category of expenditure, the fixed, variable and family expenses.

Cash

Paying everything with cash does not seem to work well for most folks for several reasons. Initially there is the danger of loss, theft, and of course it is foolish to send cash through the mail to out-of-town creditors. You could purchase money orders or buy Bank Drafts and pay bills that way. But again, there is no guiding light to tell you when the limits of that particular budgetary item have been reached, and too often cash in the pocket or purse is cash quickly gone.

The Combination Method

Using both cash and some checks in the same system seems to work best for most families. Using their checking account to send a payment to far-away institutions and to pay those obligations for which they wish to have a check as a receipt, and then using a simple cash system to pay for other expenses, works well. A popular method of paying bills that has come to the fore in recent years is the "automatic withdrawal" system wherein the creditor directly bills the customer's checking account each month. The biggest trouble with automatic withdrawal system is the critical need to be sure there are adequate funds in the checking account to cover the charges sent down the line each month. Some people can do this, and some can't.

The biggest advantage of using the combination method is:

- The checking account is easy to keep track of because there really aren't all that many checks written each month, and those that are written can quickly be scanned to see if the amount spent is within the boundaries of your budget limits.

- The cash part is self-policing. And simple. Just wait a minute. In case the concept hasn't grabbed your mind yet, let's just say it outright:

Budgeting involves establishing a system of spending limits.

I would report to you that in my own family my wife handled all our family money using this combination method, and she did a fantastic job. She paid all the "fixed overhead" items by check and handled the "variable" and "family expenses," with a nifty cash system which will be explained in the next paragraph.

Here's how to use cash as the other part of the combination system. It's easy to do, and you can keep good track of each and every expenditure. For each of the remaining "variable" and "family expense" items we took a plain envelope and headed the top of the envelope with the name of the particular category to be funded.

When my wife made a purchase in that

> (sample envelope)
> # Clothing:
> mo.amt. $_____
> Date   to   amt.   bal

category she noted the date of the purchase, where the clothing was purchased, how much was spent, and then kept a descending balance in the far right-hand column. The cash money left in the envelope should be the same as the amount shown in the balance column on the far right side of the envelope. Piece de cake.

It shall be quickly granted that pursuing this envelope system for handling cash calls for a level of compliance, the old "let's give it a try" thing, and enough discipline to stay within the budgeted amounts each week or month. Some people just don't and can't think this way, but those who were able to accept the concept seemed to prosper, and, as I mentioned before, the system worked very well in my own family for many years.

Money Management— Allocation of Funds

At this point in the loan application or financial guidance process, having seen the family's current financial situation, the next step was to figure out some sort of budget for the family, working backwards. The plan was to take their combined net "take home" incomes and apply some rather arbitrary budget percentages to that net amount in this mythical budget so the family would be able to see theoretically how they could handle their funds in a manner that met all their obligations. That would then take the pressure off, and they could stop the interpersonal sparring and bickering that money troubles bring. Please note the word "theoretically" because that is all any early budget plan is: a theory about how the family money might be handled.

To do this yourself on the easy budget form following on page 78 start at the top with the "Fixed" expenses, such as the rent, or house payment, the utilities and so on, then apply the suggested or theoretically possible percentages against your net combined incomes to get some sort of idea how your present financial situation might compare with what could be considered the average family expenditures. Once you have finished those items in the "Fixed" overhead section, continue on to the "Variable Expenses" category.

Please note when working in the variable expense section that the amounts for the various items become more uncertain. For example, how much money do you need to spend on each person in the family to maintain his/her wardrobe in an appropriate manner? What can you do but guess at the estimated amount of medical expense that will come about in the next year? Who knows? Just guess, is about all you can do. And so on with the other categories down the list.

Even though the form doesn't call for it, if you would come up with a sub-total of expenditures at this point, including the known costs in the "fixed," which are fairly easy to get at, and the guessed-at amounts in the "variable" categories, you will know about how much money you have left for the fun category in the budget, aka the "family expenses" section. As said before, "Man nor woman does not live for work and drudgery alone." Both of you marriage partners, and the children too, must have, and are entitled to have some fun out of life.

Probably the smart thing to do to figure out how much money will be left over for the "family expense" department would be to first address the "savings" issue, and say, "We are going to put aside $_____ (fill in some modest amount) each month," then see how much money is left over for the other items listed, such as entertainment, house/furnishings, auto and personal expenses and so on.

Hard news; sometimes the financial pressure is so great in a family's history it is impossible to save any money on a regular basis. If that's the way it is, then that's where it's at. All you can do is wait for expenses to lower, as time goes on, and begin your savings plan at a later date.

Hopefully, your employment situation is providing for retirement funds, and you have IRA and 401k accounts withdrawn from your income. Of course there is the Social Security system too.

So here's what to do next: The two of you sit down together, and, since you know what the fixed monthly obligations are as listed under the "present cost" column on page 78, and you have estimated the amount of money necessary to fund the variable expense items, you can arrive at the estimated amount which is left over and which hopefully will come close to fulfilling everybody's needs and desires in the "family expense" section, taking care to be fair and honest all the while. For example, if Dad gets "x" a week for spending money, then Mom also gets the same "x" a week for her fun and games too.

If you have children and are giving them allowances, be fair and reasonable with them, too, so that not only do you not show favoritism, but also the amount of money each child receives each week or month is realistic and in keeping with your overall financial situation. A lot of teenagers learn about the value of money and work effort in their early years, and many of them hold full- or part-time jobs to provide their own spending money.

Once you have gotten some sort of preliminary figures in all the categories, and everything is totaled, you will be able to see how close the "proposed" or estimated expenditure amounts come to the amount of your total net incomes.

Not infrequently, the amount of money proposed to be spent in the budget exceeds the amount of the incomes. So what to do then? Since the income amount is usually quite firm, go back over the "variable" and "family expense" amounts and see where you can make changes to make the budget balance, or come close to balancing.

I would suggest that you begin the review by looking at the amounts in the "variable" section first because, as a rule, unless you are going to take some really drastic steps like moving to a different home or quit paying the utility company and sit in the dark, you can't do much, if anything, about the "fixed" amounts, so don't worry about them. But if the amounts shown in the "fixed" column are way too far out of line with the "average" level of expense, as reflected in our percentages, then you folks might have to consider taking drastic steps to get your financial situation closer to being realistic.

For example, if our percentages say that with your total income(s) you should be paying somewhere in the area of $750 a month for rent or house payment, and you are trying to pay $2000, then you are faced with a hard decision to solve that cost over-run. Paying too much for housing is known as being "house poor." The same applies to having too high car payments.

An obvious move to balance a family budget is to secure some additional income for the family coffers, either by finding a second job, or if the wife is not working, perhaps she could help out by finding a part-time job which would provide a few hundred dollars a month, and not interfere too severely with her parenting wishes. Frequently I would see where the addition of just a few hundred dollars a month would make a great deal of difference.

From time to time, while consulting families, I would see someone who was holding down two hard jobs, sometimes even three. I never met anybody who could stand all that work. In fact, on some occasions when someone would come in and admit that they were working three jobs I almost always knew I was looking at a walking-talking corpse. It never seemed to fail that unless the amount of work being done was trimmed back to a more reasonable level that person was going to either develop some serious health problems, or die. So, be careful.

From here on, straightening out your financial situation, if indeed it does need tinkering with, is just a process of using good effective communication techniques in a negotiation process. The two of you work together as a team to solve the management "who" and "how" process until you finally get your family budget to balance. Once balanced, and you are able to keep up with the ongoing financial pressures, your marriage relationship will move to a more comfortable level. Remember:

Budgeting Involves Limitations on Spending!

Every family is different and every family financial situation will have its own sets of needs and pressures, so this suggested system of solving family money problems is just that: a suggested method of handling family financial matters.

It is entirely possible that you may not be able to execute this exact budget. But you can do some budget. All that is required is to accept the discipline and spend the time to work out whatever financial plan that will work for you, and then try to live within its limitations. If the first budget won't work, then try another, and another, until you do find one that will work.

On the following page you will find some sample percentages which will give you an idea how some sort of "ideal budget" would look in your case, if your total net take-home pay is $3,000. Obviously, once you have filled in the numbers in the "fixed" category, the rest of the amounts are simply forced to some level of livability.

SAMPLE ESTIMATE PERCENTAGES

Combined total take-home of $3,000 x % = cost goals.

Put your total income(s) here $__3000____

FIXED OVERHEAD:

Shelter: How about	25% (?) x $__3,000____	=	$____750____
Utilities:	8% $____"_____	=	$____240____
* Food	10%x $_____	=	$____300____
Payments:	15% (?) x $____"_____	=	$____450____
Insurance:	5% (?) x $____"_____	=	$____150____
Other:	? x $____"_____	=	$_____

VARIABLE OVERHEAD:

Clothing:	5% (?) x $____"_____	=	$____150____
* Medical:	4% (?) x $____"_____	=	$____120____
Contributions:	3% (?) x $____"_____	=	$_____90____
Savings:	4% (?) x $____"_____	=	$____120____
Other:	? $____"_____	=	$_____

FAMILY EXPENSES

Family Entertainment	5% (?) x $____"_____	=	$____150____
House stuff	5% (?) x $____"_____	=	$____150____
* Car upkeep	5% (?) x $____"_____	=	$____150____
Personal (his)	3% (?) x $____"_____	=	$_____90____
Personal (hers)	3% (?) x $____"_____	=	$_____90____
Other	? $____"_____	=	$_____

Percentage total 100%   Total $____3000____

As you see in that example, the total on the initial budget form did arrive exactly at the $3000 income level. This is the result of forcing the income through the stated percentages. But, there is no escaping that the reality of your own situation might be quite different than those arbitrarily assigned percentages. therefore, revised figures, and amounts, will have to be used.

Asterisks were placed in front of three items to show how variations may exist between families—for example:

Food. It all depends on the size of the family. We had seven children in our family, so our food bill was higher.

Medical. Some people are lucky and have little or no medical expenses. If you are using the "cash envelope method" and everybody stays healthy, money will accumulate in the medical envelope, which is okay, because you never know when you will need to spend it. Excess monies can be transferred and stored in a savings account until they are needed.

Auto. Depends on how many cars are used in the family, what shape they are in, and how far they must be driven each day.

So, here is your own private family budget sheet for you to begin to figure out a budget for your family (See next page). Simply list your own net family income into the appropriate column and see how it comes out. By the way, don't hesitate to take this form to the copy shop and make spares for the future.

Note that the total percentage of money spent cannot exceed the 100% limit. Only the Federal Government can exceed 100%; they have the printing presses to print more money if needed. And you don't have a press that prints money. I hope.

The only way a family can exceed their expenditure levels, as compared with their total income(s), is to transfer excess spending either to unpaid bills around town, to credit card balances or to loans. All three escape plans are flawed, and the latter two will increase the amount due each month in the "Payments" category in the "Fixed" expenses section. Worse, increasing the amount of loan and credit card balances will only reduce the amount of money that can be allocated in other categories. Really what you are doing by charging and borrowing money on credit cards, or through loans, is mortgaging the future.

By the way, a lot of people think that the Federal Government can't mortgage the future with any degree of success either, but time will tell on that one.

It's time to return to the original form that appeared earlier on page 70, titled Monthly Expenditure Schedule, which contains the two columns, Present Monthly Costs and Proposed Monthly Costs. You will see that you have already figured out your monthly expenditure levels at this time. Now you can put in the "proposed" theoretical amounts from the chart on the previous page, once you get the percentages in line with the reality of your situation. If the figures don't jibe close enough, get out your eraser and work with the percentages and amounts until you do get them all to work out.

Final thoughts about money: If you find that you simply cannot solve your

YOUR FAMILY BUDGET
Your net monthly income(s) $_____

FIXED OVERHEAD:	mo. income(s)		
Shelter: How about	25% x	$_____ =	$_____
Utilities:	8% x	$_____ =	$_____
Food:	10% x	$_____ =	$_____
Payments:	15% x	$_____ =	$_____
Insurance:	5% x	$_____ =	$_____
Other:	? x	$_____ =	$_____

VARIABLE OVERHEAD:			
Clothing:	5% x	$_____ =	$_____
Medical:	4% x	$_____ =	$_____
Contributions:	3% x	$_____ =	$_____
Savings:	4% x	$_____ =	$_____
Other:	? x	$_____ =	$_____

FAMILY EXPENSES:			
Entertainment:	5% x	$_____ =	$_____
House stuff:	5% x	$_____ =	$_____
Car upkeep:	5% x	$_____ =	$_____
Personal:(his)	3% x	$_____ =	$_____
Personal:(hers)	3% x	$_____ =	$_____
Other:	? x	$_____ =	$_____
Percentage total:	100%		Total: $_____

financial problems on your own, get help. Many communities have Consumer Credit Counseling services which are usually given free of charge or at a very minimal cost to the client, not only to community residents but also to those who live in the surrounding area as well. That would mean, if you live in a smaller town which is a satellite of a more major city, don't hesitate to contact the Consumer Credit Counseling agency or firm in that larger community.

Generally speaking, at the outset, they figure out the personal or family budget to see how much money is available to retire the bills and debts. Once they have that figure, the next step is to contact the creditors and ask if they will accept a lesser amount than the scheduled payment each month, and can they go to a reduced or no-interest basis until the debtor has his financial situation under control.

Very often creditors will accept the management offer from the credit counseling agency for two reasons. One is they know if they don't go along with the offer, the next thing they probably will get in the mail is a notice of bankruptcy, which usually means the creditor gets little or nothing. The other is that part of the agreement consists of the debtor either assigning his check directly to the credit counseling office, or promising to bring in the paycheck each and every pay-period.

The point in that direct payment to the credit counseling office is that the bills and payments are paid to the creditors directly from the office. Creditors know, with that procedure in place, they will get paid each and every month, and they won't have to continue or resume chasing the debtor as they had in the past. Some people just can't/won't pay their bills on time because often times that's the way they are (slow pay), and the reason they got into financial trouble in the first place is they weren't able to manage their personal finances.

Like General George Custer at the battle of Little Big Horn, they just spent too much time charging around. Which segue leads to a very important part of the agreement between the counseling office and the debtor: NO MORE BILLS AND DEBTS!

The counselors working in these institutions typically are experienced former employees of banks and finance companies. They know how to adjust and work with people's bills, and how to help folks balance their budgets so they can live within their means.

As mentioned above, one of the techniques they use, which would be difficult for an individual to do, is called pro-rating. Pro-rating bills and debts, means that they contact each creditor, and by agreement, partial payments of monthly amounts due are made, usually with reduced or no interest. While this process in effect appears to lengthen the time it takes to get out of debt, such is not always the case because the reduced or no-interest rate on those accounts can make up for a lot of lost time. A good side-effect of using a credit counseling service is that the entire process will tend to preserve a person's good credit rating.

Consumer Credit Counseling services do good work. There is bound to be one somewhere in your area.

Bankruptcy? Only in the MOST extreme circumstances. Lawyers will tell you that bankruptcy is the way to go.

What goes is several thousands of dollars into their pockets. A good bit more will be said about shyster lawyers and the legal profession later on when we get to the O Stands for 'Outsiders' category.

After all is said and done, the true goal, that can't be forgotten or overlooked, is to help you achieve peace and tranquility in a financially troubled marriage relationship, if such is the case. I wish there was a quick and easy way to tell you how to manage your family finances, but there really isn't.

What is so very important to you is to not let a silly thing like having major troubles over money blow away your marriage relationship. There is a solution somewhere. All you have to do is find it.

A

Stands For 'ANGER'

Anger is an emotional response that we sometimes feel when something happens that upsets us. Anger as an emotion can be a fleeting sensation like a sudden flash, or a more deep-seated and longer-lasting emotion, all depending upon several factors.

Before we launch into our investigation of anger as a problem within the scope of a marriage relationship, let's have a quick look at the entire range of human emotional responses so you will have not only some idea of their existence, but also how they fit within all of our lives.

The science of psychology tells us that as humans we have a variety of emotions available to us and, any time someone says that we exhibit seven emotions, someone else will stand up and say, no, there are 12, or 16, or nine or some other number. Be that as it may, let us concern ourselves here with an appropriate explanation of the range of human emotions.

The present-day generally accepted outline, or design, of emotions appeared in 1980 when Robert Plutchik devised his own new scheme or explanation of human emotional responses. It is Robert Plutchik's idea that there are eight primary emotions and eight 'mixed' emotions, and that mixed or blended emotions come about when two primary emotions become combined and spin off a secondary, or mixed emotion. By using the word "mixed" he doesn't mean "confused," as could be the connotation from the old saying that someone had "mixed emotions" about something which meant they really didn't know for sure just exactly how they felt about a certain issue. But by mixing two emotions together a different emotion is produced. For example mixing the colors green and blue yields the color yellow.

Plutchik's emotional design idea looks like this:

Primary emotion Mixed emotion

1. Joy
    \
     plus - yields - 1. Love
    /
2. Acceptance
    \

plus - yields - 2. Submission
  /
3. Fear
  \
   plus - yields - 3. Awe
  /
4. Surprise
  \
   plus - yields - 4. Disappointment
  /
5. Sadness
  \
   plus - yields - 5. Remorse
  /
6. Disgust
  \
   plus - yields - 6. Contempt
  /
7. Anger
  \
   plus - yields - 7. Aggressiveness
  /
8. Anticipation
  \
   plus - yields - 8. Optimism
  /
1. Joy (again)

The circle is then closed so that all the primary emotions listed in the left hand column, when combined with the primary emotion either above or below in the same column, result in the secondary or mixed emotion appearing in the right hand column.

For example, look at the list again and you can see that: Primary 'Joy' + 'Acceptance' = the 'mixed' emotion called 'Love'. Farther down the list, primary 'Disgust' + 'Anger' = 'Contempt'.

Although Dr. Plutchik did not seem to advance this aspect of his paradigm, a case might possibly be made that says if you combine two adjacent mixed emotions in the right hand column, they produce the primary emotion between them in the left hand column. For example: Mixed emotions: 'Love' + 'Submission' yields the primary emotion of 'Acceptance'. Mixed emotions: 'Submission' + 'Awe' yields the primary emotion of 'Fear'.

Perhaps more to the point, the mixed emotion of **contempt** plus **aggressiveness** yields **anger.** Can it not be then, that this emotion with which we grapple, anger, results from those two mixed emotions? As splendid as the idea is, we can't spend much time with Plutchik's emotional design layout, but, without question, he invested a good bit of effort and thought into his concept and is the leader in this field.

We are concerned with the emotion of anger as a primary emotion as it comes into play in a marriage relationship from two points of view, one being to look into the reasons that might exist which caused the anger, the second point obviously being to offer some alternative possibilities to mitigate or control the amount of anger to more tolerable levels.

Or, said perhaps more clearly: a) how to avoid being angry, and b) but if one is angry, how to control and confine the emotion to the specific issue at hand. Sometimes when a person is angry s/he has a right to be furious, but not the right to be cruel. And, that's what we want to work on.

As a matter of definition, anger, as used in this context, does not include those minor upsets which will inevitably occur in every marriage relationship. Any two people who are trying to live and work together, raise a family and do all the other things we have to do, are bound to have disagreements and differences of opinion, simply from the normal clashing of their individual and differing personalities, characters and temperaments. As mentioned earlier, everybody is entitled to a good "whine" once in a while, and sometimes airing a difference of opinion via a sudden burst of anger can prove in the long run to be a bonding event.

Anger as a personal emotion, and the tendency to quickly feel and express anger, can stem from not only a person's in-born temperament, (emotional responses) but also his pre-marital or codependent experiences as a child and young adult. However, it must be admitted that almost everyone can be driven to feel and express anger, possibly with justification, if some event, comment or circumstance happens that upsets him.

Doctor Harriet G. Lerner, has written an easy-to-read book on the subject of anger titled *The Dance of Anger* (1985), and anyone troubled with deep feelings of unremitting anger which are difficult to control should not hesitate to get and read her fine book. I might mention that her work is aimed, to a good extent, at women's issues and the problems many women have in dealing with their own anger.

Everybody has the right, and perhaps even the personal obligation, to get angry when his personal integrity and rights are unfairly violated. However, problems and troubles can come to pass if someone who could be said to be "hot tempered," too quickly expresses his anger over relatively minor incidents or perceived transgressions.

Anger can assume several paths in expression, ranging from smoldering silent submission through emotional distancing, which can be known as the "silent treatment," through ineffective constant bickering, fault-finding and endless criticism, to fighting, and other out-of-control displays. One way some folks avoid addressing the anger-producing issue is to engage in fighting about the wrong topics, and even petty retaliation of one type of another.

Just in passing, I must mention that someone who displays too much of the "silent treatment" could possibly have a personality disorder known as being passive/ aggressive (P/A). A person with P/A strives to achieve his goals and demonstrates his aggressiveness by assuming a posture of passive submissiveness. I know that sounds backwards, but the passive/aggressive personality disorder is not uncommon.

An example would be the person who, in the course of a heated discussion, would suddenly become silent and sulk or pout. His behavior and perceived disapproval would be obvious, and he quickly dampens the conversation and thereby gains the control he sought. The P/A personality disorder is all about control.

The bottom line on anger is to somehow figure out the answers to these questions: What are you angry about? Whose problem is the anger anyhow? And how is the anger being expressed?

As opposed to the passive-aggressive approach used by some, other folks are temperamentally inclined to "let it all hang out," "go bananas" and throw a tantrum. The excessive display of emotion will usually not only fail to solve the problem, but worse, all the screaming or shouting may work in reverse, so the person who is so terribly angry and puts on all this show will not only discredit himself, and his own integrity, but also can diminish or make to appear foolish whatever issue it is he is so upset about. Losing control in a fit of anger can be a very embarrassing and degrading experience.

In her book, Dr. Lerner compares an unhappy and angry married couple to a man and woman dancing together wildly and endlessly in a circle. For example, she nags because he drinks, so he drinks because she nags, so she nags because he drinks, so he drinks because she nags; around and around they go.

The number of issues that could cause such circular strife between a husband and wife is almost unlimited, but whatever the cause of the disagreement may be, once the dance of anger is begun, around and around they go, whirling mindlessly to the same inane tune (theme), with no end or resolution in sight. Who is right, or who is wrong? What difference does it make anyhow, since the goal is to reduce the anger between them and return their marriage relationship to a more balanced state.

Speaking of dancing, anyone who has ever danced in "ballroom" style with another person knows full well that a sudden change in steps or a misstep taken by one of the dancing partners will confuse the other person and the dance is interrupted, and will stop, at least for a time. Please keep this notion in mind because the way to stop any "dance of anger" is embodied in that metaphor.

Reasons For Anger

Without going into a lengthy explanation of the many possibilities for anger to appear in varying degrees in a marriage relationship, may I direct your attention to the main causes of anger between married couples.

Usually the reason for anger in a marriage relationship is because one of the marriage partners becomes dissatisfied with the other marriage partner's behavior, bearing, or perceived failing or shortfall, and sets out to change that marriage partner by using his/her own anger as the tool to bring about the desired modification. Using anger to try to affect someone else's behavior is impossible, because—and please keep this in mind—nobody ever changes anybody else unless that person wants to change. If there are changes to be made, they must somehow be made by the one who is angry.

To paraphrase Dr. Lerner, people, especially in a marriage, seem to come in two speeds: over-functioners and under-functioners. (Is this the "opposites attract" thing again?) From the woman's point of view we come to a split, a dichotomy, if you will, because Dr. Lerner points out that through the centuries women have been socialized and brought up as little girls to be the less dominant under-functioning partner in a marriage relationship. But at the same time girls, later-to-be wives, have been taught (socialized) and are expected to be the emotional over-functioners in their marriage relationship.

In the case of the male, the exact

reverse circumstance is expected: Males observe the behaviors of their father and mother as children, and are socialized in those younger years to expect to be the dominant over-functioning partner in their own eventual marriage. At the same time males are taught as children not to be emotionally responsive, so they become emotional under-functioners.

This brief chart will clearly show the conflict that exists in the modern-day Marriage Relationship schema:

From the male point of view, anger can develop because of what seems to the male to be a steady stream of constant criticism and haranguing by the woman of the house on some aspects of the male's behavior or persona. As is so beautifully explained by Dr. John Gray in his book, this feminine "correctional" trait, as he calls it, arises from the natural socialization, and also to some extent from an in-born feminine viewpoint mentioned before, which holds:

	Over-functioners	Under-functioners
Dominance	Males	Females
Emotions	Females	Males

From the female point of view, being ever cast in this role as the under-functioners from a dominance point of view in their marriage relationship, and therefore always being in the one-down position, can gall a woman to the point where she may eventually become dissatisfied and seek a more balanced dominance relationship with her marriage partner. The danger that exists is that she may attempt to achieve balance with regard to dominance in an inappropriate manner, by using her anger as the enforcing or catalytic agent. Many women will seek peace at any price. Sometimes when the price seems too high and she feels the very existence of her own self-esteem is at stake, it is possible that she will get angry, and seek to resolve the imbalance by escaping from her marriage through divorce.

Recent studies indicate that as high as two-thirds of all the divorce actions are filed by women!

Women are put on this on this earth to help support and guide their physically stronger male mates to do and be better.

Therefore, it is woman's life-task to point out to her man those various things which she sees as needing correction or adjustment in her mate's efforts or behavior. The net result is that the often sincere "help" offered by the wife is viewed as endless "criticism" by the husband. What usually happens then is incessant and abiding conflict.

This may possibly be the understatement of the year, but men don't take criticism very well, and most of the time not at all. So, the situation in a standard marriage relationship is that she thinks she's helping her man, but he thinks she's nagging and criticizing him. She is simply trying to offer constructive comments, but he thinks she is being a "know it all" and is more knowledgeable than he. Many males feel:

For every action, there is an equal and opposite criticism. Around and around they go, dancing endlessly in anger and frustration.

Of course there are countless other more potential causes for anger, but generally speaking, these two circumstances are cited as the basic causes of misunderstanding and sources of anger in a marriage relationship:

1) Women get tired of being the lesser member of the marriage partnership and don't know how to correct this unfairness.

2) Men get tired of being "helped" (seen as being criticized) by their wives.

The goal in any relationship, especially in a marriage, is to work to gain a balance between "separation" and "togetherness" and to be able to maintain an equal "I vs. we" condition. Chronic anger contains more "I" than "we," which is definitely detrimental to any marriage relationship. We shall get to some possible solutions to that dilemma directly.

Displays of Anger

In the science of psychology there exists a principle known as the "defense mechanism" which means that when someone is confronted about a problem, the recipient or target of the criticism might fight back by suddenly becoming very angry. This is an example of one of the various defense mechanisms which people use.

Defense mechanisms, which will be explained in detail later in the *Negotiation* section, involve the injection of usually irrelevant personal complaints or criticisms directed back against the person who brought up the touchy subject in the first place, and who is seen as having started the fight.

As a rule, the introduction of a defense mechanism, and the changing of subjects, will cause the conversation which was originally intended to solve or alleviate a particular problem, into a useless, mean, acrimonious and pointless round of accusations and complaints, one partner against the other, around and around, with no end in sight and with no resolution of the basic disagreement.

While anger can be displayed in wild emotional outbursts, more frequently anger is displayed in smaller doses in the form of ineffectual bickering, carping or finding fault. The marriage partners might commence doing mean little things to each other, all the while carefully avoiding any meaningful discussion about the real reason for their anger. The dance goes on.

Unfortunately, such minor skirmishing and struggling does nothing to solve the basic underlying problems. Fortunately, minor infighting does somehow manage to maintain whatever level of fragile balance that does exist in their marriage relationship. As mentioned earlier, a good "whinealogue" can sometimes help clear the air a little and perhaps, in the long run, foster increased mutual understanding.

Some Ways to Solve Anger Problems

Needless to say, the techniques to be outlined later in the sections dealing with communication and negotiation will be heavily intertwined with the suggestions offered here. The only serious twist with regard to issues involving anger has to do with the source or cause of the anger, which is most often housed in the mind of the one who is angry, and which may not even be known by the other person who is the recipient of the anger. Without any assignment of importance to these suggestions by the order of their presentment, try working with anger this way:

- Learn to translate your anger away from accusations and complaints to non-blaming "I" statements. For example instead of saying, "you always, etc. (criticism)," or, "you never, etc." learn to rephrase and redirect your wishes or complaints to yourself by saying, "when you _____(complaint), I feel so, etc, etc." Focus on how you feel. The objective here is to try to get your mate to feel that he can help you, if he will, since in fact, you are admitting that the problem is yours. That's why you feel as you do.

- Be prepared for and expect counter-moves and defense mechanisms to be offered by your mate when you voice what it is you are angry about. Stick to the subject, be cool and simply do not allow the conversation to return to the typical circular argument pattern that usually ensues when you voice a complaint related to your anxiety or anger. If the situation becomes too emotional or heated, simply call a "time out" and set another date to talk about the issue.

- As life goes, you can probably count on having to make several attempts to state your problem before any measurable success is achieved. And, of course, there are never any guarantees of a completely successful outcome anyhow.

- Keep in mind that anger can be the vehicle for self-growth and learning. If you engage your brain and approach the troublesome issue(s) with intelligence and understanding, aren't you really gaining in your own measure of self-worth? Won't your being able to break the miserable dance of anger help prove to yourself that you are capable of personal advancement and change, and also validate that you are capable of helping your mate to view you in a different light?

- Never forget that many of the problems married people have are the result of misunderstandings of positions or concepts viewed in a different manner by each partner. That's why "mirroring" or repeating what you THINK you heard will ofttimes settle a dispute before it gets going.

There is no perfect right and no perfect wrong in any difference of opinion, assuming, of course, that none of the three reasons to divorce are present. There can be many ways to view any situation, and all people can and usually do think and respond differently to any particular set of circumstances or situation. Just because you think that this is the way it is, does not, in fact, make it the way it is.

- Never make a decision when angry. Stop over-reacting and start thinking. Work hard to achieve a lower level of emotionality when embarking on a discussion with your mate regarding some hoped-for change in status or behavior. Don't be afraid to admit that you do not know the answer to the problem; rather, simply cite what seems to be the problem to you and seek your mate's assistance to find a solution. Reaction is fine, but over-reaction or emotionally over-functioning is not so fine.

- Responsibility. Who is responsible for what? We all are totally responsible for our own selves. If someone or something is making us angry then we must sit down and try to figure out why we are angry, and try to pin-point just exactly who and what is causing our anger. If you are making someone else angry, what can you do to help him through his anger; and is his anger justified? Any truly responsible person will take whatever steps it takes to eliminate, or at least to ease, any justifiable cause of someone else's anger.

- Don't ever forget one other thing: The presence of anger can sometimes be sign of mental or physical illness, especially if the onset of the anger is sudden in nature. The presence or existence of anger as a symptom of mental dysfunction is mentioned numerous times in the diagnostic manual used by psychologists and psychiatrists (DSM-IV). Two notable and rather common symptoms involving anger occur in what is called "Post Traumatic Stress Disorder" (PTSD), which is a reaction that can occur at any time after an individual is subjected to more than usual trauma or stress. Another illness in which anger might pop up could be as a symptom of the onset of Alzheimer's disease. This usually, but not always, occurs only in older people.

- Hang onto the thought: Nobody every changed anybody. If you are angry about something your spouse is doing, assuming that he is behaving within what could be said to be normal boundaries, you are not going to get him to change unless you can convince him to change himself, for your sake. You have to work on changing your own point of view and frame of mind so you will be better able to understand and therefore cope with, or at least tolerate, what ever it is that is annoying you. Do not think that you know what is best for another person. Do not lecture.

- Step back and watch your anger. Observe the behavior patterns that are causing your anger and find new options for your own new behavior. When talking to your spouse about the problem, you will find that your own self-disclosure will help break the circular pattern of argument which goes nowhere. Shift from: "You have a problem," to "I have a problem," then tell your spouse (self-disclose) what your problem is, clearly and unemotionally.

- Keep the principle of general codependence in mind, and also remember the strong influence the behavioral standards of your mate's original family, and your own as well, have on both of you. As the child is brought up, so will the adult behave. Watch out for events or anniversaries which might trigger errant behavior, and if angry or unexplainable arguments come up, don't respond, simply decide to "wait it out."

Perhaps the best ever one-line explanation or definition of anger comes from a

Robert Ingersoll who said :

"Anger Is a Wind Which Blows
Out the Lamp of the Mind."

Psychology has identified certain behavioral conditions which are considered to be Personality disorders. Extensive discussion and explanation of personality disorders comes along a little later in this text, but it wouldn't hurt to keep the existence of these disorders in mind. The good news is that there are psychotherapies available which can usually overcome a dysfunction.

Okay, here's how to stop the "dance of anger" in your household:

Do you remember the example of the couple engaged in what is known as "ballroom dancing" wherein, usually in a close embrace, both people dance the exact same steps to the music and whirl around and around in perfect sequence? Well, the perfect way to stop a circular "dance of anger" that you might find yourself getting sucked into, is to step on your partner's foot, as it were, and do NOT react in the same typical fashion as you usually do! Rather than lash back, agree with him. Instead of crying, become thoughtful or questioning. Rather than shout or rave, tell a joke! Do or say anything you can think of to be unpredictable and thereby upset the beat of the dance.

Instead of stepping on your partner's foot, **step on his brain!**

You will find that once your circular and predictable "dance of anger" is interrupted, progress can be made by both marriage partners with regard to

DO	DON'T
Deal directly with whatever is causing your anger.	Gossip or "triangulate" your pain, and get others involved.
Speak up if the issue is of importance to you.	Put off or dodge talking about issues that are important to you.
Get at it in a timely and reasonable manner.	Use "I feel" language. Do not attack your mate.
State very clearly what it is you want.	Make vague requests.
Realize we are all different.	Unfairly fight back with labels.
Realize that each person is responsible for himself.	Try to tell someone how he should feel.
Take your time to think and clarify your position.	Engage in "intellectual" debates which go nowhere.
Give every benefit of doubt.	Strike back when you are angry.

the cause or reason for the disagreement and anger. In conclusion, here are some "do's" and "don'ts" when it comes to coping with anger:

Two Final Don'ts

Don't allow your anger to live too long and get you into a state of total incompatibility, which is one of the three valid reasons to divorce. And, don't expect change to come about from one or two exchanges.

Anger, when it exists in a marriage relationship and as it certainly does in virtually every divorce action, is simply an emotional response to an event or stimulus. Obviously, the best course is to solve the problem that is causing the anger. A problem solved, or at least diminished to a more acceptable level, will then lessen or remove the anger.

One final thought: Too frequently one hears someone complain about his spouse's anger by saying "It's his problem, not mine." How incorrect and stupid is that thought process! If your spouse is angry about something, the anger is your problem too and don't you ever forget it, and you had better do something darn quick to alleviate that anger or you will live to regret it. Too many people get divorced simply because they are angry.

Remember:
Contempt + Aggressiveness = Anger

You can get over anger. You can't get over a divorce, and neither will your children.

R

Stands For 'RELATIVES'

Problems over relatives within the scope of a marriage relationship are common, and in fact relative trouble is one of the so-called "Big-3" areas of difficulty that can contribute to marital strife and even an eventual divorce. Please recall that the three most frequently cited areas of conflict in marriages are money, sex and relatives. How fortunate that two of the "Big-3" marriage problems appear early in the text.

I shall approach the issue of relatives from three points of view. One is to perhaps unnecessarily identify who a relative might be; second is an inquiry into how the relative or relatives causing trouble got into the position of being able to be a source of friction between the marriage partners; and finally, a two-part look into what reasonable steps can be taken to lessen the influence of troublesome relatives on a marriage relationship.

Obviously many people can qualify as being relatives, including parents, uncles, aunts, brothers, sisters, grand-parents, in-laws, out-laws, and in the case of a re-marriage situation, all of the above assortment of legally and blood-related persons on both sides of the previous marriage, plus any children from previous marriages. In addition to that assortment of characters, there also could be other people who are simply allowed into the family circle, and while they may not have legal status, they still might be close enough to the family to be able to influence various aspects of a marriage relationship.

With regard to the second consideration (how the relative came to be in a position of power in the first place), a likely explanation is that one or both of the marriage partners failed to realize or recognize the strong influence and the amount of power that the relative or relatives have over the individual affected. While it is true that two individuals who are "going together" prior to marriage will probably get to know their prospective marriage partner's relatives to some extent, it is nonetheless likely that the level of influence which might eventually be exerted by the pesky relative(s) will not be recognized.

On the other hand, if a person perceives that the prospective marriage partner holds too close ties to the parents or other relatives, then caution and some determination of the depth of the relatives' influence into the planned new marriage relationship should be ascertained, and solutions need to be negotiated prior to the marriage.

For example, it could certainly be an error of significant proportions if one of the soon-to-be marriage partners thought to himself that his intended, his dear betrothed, was too attached or dependent on a parent or other relative, but chose to overlook or discount the devotion by the other partner to the relative, hoping, or assuming, that the exhibited affection and obedience to the relative would simply disappear on the wedding day. The hopeful partner may well be in for a big shock.

Realistically speaking, the foregoing paragraph is probably just a dream. When people are "in love" and planning marriage, they are usually not focusing on anything outside the sphere of their own intimacy. The reality of eventual relative-trouble is about the last thing they have in mind. Another real possibility which might exist is that a relative who possesses a meddling, intrusive and, therefore, troublesome nature, could be, as they say, "lying in the weeds" waiting to see if the marriage actually does come about before playing his card. Really then, how would it ever be absolutely 100% possible for one marriage partner to know for sure that a relative is going to be a problem until after the marriage vows are spoken, and by then it is too late.

Perhaps a good rule to remember, is, that families are a lot like fudge; mostly sweet but there are always a few nuts in the mix, so watch out for them.

Another possibility that could precede intrusion by a troublesome relative might be some later-on or post-marriage impression or conviction by a relative that his help was, for some reason or the other, desperately needed to straighten out perceived behavioral errors or shortfalls with regard to one of the marriage partners. This ill-conceived perception would dictate that it somehow became his duty to interfere and "guide" your marriage relationship in the right direction, and therefore on the true path to happiness.

Still another possibility could be that the affection of a person newly-married for a parent or relative did not bloom until after the wedding ceremony. This might be a little hard to believe, but some people never get homesick until after they are married. As weird as that may sound, the possibility exists—and history tells us—that a very close attachment to a parent or family member which remained unfelt or unacknowledged in an earlier era may suddenly blossom at a later time, like after a marriage. In the science of psychology this phenomenon of an offspring's failure to separate from a parent or parents is known as the failure of "Differentiation."

Differentiation is defined as the normal function of a person to develop his or her own identity at the appropriate time in life when such independent development of one's own personality and individuality usually occurs.

In the companion book to this work entitled *Some of the Reasons We Behave the Way We Do*, time and space are given to this subject of differentiation, with extensive specific reference to Erik Erikson's developmental plan, which states that somewhere, from age 11 to age 18, it is the natural and normal life-task for a young person to develop his own identity and to not get caught in the "Mommy's little boy/girl" or "Daddy's little girl/boy" trap. The failure of an individual to accomplish this parental differentiation and to achieve the normal separation and personal development of identity will forebode and almost guarantee a lifelong history of personal and inter-personal difficulties, and especially in the marriage relationship.

Unfortunately, it is difficult for the untrained eye to identify a potentially troublesome relative prior to one's marriage. Even more difficult and unfortunate is a post-ceremony discovery of the mate's attachment to another person, usually a parent, which would probably manifest itself by too much apparent closeness and dependence on the parent or relative by the now-grown child. Said another way, the psychic umbilical cord was never appropriately cut at the normal time, and in the normal manner. Some would say that the person never grew up.

The conclusion is that not all relative-trouble is the fault of the relative. It can also possibly be the fault of the marriage partner who has failed to differentiate from his parents or relatives. However, if such difficulty as this dysfunction called relative-trouble does occur in your marriage, something must be done in a timely manner to alleviate the stress. A lot of divorces have relative-trouble written all over them, yet this waiting disaster is rarely recognized and most certainly not admitted.

Some Possible Solutions For Solving Relative Troubles:

1a. Differentiation: You find out or figure out that your spouse has failed to differentiate and to normally separate from the parent or relative. The problem, as it seems to you, is that your spouse is overly attached or dependent upon his relative who seems to be exerting too much influence, not only on your spouse but also on your marriage relationship, and therefore on you. You feel hurt, left out, overlooked, intruded upon, and not able to make your own decisions.

If this is the case, then before you blow the whistle and launch into an effort, or maybe even a tirade, to straighten out your mate, maybe you should stop and remember that everyone has a right to his own personal relationships as long as they are not cumbersome, intrusive or destructive to your marriage.

Perhaps if you come to realize that you just wish the attention your spouse is paying to someone else was aimed solely at you, then maybe you should admit that you are jealous of the attachment. There is a good chance you should simply accept your spouse's relationship with that person for what it is, just another friendship to which your spouse is entitled and can have if he wants. Assuming, of course, as mentioned above, that the contact with this other relative is not, in fact, destroying the fabric of your marriage relationship.

Anyone can stand only so much of the "Daddy or Mommy says" stuff. But the real question is, are you just fussing over their relationship, or is it really a problem? And how much stress is the attachment to the relative really causing? After all, no one "owns" anyone else, and maybe your spouse really needs that level of closeness with the relative at this time in his life.

However another alternative condition or situation may exist: There is the real possibility that your mate doesn't even realize your concern, or that you are in some pain over his relationship with the relative(s) because you have not told him of your concern and how you feel. If this is the case and you are suffering in stony silence, then the problem is yours. You are the one who is unhappy and it is up to you to find a solution. You cannot ask and expect your mate to solve a problem he doesn't even know about. Very few humans are accurate mind-readers.

Of the many ways this sort of a problem can be solved, above all don't assume the cloak of martyrdom; don't lash out; don't draw any lines in the dirt; don't issue any attack orders; don't issue any either/or ultimatums, and don't start a "taking sides" program where it's you good guys versus those bad guys. On top of that, once you have started on a path of problem resolution, don't expect immediate or complete results. Intruding into someone else's emotional involvement with a relative is a tricky process and can be very time-consuming.

The obvious solution to the situation is to simply initiate a conversation, or series of conversations, conducted in the correct manner and time, with the intention of conveying your feelings. Tell him that either you feel he is too emotionally involved with the relative, or you feel the relative is being allowed to intrude into your marriage too much.

Don't directly complain to your spouse about his/her involvement with the relative unless you really have to. But if and when you do decide to complain, use only "I" statements, as you tell your mate about how his attachment makes you feel, and how you are worried about the relative interfering in your marriage. Never, ever head off in the "you always . . ." or "you never . . ." accusation and attack pattern. If you find you are unable to control the conversation, or the exchange becomes too heated or emotional, call a "time out," by saying something like, "I can see this isn't a good time to talk, so let's set another time when we can visit about this issue, which is really very important to me," and have another go at it later.

Especially note this: Remember to add some positive inducements. In psychology it's called "positive reinforcement."

Compromise where and whenever you need, and expect a wealth of defense mechanisms as well as countermoves and accusations. I've said it before and I say it again, in life we don't get what we deserve, we get what we negotiate. Resolution of a relative problem is just another episode in the long negotiation session that is called life.

'Tis a bit of a pity that the section on negotiation is farther off in the text, but by the time you get to that section, maybe you will at least have a grasp on the basic principles of the technique, and on the use of effective communication skills.

In addition, when you get to the section under **G** which stands for general codependence, you will find that one of the more distressing symptoms of that dysfunctional behavior pattern is known as the "don't rock the boat" attitude, which holds that no matter how bad things are, never change anything. So if your mate resists or rejects your suggestions about his behavior and attitude towards the relative, what you may have encountered is that old "don't rock the boat" syndrome, and you will need to deal with the general codependence default before you can deal with the problem.

1b. What if you are told that it is you who has somehow failed to differentiate from your parents and find yourself being the recipient of complaints from your spouse about the perceived negative influence in your marriage relationship by one of **your** relatives? Read the foregoing 1a. over again and go look in the mirror. If it is your own relationship with a relative which is causing stress within your marriage, don't hesitate to take what ever steps are needed to remedy or adjust the situation to that point where your spouse will feel more safe and secure. Be reasonable. Keep your priorities in mind. Negotiate. Compromise.

You might find that the solution to the problem lies simply in timing or adjusting rituals. You should be able to quite easily adjust the involvement with the relative, as far as your mate is concerned, by changing some of the things you do together, and get to that point wherein the spouse will no longer be as upset or disturbed. For example, a daily phone conversation which occurs when the time might better be spent with your mate could be put off until later, or earlier.

Perhaps a visit, which is regularly scheduled either to or by the relatives, can be moved to a more random or uncertain time or condition so neither you nor they will always be showing up at a predictable time on a certain day. Some people hate to get locked into a fixed and predictable routine.

2a. What do you do when the problem is a lack or failure of differentiation by a relative(s)? The reverse instance in that it is the relative who needs or demands more attention than usual from your mate. Or from you. As a rule this circumstance occurs when a relative refuses to "let go" of their child-now-adult, and continues to involve themselves in the personal and family situations or decisions which are none of their business. Sometimes the child/adult, your own spouse, realizes the existence of this oppressive intrusion, but goes along with and/or tolerates the unwanted advice and intrusion in order to avoid hurting the feelings of the relative.

Whether or not the meddling of the relative is a serious problem is a decision that only the non-involved marriage partner can make. But if the non-involved marriage partner decides there is a problem, then, by golly, there is a problem, and the bad news is that it is the problem of the marriage partner who has the relative hanging onto them.

To specify a circumstance: Say the wife's parents are too involved and are meddling in the marriage relationship, and the husband resents their intrusion, then obviously both marriage partners have a problem. Simply telling or demanding that she tell her own parent to "get lost" is asking too much. On top of that, three possibilities exist. One is that she may not even realize the parental intrusion is causing a problem until you tell her. Another is that she may not care if it is a problem for you; and the third is that it may be just too difficult or painful for her to solve your problem for you.

The ball is in your court. If there is a problem, then it is the one who is unhappy, the non-involved partner, you, who must solve or bring about a solution of the problem for yourself, and ultimately for your own family.

There are many courses or directions of action to solve such an unfortunate circumstance, but here I offer a course of action which should work, if given the time and patience it may take to resolve such a problem.

First; have a conversation with your mate and tell him how you feel about the meddling relative. Keep in mind, and don't hesitate to tell your marriage partner that **your feelings are not negotiable!** Tell him you have made this decision for yourself and that you realize the seriousness of the situation. There is always a very real possibility that your mate will deny the intrusive influence of the relative and may undertake to initiate counter moves to try to protect the relative. Your mate may fend off what is initially perceived as a personal attack. Alas, once again, the old "don't rock the boat" syndrome. But, be firm and resolute, and continue the conversation in this vein: (MP = marriage partner)

MP 1: "Honey, I need to talk to you about some feelings I have about your folks intruding a little too much in our lives, and I need to do something about the situation." (Note: Do not attack the relative. Talk only about the situation that bothers you, and do not let the conversation deteriorate into a pointless argument about some other subject.)

MP 2: "What do you mean?"

MP 1: (calmly and coolly explain your feelings) Say, "I feel . . . " "For us . . . " "I need . . . " "Please help me to . . . ," and so on. Be careful to use only internalized "I" comments directed just to yourself. Use "I" language and not "you" or "they" language, and again, do not attack the relatives. Proceed to state as clearly and calmly as you can just what the problem is, in your view, and what it is that you hope can be adjusted or adopted in the relationship with the relative which will take the pressure off yourself.

MP 2: (Who knows what might happen? The marriage partner might agree with you, or he might get mad, use countermoves, and maybe even launch an attack on you personally along with a wondrous display of multiple defense mechanisms.)

MP 1: If the MP agrees with you, then all you have to do is mutually devise some workable solution to solve the problem. Decide together to either simply make the necessary adjustments yourselves without confronting the relatives. (Good course.) If you find the indirect approach won't work, then you might have to confront the relatives together and explain to them how things are with you, and how your relationship with them will actually be better in the long run once the problem is resolved.

If the MP doesn't agree, or wants to argue with you, then you might consider saying something like: "Look, honey, I'm sorry that you are taking it in this manner; I'm not trying to make you mad, but I have made a decision for myself, in the best interests of our marriage, which is the most important thing in my life, and I am going to talk to Mom or Dad (or whoever) and tell them how I feel and try to work out a better relationship with them, at least in my view." Of course, the eternal point here is that you have the right and even the duty to make your own life-decisions, and in this instance all you are doing is fairly advising your MP of your decision.

Do not allow yourself to be bullied or dissuaded by any display of anger or threats. Self-assertion is often quite painful and scary, but be firm and determined to bring about a solution to what seems to you to be a problem. More about self-assertion later.

If it is difficult for you to assert yourself, before you try the conversation with Mom or Dad, or whoever, look in the index under "self-assertion" and read that section. Not everybody automatically has the grit to "speak his piece" without some training.

And so the stage is set for you to talk with the relative, or relatives, and that conversation probably won't be much more fun than the visit with the spouse, but which confrontation, if held in the correct setting and time, and conducted in a straightforward calm manner, could sound something like this: (REL=relative)

MP 1: Mom (or Dad, or relative) I've got to talk to you about something that I hope won't hurt you, but I feel you are involving yourself(ves) in our marriage relationship a little too much, I almost feel a wedge is being driven between (other MP) and myself, so I'm scared.

REL: "What do you mean?" (perhaps angrily)

MP 1: At this point simply and clearly explain what it is you want. Fewer calls? Don't just "drop in" on us without calling? Don't tell us how to raise your grandchildren, etc. Say, "I'm doing the best I can, I don't do everything right or the way you would, or have done in the past, but I'm me and I'm living my life the way I want to." Focus only on your feelings. Do not attack the relative. Do not say, "you always . . . etc " or "you never etc, etc."

Here's a possible ploy you might use: Ask them about their own childhood(s). Ask them about their parents. Ask them what shortcomings or changes they feel they might have made in the past in raising your mate. Be firm. Be cool. Don't cave in. Don't get mad, no matter what. If the conversation gets too heated or emotional, say, for example, "I can see this isn't a good time to talk about this, so let's talk again next week. I'll call and make a date so we can have coffee and I'll try to explain my feelings then."

Focus on your feelings. Take your time. Realize that this conversation you are trying to have with them may not the best turn of events in the relative's life and that they could be very afraid of losing contact (control?) with their "child." Don't expect immediate results, and be kind.

If you will proceed generally in this manner and the relative(s) are nice normal people, eventually you will succeed, and in the end, you'll probably have a much better relationship with them. On top of that, once your mate sees how things are going and that you are willing to fight for your marriage, you will also find a closer bond developed between you, because he will find new respect for you taking care of your own problem and fighting for, or at least having the gumption to stand up for your family, of which he is the primary element.

The foregoing conversation, which is only a suggested possibility, is based on the assumption that the relative(s) are nice normal people and can be reasoned with. Unfortunately, such is not always the case because there are some people in this world who are known as "irregular people," which topic moves us to the next possibility.

2b. Differentiation: 'Irregular people'. Psychologist Dr. Joyce Landorph, wrote an outstanding book titled *Irregular People,* which is very likely available at your public library or at a bookstore. In her fine book, Dr. Landorph clearly lists and explains the characteristics of what she calls "Irregular People."

Briefly stated, the gist of her book is that there are some people who are simply "irregular" in their interpersonal behaviors and manner of communication. She further sets out that everyone has at least one "irregular person" in his life. Too bad, but probably correct.

So, who is an "irregular" person?

According to Ms. Doctor Landorph, an irregular person is a bully-type individual who is completely outspoken, frequently rude, unkind, fault-finding and mouthy. He seemingly never fails to launch an attack with a biting criticism or demeaning comment intended to hurt someone else's feeling such as:

"How can you live with such a pig?"

"Don't you ever vacuum?" (or dust, or . . . .)

"I can't understand how you can let your children . . . "

"What you need is . . . "

"Why didn't I know . . . " (like they were entitled to know everything you are doing)

"Well (sniff), I certainly don't understand how (or why) you could etc. etc."

"What you should do is . . ."

"How can you live like this . . . etc. etc."

"Well, I thought . . ."

The list could go on and on, but you are getting the idea aren't you?

Irregular people, in order to maintain what they see as control over someone, feel that they can say anything they want to, at any time they want to say it, and get away with their cruel remarks. Irregular people do get away with their mean barbs and cuts; but, only if you let them.

That's the key: If you let them.

Worse than that, irregular people never seem to realize or even care that they are hurting someone's feelings, and according to Dr. Landorph, they never will care who they hurt, nor will they ever change their obnoxious behavior or attitudes as long as they live. There isn't one blessed thing that you or anyone else can do about the way they behave.

Doctor Landorph says that we all go through our lives enduring the continual bullying and abuse from our own 'irregular person', usually due to incorrect thinking on our part. We seem to feel that the abuse we accept from this person is really what we deserve because we think we are somehow inadequate or at fault.

Of course, once you know about irregular people then you can realize that the problem doesn't lie with you or anybody else, but only with the poor irregular person who has his own insatiable and perhaps irrational need to dominate someone or some situation for unknown reasons. The way they achieve their domination, which can be either real or imagined, is by being obnoxious. Endlessly obnoxious. These irregular people have found that by being rude, crude and uncultured, they somehow can "get their way" and make others feel badly. This they dearly love, because they then foolishly think of themselves as superior.

The companion book to this book, titled *Some of the Reasons We Behave the Way We Do*, includes extensive analysis of the subject of personalities and personality disorders which you will find fascinating. Some would propose that an irregular person is afflicted with one or the other, or several, personality disorders, and indeed, such might be the case.

Bad news summary: an "Irregular Person":

a) does not realize he is "Irregular";
b) will not change his own behavior to any sort of normal pattern, no matter what you do or say.

If an irregular person changed to more normally civilized levels of behavior, he would then be afraid of losing, or feel that he had lost control over whomever it is he is trying to dominate. The need to control and dominate others is of prime importance to your everyday irregular person.

Hopefully you don't understand the above part b) because, heaven forbid, if you do understand such irrational behavior and it all makes sense to you, then perhaps you are an 'irregular person' yourself. Perish the thought.

The point of inserting this discourse concerning 'irregular people' at this point in the text is the possibility that the relative who is causing trouble in your marriage relationship just might be an irregular person. If so, then there really isn't a thing you can do about changing him, or ever having any sort of rationally therapeutic or correcting conversation with him. Neither you nor anyone else can solve an external problem with an irregular person. A problem with an irregular person can only be solved internally on your own and within yourself, by utilizing one of, or a combination of the following suggestions:

1) Simply resolve to ignore his caustic and unkind remarks. Unfortunately, this course is easier said than done because frequently the person who is delivering the tongue lashing is someone who is cared about. But, overlooking the barbs and arrows is a possibility if one has a grasp on what is called "Rational Emotive Therapy" (RET). The "Rational Emotive Therapy" concept was developed a number of years ago by a famous psychologist named Albert Ellis. RET, listed in the index, will be fully explained later in this text. But briefly stated, using RET as your own defense mechanism involves the

pre-conditioning of one's self to control responses to the behavior of others.

2) Lash back. Being constantly on guard and prepared to counter unkindness with unkindness is certainly no fun and no way to live. Having a continuous and ongoing family fight could in itself be ruinous to a marriage relationship.

3) Avoid the irregular person. Stay away. You are entitled to and deserve your own peace and sanity, and you simply don't have to put yourself in harm's way by ever even seeing the irregular person. Of course, such a plan of action can cause friction between the best of marriage partners. But from a priority point of view, the most important aspects of life are your own well-being and welfare and the happiness and solidarity of your marriage.

In conclusion, don't let either the intrusion of a relative of yours, or of your marriage partners, spoil your marriage relationship. Life is too short and a good marriage is too precious to be placed in jeopardy by a meddling relative.

R

Stands For 'REVERSALS'

A Reversal, as defined earlier in the explanation and definition section, is any significant occurrence which happens outside the normal range of life's usual day-by-day events. Reversals obviously can come in two varieties, good and bad, and then within all the in-between intensities ranging from extremely good, to catastrophically bad. The issue in a marriage is what effect the reversal, be it real or perceived, can have on the relationship.

As we all know, occasionally a reversal will occur which at first appears to be a total disaster, but, later on, the event turns out to be a blessing. Conversely, it can come to pass that an event happens which appears to be in the bonanza class can turn out to be a real bummer. One never knows for sure how a reversal will eventually turn out, only that reversals happen to everyone.

In keeping with "Murphy's Law," which holds that if anything can possibly go wrong, it probably will, "bad deals" as reversals seem to be more prevalent in life than "good deals." But, to be more explicit, here is a brief sampling of some of the types of reversals that can happen on both sides of the fence:

Bad Deal Reversals	Good Deal Reversals
A death	Make too much money
A business failure	Win the lottery
Job loss	Get a big inheritance
A serious illness	Success in career
Financial loss, a serious accident	?
Fire or flood	?

Please note that I'm not talking about the inclination some people have to over-react to minor events. Some folks can handle the big events in their life, the disasters, better than they can handle small events, such as burning a roast, or getting a parking ticket. Consistent over-reaction to seemingly minor occurrences and perceived disasters might be a personality disorder known as "histrionics." Or, maybe the individual simply uses the minor event as a ruse to get more attention.

Trying to live with someone who goes ballistic every time some little thing runs astray would be quite uncomfortable not only for the one who gets very "worked up" over minor events but also for the person who is trying to live with someone in a constant state of uproar. At this point in our consideration of the marriage relationship idea, I am going to be talking just about major-type reversals.

For example, a very knowledgeable and experienced bankruptcy attorney stated that in the case of a personal or business failure resulting in a bankruptcy in which substantial financial losses were sustained, from 75% to 80% of the time the people involved get divorced. That is a whopping 50% increase in divorce over our normally awful 50% divorce rate in the United States, making the overall divorce rate of people who go through a catastrophic financial loss a screaming 75%!

Another example: In a syndicated and copywritten article which appeared in the December 16, 1992, issue of our local newspaper, there appeared a letter to one of those home-grown advice-to-the-lovelorn columns from a woman who related that since their two-month-old child had died a few months earlier of apparent "sudden infant death" syndrome (SID), she and her husband had been drawn apart, and were, at that point in their lives, completely at odds. The lady writing the letter sought advice to help avert what seemed, to her, an impending divorce.

Still another example: The September 5, 1993, issue of the same newspaper carried a brief article concerning the story of an Iowa couple's son who had been kidnapped 11 years before while delivering newspapers in the Des Moines area, never to be heard from again. The article quoted the couple as saying 'the stress of their 12-year-old son's disappearance contributed to the breakup of their 26-year marriage.'

The paper quotes the mother, "The situation is, that we've (as husband and wife) grown so far apart it is impossible for us to be together." The tragic aftermath of a horrendous reversal.

Why does a disastrous reversal so frequently result in, or seem to cause, the breakup of a marriage? Why is it that just because, for example, a child becomes terribly injured or dies, a person lost a job that he thought he had for life, a business failed, a flood happened, or a fire, or any substantially adverse event happens, does this setback seem often to be a proximate cause of the death of the marriage of the couple involved?

With regard to opposite good-side reversals, why is it that when a couple falls on good times and enjoys more-than-expected financial success or increased social status, so frequently they seem to lose their balance, change behaviors? And it isn't very long until you see their names in the newspaper in the divorce column?

Brief concession: As mentioned above in the instance of the family of the young lad who was kidnapped, the people themselves admitted that the reversal only "contributed" to their divorce, and such may indeed be the case. A reversal may be the "last straw" which might bring an end to an already troubled marriage. The obvious warning embodied in this premise is to work diligently to keep as many problems under control as you can, so that when the reversal happens, as it most surely will, you will be as well prepared as you can hope for.

Never forget this: It's an absolute given that every marriage relationship has troubles in it, to some extent. Anybody who tells you that he's got the always agreeable, perfect, blissful marriage and "everything is peachykeen and wonderful" is either a liar of the highest order, or a person who is a great big bully, or some poor soul being completely bullied.

The last person who told me with a straight face he had a perfect marriage, with nary a squabble or problem, got caught in bed with his neighbor's wife about a week after he told this fantastic lie, and you can just bet he very quickly knew all about trouble.

What is the problem? The problem is that when an already shaky marriage encounters a sudden shift in status of some sort, and a state of imbalance or instability enters the marriage relationship, the destabilizing influence frequently proves to be too much for the already unsteady relationship.

But is the reversal really the primary problem? That all depends on the basic status of the relationship and whether or not good and sufficient preparation has been made by the marriage partners to anticipate those guaranteed-to-happen life-events.

If a reversal occurs that seriously upsets and disturbs the marriage, it is a problem for both marriage partners, and the two of you must join in solving and re-establishing the balance lost in your marriage relationship.

Background: A famous practicing psychiatrist in Vienna by the name of Viktor Frankl got ensnared by the German people in their wholesale slaughter of millions of innocent people in Europe in the WWII era, in the event which is now known as the Holocaust. Doctor Frankl spent three years in German concentration camps, enduring unbelievable privation and brutal treatment by the German guards. He was living right on the outskirts of hell. How he ever managed to survive is an incredible story of human strength and determination.

But, by some collection of sheer determination, miracles and luck, he did survive the ordeal, and was finally liberated by the Allied troops when they over-ran the infamous Auschwitz concentration camp. Of course after three years of that brutal treatment, he was a sorry example of humanity, as were all his fellow prisoners, many whose only crime was being Jewish, as was the case with Dr. Frankl. But somehow, some way, he lived through all that, and from his subsequent teachings, we are shown the way to find some solace and understanding in our own personal struggles with reversals.

Out of this gigantic reversal in his life,

and being a psychiatrist, Dr Frankl (1905-1998) came up with a very important variation of an older psychological idea or theory known as existentialism. The essence of existentialism encourages people to deal with whatever circumstance that occurs in their life.

In short, to deal with the here and now, as the here and now does exist, and to move forward in their lives. We didn't say anyone had to accept or to approve of the reversal, but just to plan to survive and cope. Doctor Frankl called his new and exciting variation of existentialism "logotherapy," which is derived from the Greek word *logo* which means "meaning," and "therapy," which means "to treat."

Thus it is the goal of Frankl's logotherapy to help people figure out the meaning or purpose of their life, and once that purpose is fairly well determined, then to learn how to cope with their life-events and reversals as they occur. Especially vulnerable to inciting tragedy and doing really dumb things, like divorce, are those people who have run aground on some reef of disaster or disappointment, who are feeling lost, and think that they are not making much headway in their lives. They simply have not figured out the meaning of their own life.

The basic premise of Viktor Frankl's idea is, no matter what sort or variety of reversals come up in our lives, we must all keep our focus on the future. We each have an obligation to try to find the meaning of our lives and not to focus solely on ourselves and our own feelings or circumstances, as life's reversals roll over us. Doctor Frankl says in his book, titled *Man's Search for Meaning,* "Don't expect anything from life, but try to figure out what life expects from you."

Doctor Frankl's book first appeared in 1959, over four decades ago, and more than three million English-language copies have been sold. The book is divided into two sections. The first part tells of his struggle to stay alive in the concentration camps. The second part explains the essence of his logotherapy concept.

A gripping section in the first part tells of a particularly moving incident which happened in the concentration camp. As Frankl begins, "It had been a bad day." This serious understatement brought about a meeting of inmates later, and Frankl was asked to speak to the other prisoners. Although he described himself as "sick, cold, hungry, irritable and tired," he did make the effort to address and give encouragement to the others huddled in their "earthen huts."

Doctor Frankl says he began his opportunity to extend his thoughts of encouragement to the other freezing and starving prisoners by mentioning "the most trivial of comforts." He pointed out they were all still alive, and had a roof of sorts over their heads. They got fed once in a while, and most importantly they all "had reason for hope," He continued talking about the future, that they all had reason to expect that their health, their families, fortunes, professional abilities and position in society were all things that could be achieved again, or restored. The lesson? No matter how bad things are today, always look ahead to better days.

In the second part Frankl really hits the nail on the head by listing the four things in life that he felt did put meaning in life. The four are listed, not in any order of importance, but as important in themselves. One finds meaning in life by:

loving someone
taking care of someone
creating something
overcoming adversity

In the course of the book Dr. Frankl talks about how fellow prisoners could almost tell when another inmate was going to die, either by sickness, inciting a fatal beating by the guards, or suicide. The key, he discovered, was seen in their eyes: They gave up hope.

To give up hope means death whether you are locked up in a concentration camp, terribly ill in a hospital, or to paraphrase the idea, in an ailing and troubled marriage relationship. To give up hope and to lose determination to succeed in your marriage, can certainly predict the eventual death of the marriage relationship. The final chapter in this book deals with hope.

One of Frankl's quotes I admire so much is:

"That which does not kill me
makes me stronger."

Paraphrased, that could read:

"That which does not kill our
marriage makes it stronger."

So, how does one handle a reversal? The number of various methods a couple could use to keep a reversal from destroying, or badly damaging, their marriage relationship is quite lengthy, but in the interest of brevity we shall take a look at two possible therapies or plans to cope with a reversal which should be quite easy for you to use when coping with a reversal.

Stress Inoculation

The first procedure utilizes psychologist Dr. Donald Meichenbaum's "Stress Inoculation" idea, which is a plan widely used by therapists to help those who are inclined to over-respond to stressful events. Briefly stated, Meichenbaum's "A-B-C" concept is a good idea and one that you can use to prepare yourself for the reversal that you know will come along some day. But who knows what or when? A comedian is quoted as saying that if everything seems to be going your way, you are probably driving on the wrong side of the freeway, going the wrong way, and in the wrong lane. Here is Meichenbaum's "A-B-C" way to handle the stress of a reversal:

A Action. The actual reversal, the event. What happens. The disaster or the bonanza. The basic idea is for you marriage partners to plan for, to expect and talk about the inevitable "what ifs" of life and your marriage. By anticipating and counting on a reversal happening, you won't be so surprised and/or devastated when your turn finally comes.

B stands for what it is that you want to think when the reversal happens, the BELIEF of what has happened, or how you view the impact of the event, and how it affects you and your marriage. In this phase, people who are smart "inoculate," or immunize themselves from disaster and inappropriate thoughts, by pre-thinking and planning how they will react when the disaster happens. Think about how you want to respond when the reversal does occur so you won't be caught off-guard and say some stupid things, or jump to an incorrect conclusion. Keep as many of the 20 issues in your marriage relationship in good order and under control as you can so you won't be dumped into a "last straw" frame of mind and let the reversal whip you.

C stands for the consequences of the reversal. Try to decide, or at least think, before the reversal occurs, how you and your marriage relationship will be when the consequences of the reversal are all that is left. Trust that your marriage will be stronger and better after the disaster, and the two of you will hold together and plan to react in as positive a manner as you possibly can. In the case of a good-side reversal, plan to keep your family and marriage relationship as the most important factor in your life (outside of yourself) and simply refuse to be led astray by new influences or new people.

In short, plan ahead and imagine what actions you are going to take in response to the reversal, once you fully understand just exactly what has happened. Keep in mind that neither the pain nor the joy of a reversal will last forever. If you suffer a negative reversal, don't forget that it might take some time for the two of you to recover, and you probably won't recover from the pain of the reversal at the same rate. If you are lucky and have a positive reversal, keep calm and remember from whence you came. Try hard not to change your behavior patterns. Maintain your balance personally, in your marriage relationship.

To get to the second of the two possible avenues to cope with a reversal, consider the work of Dr. Elizabeth Kubler-Ross, who has spent her entire life and medical practice working *On Death & Dying* which, by the way, is the name of her now-famous book. Your knowing what she found out about the predictable psychological steps people go through who are facing their own impending death could well be applied and pertinent to our discussion of reversals, and could help you pre-condition your own reaction or response to any type of reversal that might befall you.

Doctor Kubler-Ross says that people go through five stages when they come to the point of facing their own impending death. The direct application of these five stages to our consideration of reversals is that each of the stages could be expected to occur in the mind of anyone who suddenly and unexpectedly encounters a reversal. Here are her five stages as she found they apply to someone who learns they are at death's door:

Stage 1. Disbelief—shock
Stage 2. Anger
Stage 3. Bargaining
Stage 4. Depression, and finally,
Stage 5. Acceptance

To take her five stages and apply them then generally to any reversal as it happened, good vs. bad, your reaction could be:

	Bad reversal	Good reversal
Shock:	Being stunned. Disbelief	Ditto.
Anger:	At God, bad luck, or others who seem to be responsible. Why me?	Wild feelings of joy, which is the opposite of anger.
Bargaining:	Trying to "make a deal" to get out of the problem	Feelings of insecurity. Fear that the good fortune will go away.
Depression:	Inability to accept what has happened.	Sustained feelings of unwarranted power.
Acceptance:	Finally accepting the awful thing that has happened.	Realizing that the good fortune happened but you're are not going to let it ruin things.

And then in both cases, moving ahead with life.

Doctor Kubler-Ross adds, in the bad news department, people will and can individually move through the five stages in differing manners, speeds and order. That is, a person might try to bargain his way out of a mess before he gets angry. Some folks will be depressed for a long time, others will not have time for a prolonged period of depression, and whip right through the stage. Much will be said later about the dangers of a "deep depressive episode." But it is her contention, that one way or the other, at one rate or the other, everybody passes down the same road.

These stages are pretty much self-explanatory, but if further information is desired you can certainly find Dr. Kubler-Ross' book at your library or bookstore, and make your own conclusions or patterns for dealing with reversals. A case can be made for equating death with divorce. In either event, a person's own reactions to either disaster will fit into the Kubler-Ross schema.

Again, don't forget that nothing lasts forever—not even your troubles. Reversals, be they of the good or unfortunate variety, can indeed be very bad or even disastrous for a marriage relationship, so watch out for them. Talk over and plan with your spouse how you hope to handle a reversal or series of reversals if that is the way they will come at you.

Don't be afraid to play the old "what if" game that was mentioned earlier. Talk with each other about what will be done if . . . . How can we handle _____? Your just sharing each other's fears and dreams will bring you closer together.

Dream of the best and expect the worst. Stay alert and vigilant, and when a reversal happens, hold on with integrity to the basic values that have held you together so long. Indeed, forewarned is forearmed. (Boy Scouts of America)

I

Stands For 'INTEGRITY'

Integrity as an issue of concern and as one of the 20 categories in the Marriage Relationship concept can cause a married couple a great deal of conflict and trouble. But first let's review the definition of the word "integrity" as it appeared earlier in Chapter Five, just in case the explanation given there was not completely clear.

The word "integrity" has several different definitions, and if you take a peek in your dictionary you will find that, in addition to the usually-thought-of meaning of being honest or telling the truth, there will also be reference to the idea that the word "integrity" includes "consistency." Within our Marriage Relationship concept, the important connotation relates to parenting and making family decisions. Other words or phrases that convey the idea of being consistent include acting in concert, being mutually supportive of each other, predictable, up-front, unified in thoughts, words and actions, loyal, and acting as a single family unit rather than two separate entities. And simply "hanging together," especially on those matters relating to the marriage relationship, and important family concerns.

It is this "unified family action" concept embodied in the definitions of integrity on which I am primarily focusing, because a failure of integrity within a marriage can be a serious problem. Telling the truth or being honest is not included within this brief discussion of integrity.

Other meanings or implications of honesty within any marriage will be covered much later when we get to the **H**, which stands for honesty, later on in the word "relationship."

A good example of integrity is a brief consideration of an airplane, which works like this: The wing of an airplane is said to have integrity with the fuselage or cabin, the tail pieces, the motor and propellers, control surfaces, and the pilot who is flying the plane. All the parts work together, and as a result of their coordination and consistent interaction, the airplane flies successfully, and is then said to have integrity.

In other words, an airplane works because all the various components operate together. The question is not which single or particular part is needed most because they all are critical in their own right. What is crucial, is that everything works together in a unified manner.

There is no difference between that description of integrity as it might apply to an airplane, and a marriage relationship. In order for this delicate human relationship to work, each one of the 20 components not only has to work on it's own, but each component must operate and be in accordance with the other 19 categories of the concept.

Here is a true and classic example of a lack or failure of integrity in a couple's relationship: Bob and Betsy have a daughter named Abigail who seems to run with a wild crowd, stays out late, and whose behavior causes Bob more concern than it does his wife. But since Bob and Betsy do not agree on how to handle this situation with their daughter, they are in conflict, and therefore have a failure of integrity in their family.

The net result of their not being in agreement with regard to their daughter's situation is that the parents are not behaving in concert and with consistency, which is not only disruptive and stressful to their marriage relationship, but also confusing to the daughter. Young people want, and need to live in an atmosphere of harmony and constancy. Youngsters need to know and have respect for the family rules, what the parents stand for, and importantly, what they will stand still for. In other words, some expected boundaries of behavior must be established.

A comedian once said, "The best way to keep kids at home and happy, is to make the home a pleasant place. And, let the air out of their tires." Perhaps extreme with regard to the tires, but certainly true with regard to the atmosphere in the home.

The truth of the matter is that the family which had this exact true-life situation in their marriage ultimately ended up in divorce. One cannot fairly say the failure of integrity with regard to their daughter was the only cause of their divorce, because most certainly there were other areas of conflict in their marriage. But, at this point in time, there is no question in the minds of the parents, but that the failure of family integrity was a factor in their divorcing.

Who knows which conflict is the last straw and it's hi-ho, off to the attorneys we go. To this day I still wonder if the daughter ever knew, or knows, or would be able to admit that her errant behavior was part of the final reason for her parent's divorce. And, if she ever did know or had to face that she had a hand in bringing about the end of her original family, how do you think she would feel about that?

In addition to the foregoing example of a failure of a family's integrity, there is still another aspect embedded within the idea of integrity that needs attention, and that is consideration of the commitment that each of you made, not only to each other, but also to your marriage relationship.

That day the two of you got married and exchanged all those vows, you made a commitment not only to each other and to your marriage relationship, but you also made an implied agreement to work together, to the best of your ability, without exceptions throughout your married lives. You remember, don't you " . . . in sickness and in health, for better or for worse, until death do us part"?

The commitment to work together with integrity, along with the stated end-date of the marriage vows, "'til death we do part," is the very essence of every marriage contract. If you have a failure of integrity, then you must rely on the strength of your commitment to each other to solve whatever problem(s) are troubling you in order for your marriage to continue to exist.

Obviously one of the major difficulties of marriages in these days is the too-often absence of unending commitment by the marriage partners to each other and to their marriage vows. Every marriage relationship has its periods of tough times. There are always conflicts and differences of opinion between marriage partners, and it is HOW these disagreements are handled that will predict the success or failure of the marriage.

Judith Voirst wrote in an article in *Redbook* magazine:

> "One advantage of marriage is that, when you fall out of love with him or he falls out of love with you, it keeps you together until you fall in love again."

Wait a minute: Nobody ever said that you and your spouse have to see eye-to-eye on everything, because that's not the way we humans are put together. Some amount of conflict in anybody's marriage relationship is inevitable and even desirable, to some extent. Through disagreement and subsequent discussion about differences of opinion between marriage partners over family policies and positions, mutually acceptable points of view will eventually be found and agreed upon.

At the same time, the very disagreements and the following discussions not only will lead to this necessary family unity, but also, through the process of deliberation and negotiation each person will gain a better understanding of his mate, and perhaps of himself. The process of debate and intelligent discussion will also affirm their commitment to each other and their marriage, and as a happy side-effect each marriage partner will confirm his own identity, as he must.

Chorus from, *The King And I:*

"Getting to know you, getting to know all about you."

So, what is the problem? The marriage partners disagree on an issue of significant family importance, and this difference of opinion or position needs to be resolved or negotiated to a level of mutual understanding and agreement. The conflict or difference of opinion, whatever it may be, is a problem for both marriage partners, and the solution must be jointly found and agreed upon.

Neither one of the marriage partners should ever be allowed to solve a basic difference of opinion with regard to family matters on his own terms. If the solution to a difference of opinion is one-sided—that is, if the outcome of the disagreement is at the sole discretion or is the decision of just one partner—then there does not exist within that marriage relationship a negotiation arrangement, but a dictatorship.

Several aged clichés could be appropriate here: "If you don't pull together, you'll pull apart." Or how about: "If you don't hang together you'll hang separately." Take your pick.

The solution to a failure of integrity, hopefully not a failure of commitment, must be mutually sought in a calm and rational manner.

The first thing to do is to clearly identify the problem and admit the rift between the two of you, and decide then and there that somehow you are going to find some middle ground, and an agreement that you can both live with. Don't "stuff" the problem and hope the disagreement will go away. Like old garbage, a problem once identified can be left for almost any length of time and upon returning to the same issue, the problem will still be there.

Qualification: We are not including disagreements or differences of opinion that the two of you may have over strongly held personal beliefs, such as politics or religion or any other issue which is usually a part of a person's codependent background. As a rule, strongly held opinions have been part of a person's make-up for a long time and you should have known that your spouse held these opinions before you got married. How can you cause trouble over them now?

Here is the way to handle strongly held personal opinions or positions: Don't talk about them. Ever. Those who have been married for a time know full well that there are always some areas of conflict, or some topics of conversation that one simply cannot successfully bring up for discussion without getting into a silly argument. Therefore, one has to live with a strongly held opposite opinion or position of his marriage partner, whether he likes it or not. Silence can indeed be golden.

Whatever particular solution or compromise is best to try is the one that surfaces after a cool, calm discussion, and thorough airing of the facts as individually perceived, and an explanation of the reasoning behind each party's point of view. If the issue is of vital importance and emotions or feelings tend to run too high, and time is not critical, take one of those famous "time out's," and continue the discussion at a later time.

Solving a knotty and contentious family problem can take a series of several sessions to achieve a mutually agreeable compromise. A compromise is always possible, and a tentative solution to the problem needs only to be implemented, perhaps on a "let's see if this works" basis to see if the answer does indeed pan out.

If the attempted solution doesn't work, sit down again, and try to figure out where the flaw in the thinking might be, and try a different tack. If that one doesn't work either, try another one, and another one, and another one, until you do find a solution that seems to solve the problem and is mutually agreeable.

Nowhere is it written that the two of you must be in total agreement on everything all the time, or that the first attempt to try to solve a problem will be an instant success. Experience has shown, time and again, that very frequently the first attempt or two at solving a problem can miss the mark by far enough to cause a re-load, and then more attempts are required until success is finally achieved. Above all, don't give up.

And finally, also embodied in this issue of integrity is the idea of respect, which is a very important concept to be dealt with a little later when we get to the word

"Relationship" because the first **R** in that word stands for "Respect." But, as the concept of respect is intertwined in the integrity idea, what is important is that you both have respect for each other's feelings, thoughts and ideas, and if you "don't get no respect," as Rodney Dangerfield says, you got trouble.

So, even though you might not totally agree with the position of your spouse, at least you have to admit and respect his opinion, and if the division of ideas or attitudes is a little too far apart, then you've got your work cut out for you to get some measure of modification on both your viewpoints until you can get to the middle ground and hit on a solution. Note the word "both."

You don't know everything and neither does your partner, but if you work together with integrity and steadfastly hold to your commitment to each other and to your marriage relationship, you can work through a lot of really tough spots. It's that old saw about, "Two heads are better than one." So once you figure out where your spouse is coming from, and you can effectively explain your position on the matter, and having duly removed as much granite from your heads as is humanly possible, you can work out almost any problem to a mutually satisfactory conclusion. At least, for the time being.

It is said by some males that there are two ways to argue with a woman, and neither one works.

Females counter by saying being a woman is very difficult, since it consists mainly of dealing with men.

Keep in mind that what you want is a "Win/Win" solution to solve a problem with family integrity. That is, everybody wins something and there is no "loser." Neither marriage partner has to completely give in and end up saying "We'll try it your way," because then if things go awry and the attempted solution fails, the role of "loser" moves from the one who gave in to the one who bullied his opinion through the false negotiation.

Remember, to negotiate means to compromise.

Do you recall the part cited earlier from John Gray's book, about how men and women approach and solve their problems in different manners?

Men won't talk about a problem until they have their solution, and women won't come to a solution until they have talked about their problem(s).

Around and around we go. The trick in any marriage relationship is to always work together, and you can work together if you will just try.

A

Stands for 'ABUSE'

As set out earlier in Chapter Five, abuse as a category of concern within our Marriage Relationship concept is one of the only three reasons for a divorce. To refresh your memory, the three reasons to divorce, not listed in any order of importance or anguish are: infidelity which cannot be stopped or tolerated; total incompatibility; and abuse, physical, sexual or mental. And so, we begin our investigation of the types of abuse.

Physical Abuse

Restating the previously provided definitions from Chapter Five, please recall that physical abuse is defined as any hitting, striking, hurting or otherwise causing a significant level of physical pain and distress to any member of the family. The spanking of a child quite gently, even if somewhat firmly, on the bottom as a reinforcement in the process of disciplining the child is not physical abuse. The delivery of hard blows to any person or child in a manner which causes real pain and distress is physical abuse, even if the spanking or hitting acts are thought of, or intended to be purely disciplinary. **Striking a child or anyone else in the face is always physical abuse.** Never, ever, ever, can either spouse hit, or physically injure his mate in any manner whatsoever.

Incidence of continued or persistent physical abuse is a serious problem and demands the immediate attention of every member of the family, with maximum confrontation and intervention.

Any person in the family who is aware of instances of physical abuse being perpetrated against another member of the family has a moral obligation to immediately intervene and stop the abuse by any means possible. Without exception.

Solutions to problems of abuse can be, on the one hand, terribly obvious in that it is the right and the obligation of anyone being personally abused to get away from his abuser. If someone else in the family is being abused, say a spouse, or a child or an older person who cannot look out for or take care of himself, the responsibility for getting the abused person(s) away from the abuse, and the abuser, is the responsibility of other members of the family.

The victim(s) must immediately be moved out of harm's way, and the appropriate legal authorities informed.

Most communities have agencies that deal with and help in instances of abuse, and provide "hot lines" for advice and quick intervention. Many cities and towns have safe-haven shelters for victims, and these locations should (must) be used upon the first incidence of any physical abuse.

If anyone in any way, shape or manner thinks that help is needed to either save one's self or to save someone else, err on the side of asking for the help. Sometimes contacting a clergy-person might work, but in severe or prolonged instances of beatings or sexual abuse, law enforcement authorities must be contacted, and if they fail to respond, then get in touch with a psychologist or a lawyer, call the appropriate city or county social service agency, or the county legal aid offices.

Once the abused person is out of harm's way, then comes the difficult part of the physical abuse issue, which is working with the person who was abusing someone else, the perpetrator, the abuser, who needs and deserves, if not being jailed, immediate and intense psychological therapy. Such drastic steps as those suggested above might seem to be an over-reaction, but the damage to the victim of any manner of physical abuse cannot and must not be under-estimated. Long-term psychological trauma to the victim of physical abuse is not at all uncommon. Getting the abuser to stop beating or abusing the victim is only the first step.

Most importantly: If you are unfortunate enough to encounter these circumstances, do not **EVER** put the victim back into harm's way again, as far as the abuser, the perpetrator (aka "perp") is concerned. Sometimes psychological intervention can cure a perpetrator from his abusive behavior, but not always. Extreme care and caution must be employed to assure that no chance can ever occur of the abuse being repeated.

Quick action, and being absolutely resolute to either save one's self or save another family member or members from being physically abused, is the key answer to solving the occurrence of physical abuse. Nobody, but nobody, needs to stand for any level or amount of physical or sexual abuse.

Sexual Abuse

Incredible as it may be, the increase in reported cases of sexual abuse is staggering. Stories appear in newspapers and on television almost on a daily basis of horrible and unspeakable cases of the sexual abuse of children. Precise and detailed definition of the processes and problems of sexual mistreatment of children shouldn't be necessary. Once an occurrence of sexual abuse is known, it is a problem of the utmost importance and must be dealt with immediately by using maximum confrontation and intervention. Any instance of the sexual abuse of any member of the family is the problem of every member of the family.

Just imagine the mental anguish and fear a sexually abused child must endure in his young life, sometimes for years and years, at the hideous prospect of facing continued molestation, night after night, in his/her very own home. The rules of logic tell us that we cannot say "all" of anything, but in this case, beyond any shadow of a doubt, you could say that all children who are the victims of sexual abuse are scarred for the rest of their lives.

Any family member who has knowledge of the incidence of sexual abuse, and who fails to intervene and stop the commission of that crime, is as guilty of the abuse as the psychopath (nut case) who is actually committing the crime. In legal terms this is called "conspiracy," being an "accessory," "aiding and abetting" and "depraved indifference" to the crime. In psychological terms such culpability is known as "enabling," or "facilitating" the evil behavior. No matter how you slice it, if someone knows a crime is being committed and does nothing to stop it, he thereby becomes a partner and accomplice in the commission of the crime and is liable for the same legal punishment as the perpetrator. One of the frequent by-products of a divorce and subsequent re-marriage is the sexual abuse of the young step-children.

Incredibly, sometimes even with the knowledge and thereby tacit approval of the little girl's mother! Re-marriage, which tragically can involve sexual abuse of step-daughters, is a subject covered earlier in the chapter on The Wages Of Divorce. Any incidence of sexual abuse must be stopped immediately and some of the steps available to stop sexual abuse include:

a) First and foremost, get the victim out of harm's way and away from the abuser immediately. Stay with the victim at a shelter whether it be a relative's house or a "safe-house" refuge for abused persons as mentioned above.

b) Contact the police; contact the sheriff's office; contact the appropriate county social welfare departments; call or contact a therapist; contact a psychiatrist or psychologist; contact the district or county attorney's office; contact a clergy-person, or anyone who you think has some legal authority and can be of assistance not only in saving the victim from continued abuse, but also to assure bringing the perpetrator to justice.

The possibility exists that those two alternatives could occur in reverse order in that one might first have to contact an authority and find out where to take the victim. But, no matter in which order those two eventualities might occur, do something immediately! There are no other alternatives.

Do not confront the perpetrator.
Do not attempt to warn, try to reason with, or threaten the perpetrator.

Keep in mind at all times that anyone who would sexually abuse a child, or another adult, is a mentally sick person, obviously dangerous, and needs as well as deserves whatever legal prosecution is pertinent. Psychotherapy is not always successful on perpetrators of such heinous acts of sexual abuse. One cannot assume that just because the perpetrator is in therapy or has been in prison, that they are cured, or, for that matter, that they are "getting better."

Present-day news reports frequently tell of instances wherein persons convicted and imprisoned for crimes of the sexual abuse of children will return to their child-molesting ways upon release from prison.

Recent legislation, known as "Megan's Law," has mandated that convicted sex criminals must be registered with the appropriate local authorities upon their release from prison and return to society. Neighbors of these criminals are notified that a sex offender is living in their area, and you can just guess how they feel about that.

The visible evidence of official concern about the real possibility of repeat sex abuse by known offenders should be enough warning to any right-thinking person that to leave, or return known victims to the scene of abuse and therefore back into the presence of a known perpetrator is not only stupid and thoughtless but possibly even criminal behavior on the part of the custodian or caregiver whose responsibility it is to look out for the victim.

Any attempted solution of a case of sexual abuse must not fail or be put off. Constant vigilance and never-ending suspicion must forever reside in the minds and lives of the caregivers, the protectors of the abused. One's wildest imagination cannot envision a caregiver or caring relative's giving up their life-saving efforts after a failed attempt to protect and safeguard victims of sexual abuse. But if, when trying to get help from some police agency or supposedly responsible social services department, you run into one of those agencies whose response would be something like, "Well we can't do anything about it today (tonight) (this week)," or "You have to send in a report before we can do anything" etc., etc., do not give up and say, " . . . oh well." Do something! Immediately!

Mental Abuse

As set out in the definitions section, mental abuse occurs when one person or several persons, steadily and over a long period of time with determined persistence, aim a continuous stream of talk or actions toward another person, with the intent being to demean and humiliate that person. The goal of an abuser like this is to destroy the self-respect and self-confidence of the person or persons being mentally abused.

The intention of the abuser is important in this instance. Please keep in mind that we are referring to abuse which would fall outside the normal ranges of simple criticism or sporadic complaining, which we all seem inclined to include in our interpersonal relationships from time to time.

If we can agree that the above description is the definition of mental abuse, then it must be said that no one has to endure mental abuse indefinitely, because nobody has to stand idly by and let someone else maliciously set out to destroy the self-esteem and personal integrity, either of himself or another family member. While mental abuse is not a criminal activity, as are the other two types of abuse mentioned, continued severe mental abuse can possibly be as damaging in the long run to the recipient of the maltreatment as physical or sexual abuse.

Two problems can occur and cause trouble and confusion in deciding or ascertaining whether or not mental abuse is actually occurring, in that the mental abuse is:

a) frequently not apparent to the poor person or persons being abused because they have been abused for such a long time they simply don't know any better than to take it, and

b) having so surrendered and accepted the abuse as their lot in life, eventually the abused person incorrectly thinks he deserves to be abused. Their "self" systems have been badly damaged, which was the intention of the abuser all along; and, as victims, they are unable to think clearly and take control of their lives. Women are particularly inclined to fall into this trap, and can be seen being the recipient of brutal mental abuse from their husbands for years and years.

If you feel you are being mentally abused, and this is a pretty hard thing to do, try to realize that the person who is mistreating you is having his own set of problems, and the way he is trying to solve his own problems is by abusing you. That statement doesn't make a lot of sense to normal people.

But the case can be made that by abusing you or someone else in the family he is trying to say something, and maybe even crying out for help in this curious manner. His buried hope is that you will get fed up and bring about a crisis or confrontation which will result in his getting help for whatever is troubling him. An abuser is generally unable to do anything corrective on his own.

In the case of spousal mental abuse, if you are the victim, you probably owe it to your abusing spouse to try to get him straightened out, and thereby accomplish two things at the same time. One, of course, is to take the pressure off yourself; the other is to help him come to grips with whatever psychological or possible physical problem that is causing his errant behavior.

Actual case history: Betty was the target of a great deal of spousal verbal abuse and inconsiderate behavior, day after day, month after month, by her husband, Bob. All verbal abuse, no physical abuse. So one day, after nearly 22 years of marriage, Betty had had it up to here, and moved out. Not that her moving didn't get the Bob's attention, but she really made an impact when the sheriff turned up on Bob's doorstep the next day and read him the notice of service which said that his wife Betty had started a divorce action.

Here in Iowa, as is the case in many states, in the early stages of a divorce action, it was legally mandated that both parties must attend marriage counseling-evaluation sessions. When the sessions are completed, the counselor makes a report to the court regarding his impressions of the prospects for any continuation or reconciliation of the marriage in question.

Betty attended the first counseling session by herself, as directed, and told the counselor what their marital problem was, as far as she was concerned, that is, Bob's constant unkindness, his attempts to downgrade and humiliate her, and how poorly and meanly she felt he treated her, both at home and in public. All of the allegations and complaints by Betty were, unfortunately, true.

Then it was Bob's turn to talk to the court-appointed counselor. Of course Bob told the counselor he didn't have any idea at all what Betty was so upset about. He was lying, because Betty had told him on frequent occasions just how unhappy she was with his apparent attitude and treatment of her. So the therapist, having been forewarned by the wife as to what her primary complaint was, simply dismissed Bob's "presenting" defense of ignorance and innocence, and thereupon launched into the crux of the trouble, which was to convey to Bob that the problem was the way and manner in which Bob was treating his wife and therefore abusing her.

Bob was devastated. He said that he didn't realize the impact of his behavior and that he was terribly sorry, and he really was. He asked what could he do to make things right and get his wife back and get their marriage stabilized again?

A piece of cake. The therapist simply taught Bob in a few easy sessions how normal people treat each other in life and especially in a marriage relationship, using the therapy known as "modeling" in the psychology trade. And that was all there was to that. Sometimes people simply have to be taught how to behave. Well, Bob practiced kindness and courtesy #101, bought flowers and candy, and in due course Betty moved back home and they lived a much more normal and pleasant life. Ah, but doth this not smack of "general codependence" again?

As the counselor reasoned, and so then did Bob discover, Bob's errant and inconsiderate behavior involving his constant carping and finding fault with his wife was a behavior he learned when just a child as he watched his father, who was his role model, abuse his mother in the same fashion.

Bob was behaving just as he was taught. The chance exists, even if slight, that Bob did not fully realize how shabbily he was treating Betty. The question that then begs to be asked is: Why did Betty put up with the abuse for such a long period of time? You may refer to earlier explanations for why people tolerate mental abuse.

A sad footnote has been added to their story in recent times, because, as the history of their relationship unfolded following their reconciliation, it came to pass that a contributing factor to their marital strife was that Bob had a cancer developing in his body, which ultimately proved to be terminal.

The connection between a person's health and his behavior (especially a sudden change in behavior) only proves that the physical as well as mental health of each of the marriage partners is a critical component of their everyday lives, and how they get along.

If you are having marital problems, a good suggestion is that both marriage partners should have a complete physical examination and be as sure as you can that there is no underlying physical disorder which could be a cause of your distress.

Mental abuse is a serious problem that must be solved, if not by the person being abused, then by other concerned family members who might have knowledge of the ongoing mental mistreatment, especially if the abuse is directed at a child or children or elderly persons who cannot take care of or defend themselves. Any situation of mental abuse must be addressed as early as the pattern is noticed, and must not be allowed to continue to a point of collapse, as in the true case of Betty and Bob above.

If you feel you are the recipient of mental abuse, or you observe the mistreatment occurring to some other member of your family, one of the following courses would be appropriate:

a) Somehow get the attention of the offender and by using good negotiation and communication techniques, clearly tell them of your displeasure at the way you or some other member of the family is being abused. Pull no punches.

b) Explain carefully and firmly that the abuse must not continue, and that the issue is not negotiable. Explain that mental abuse can be corrected and/or eliminated, often by his simply accepting your complaint, and by the two of you working together to find new ways to treat each other. Sometimes abusers will try to escape their guilt by diving into a pool of denial; they may even turn your accusation of abuse around to attack you or the other person who is complaining and trying to bring an end to an unpleasant abusive situation.

c) In the worst case scenario, as in the true-life example above, if the abuser just doesn't "get it," stays in denial and will not accept the responsibility for his actions and/or will not do anything to modify the abusive behavior, then the necessary effort must be put forth to bring the poor situation to a quick end, probably with the help of outside intervention. But first, the victim(s) must be moved out of harm's way in the same manner as set out in the two previous types of abuse.

Remember the story told just above where the underlying causes of abuse were both codependence and illness.

Hopefully, a series of sessions with a therapist will be enough to solve the problem as the therapist shows the offender how to behave with civility, how to address other people and how not to constantly try to drag down or demean others to what he perceives as his own low level of insecurity.

Abuse, as defined herein in the above three categories of happenstance, is indeed a reason to seek escape from marriage via the divorce courts. Failure to act and to find happiness in one's own life, or to help someone else escape abuse, perhaps a child, could eventually result in the circumstance we call "total incompatibility" in our Marriage Relationship concept, and that condition is also a reason to divorce.

Instances of mental abuse can be stopped, and the sooner the correction process is begun, the better off everyone will be.

However, if the abuser is agreeable and does manage to overcome the abusing ways, then what is the point of divorce? Divorce as such should not be a form of punishment for past sins, and, by the way, didn't you say "for better or for worse, in sickness and in health" that day? Abuse carried to extreme forms is a sickness in the mind of the abuser. If the abuser can regain his balance and mental health, then wouldn't it be appropriate to pick up the pieces of your lives, and go forward with your marriage relationship?

People can get over sickness, and lives and relationships can be mended.

G

Stands For 'GENERAL CODEPENDENCE'

Hopefully the concept of codependence, as explained earlier in Chapter Four, made sense. However, if there is still uncertainty in your mind about this concept I urge you to revisit Chapter Five and re-read that information until the notion fits comfortably in your mind and you gain a clear understanding of this thing called codependence. Please remember that this issue of codependence comes in two varieties, one being what is called "addictive" codependence, which involves an individual's loss of personal control in the use of substances or behaviors; the other is a general behavioral-type malfunction which I call "general" codependence.

Briefly restated, general codependence is defined as simply all the garbage, or dysfunctional behavior, that is passed down through the generations by family traditions and rituals. As you will see, this issue of general codependence is of such a critical nature to anybody's marriage relationship that I shall devote considerable time and space to the subject. You must know about and understand the impact that general codependence has on your own marriage relationship.

Before we begin, a quotation provided earlier in this text is worthy of repetition as a good generalized definition of general codependence:

> "General codependence is a dysfunctional pattern of living and problem-solving nurtured by an unwritten set of family rules."

A brief disclaimer: There most certainly are some good types of general codependence, such as a family teaching and training their children to be kind, generous, friendly and personable. But for the purposes of our marriage relationship discussion, general codependence, as we are discussing it here, deals primarily with the negative or down-side types of family behaviors. Therefore, within the concept of the Marriage Relationship idea, general codependence is usually not a good thing.

Your knowing about, and being able to recognize, the symptoms of general codependence should not only help you detect a codependent situation as the source of a problem in your marriage, but also, you can then try to solve or lessen the impact of a non-understandable behavior by trying some of the various solutions that are offered. If the solutions suggested in this book don't seem to work, hopefully you can engage your brain and come up with your own answer(s) to cope with a troublesome situation.

The really bad news is that every family, and therefore every person, has to some extent a state of general codependency woven into his life.

Since people already have their own set of ingrained dysfunctional and codependent behaviors, we all come into a new marriage trying to meld or shift our original family's codependent behaviors with the new marriage partner's original family codependence structure. The mixing and mashing of these two sets of original-family codependence conditions then establishes a whole new set of general codependence rules and rituals to which the children of the new marriage relationship are then codependent.

Unfortunately, except for mental health professionals, not too many folks in the general public know much about either type of codependence, and that each of us is codependent to some extent. Nor does the general public realize the tremendous effect that carried-forward general codependence behaviors can have on a marriage relationship.

Good news! The chains that hold individuals and families in the grip of general codependence can be broken, and the vicious circle of errant and dysfunctional behavior can be stopped.

The first thing I want to do is to list is some of the more common symptoms of this general codependence thing, so that when you do bump into a particular symptom, hopefully you will be able to recognize the condition. Once you know what you are up against, you can realize that the root source of the problem is not necessarily within yourself, but is a behavior or thought pattern which your spouse codependently brought from his original family.

After displaying the partial list of codependence symptoms, in the upcoming paragraph, I shall offer some of the different ways you might try to alter a particular pattern of dysfunctional codependent behavior.

Maybe just your coming to an understanding of a weird or annoying behavior will be enough to allow you to live with it, once you know the "why" of it all. But, anyhow, here is a partial list of some of the more prominent symptoms of this state called general codependence:

1) problems with interpersonal communication
2) inability to display an emotional response in a normal manner
3) inability or unwillingness to talk about problems
4) triangulation, or always getting someone else into the mess
5) too high expectations and demands on others
4) being too selfish or too unselfish
7) "Do as I say and not as I do."
8) never, never have fun or enjoy yourself
9) don't rock the boat

Of course there are other behavioral codependent variations in existence, but that list of the nine typical and more prominent symptoms should be enough to demonstrate what this thing called general codependence is really all about.

Before we charge into the solution phase, please let it be understood that in these few short pages I can offer only a small sampling of the many possible solutions that might be available to solve not only the problems listed above, but also any other dysfunctionally codependent condition or situation. There are lots of books and a multitude of good informational sources available, not only in the public libraries and book stores, but also via tapes advertised on TV, in magazine articles and other media sources, which offer their own possible solution(s) to specific problem areas.

Here again in the same order as the foregoing listing of some symptoms is a sampling of possible explanations and a few offered solutions:

Symptom #1. Difficulty with interpersonal communication

Unfortunately, this is one of the most common complaints and a very critical consideration in the life of every marriage relationship. To begin with, there are two main types of communication. One is the spoken word and how those words are delivered, the other being the non-verbal communications, which are the physical movements we make which can convey and reinforce an emotion, or a message. These physical movements include the phenomenon popularly known as "body language," wherein body movements and positions or postures can consciously or unconsciously impart to an alert viewer what emotion or message is being broadcast, without benefit of speech.

Verbal Communication Problems

Many people feel that verbal communication is the most important aspect of a marriage relationship. There is little doubt that such is the case. However, just being able to communicate does not insure that problems will be solved. Lots of times, husbands and wives communicate in their own manners, without either person having solutions to problems in mind. The goal of my Marriage Relationship concept is to offer some solutions, and as well, to offer some insight into the basic human communication process.

From a general codependence point of view, the truth of the matter is that we are probably going to communicate, or not, with our spouse in the same manner and form as we saw our parents interact with each other when we were growing up. In addition to that powerful influence, each person has his own personality, temperament and character, and as you will see, these three personal traits also contribute to the overall ability or failure of a person to communicate effectively.

And then we come to what is beyond the shadow of a doubt the biggest problem of all in male/female communications and that is the well known and generally accepted fact that men and women do not talk or communicate on the same plane, and therefore are not on the same level of general understanding.

Many outstanding books and tapes are available on this subject including the works of Deborah Tannen, and John Gary. But let me refer again to Dr. John Gray's wonderful book, *Men Are From Mars, Women Are From Venus,* wherein the obvious message is that men and women talk to each other as if they are from different planets.

Men and women might talk the same language whether it is English or Spanish or whatever, but what a woman says to a male will be interpreted by the male in the his manner, and what a man might say to a female will be interpreted and processed in her own manner. The really bad news is that the two manners of communication are not very close to being alike unless the message is completely clear and direct. Females talk to each other and understand one another. Males talk to other males and expect them to understand what is being said. And they do, by and large.

Here is the big difference between the sexes: When it comes to vocal communication, women usually tend to communicate in a round-about and indirect manner. Females do this because as little girls they were taught or socialized to not tell Daddy exactly what it is they think, or are trying to say, because if they did they would be impolite, or perhaps even not lady-like. Men, on the other hand, are taught as little boys to speak directly, and to try to say exactly what they mean to say.

Unfortunately the indirect female manner of communication is not understood by most males and this misunderstanding causes a whale of a lot of trouble between husbands and wives.

For example: A man and his wife are driving home after an evening out. She would like to stop and have a chocolate sundae or a cup of coffee, so, in her indirect female manner she says to her hubby, "Honey, would you like to have a chocolate sundae or a cup of coffee?" He hears what she has said, and after thinking her offer over for a second or two, he decides that a sundae or a cup of coffee doesn't happen to sound too good to him at this time. And since he is a male trained to take communications or spoken messages directly at face value, he simply replies, "No."

She is hurt. Miffed. Why, she thinks, doesn't he ever consider what I want?

Answer: If he knew that she actually wanted a chocolate sundae or a coffee there's almost no doubt that he would have been more than happy to oblige her desires and he would have stopped for a treat. But, since he didn't realize or understand that she wasn't able or inclined to directly state her own wish for a treat, he missed the entire point of her communication. She asked, did HE want to stop? And he didn't, so he said no.

Question: Why didn't she say very directly, "Honey, this has been such a fun evening, I would like to stop for a cup of coffee and visit a while"? Answer: Because that would be a direct statement and, once again, generally speaking, women are trained not to make direct communication statements to males.

Another true example: A lady calls male friend (me) and invites him to go to an event. Male says yes, but senses that something is being left out of the conversation. After some sparring and thrashing, male friend (me again) having been trained in the fine art of femalistic indirection in communication says to female,

"Ask David (her husband who was sitting there listening to the spinning conversation) what it is you want to tell me that you can't." She turns to hubby David and says, "He (me) wants to know what it is I need to tell him." In the background I hear her husband, David, say, "Tell him to make his own reservations." She says back on the phone to me, "David says to call and make your own reservations." She simply could not bring herself to make such a direct statement, almost an order, to another male. Women simply do not talk to males in that manner on Venus. Or to a great extent on Earth either.

Perhaps your realizing this huge difference in styles and manners of communication will help you understand the source of some of the communication problems in your own marriage.

Time and space in this text limits how much can be said about this issue of communication, but, as mentioned above, in addition to these words of wisdom, there are countless sources for additional information about developing and managing effective communication techniques in a marriage setting. Here are some generalized suggestions in the acronym form, using the word "talking."

T stands for talking. Keep talking to each other. Don't use the silent treatment as a weapon in a family dispute. Set aside a few minutes or a specific time every day for you and your spouse to talk. Just talk like you did when you were courting. Keep in touch with each other and each other's world, especially after the family arrives when too frequently each marriage partner seems to go his own way.

A stands for attitude. Watch out for negativism. Watch out for seeming to frequently put your spouse on the defensive. Talk about things and events and activities that are pleasant and of mutual interest, not just kids, or work or problems.

L stands for length of conversation. You don't have to talk for a long time or even a set period of time, but plan to spend the dedicated minutes together each day focused on each other and the interests in each other's life. Cooking classes? Skiing? Flying? Bridge? Tennis? Golf?

K stands for knowing and planning what it is you want or need to talk about. One of the great things about the mystique called "intimacy" is the ability to talk to each other about almost anything without getting into a fight. As mentioned earlier, if there are some subjects that you both strongly disagree on, don't talk about them. But if you need to talk about your sex life or the family finances then, do it, but be sure to use the techniques of good communication with "I" statements. Explain how and what you think about the issue coolly and calmly, and stick to the subject.

I stands for the need to investigate each other's viewpoints before you both try to come to a conclusion or negotiate a settlement of a problem. Take time to carefully explain where you are "coming from" on the subject. Listen very closely, and try to understand your partner's point of view. There is certainly more than one way to look at things and circumstances, so have an open mind and try to be flexible.

Some people think that a mind and a parachute are a lot alike: Neither one works unless it is open.

N stands for never. Never attack your spouse in these conversations. Do not begin the conversation with "You always," or "You never." When women say, "Let's talk," many, if not most, men immediately think, "Oh, oh, here it comes . . . she wants to talk (criticize me) about something I've done wrong," and think they smell a lecture coming. Remember to stick only with the "I" statements and avoid critical statements which begin with "You". It doesn't make any difference if the criticism is obvious or subtle, it still hurts.

There is an old saying which goes: "Sticks and stones may break my bones, but cruel words will break my heart." So, if you stay away from "you" statements and, therefore criticism, your marriage partner will realize they have nothing to fear from the daily conversations, and will freely join in.

G stands for being gentle. Give compliments. Praise each other's qualities in public, as well as in private. Help each other. Be kind. Relationships are built or eroded in little steps, so if you are a staunch supporter and friend of your spouse, no matter what, through thick and thin, you will soon find that he will be your supporter and friend, too. One of the keys to a happy marriage relationship is that, through your mutual education of each other, and with gradual gentleness, a wonderful bonded friendship can be formed.

Closing this section, mention needs to be made of Dr. Deborah Tannen's great book, titled *You Just Don't Understand,* in which she brilliantly outlines some of the very same points made by Dr. Gray in his book, but from a feminine point of view. Both books are very easy to read, and can prove to be very helpful to your Marriage Relationship.

Non-verbal Communication

In recent years more attention has been paid to the study of body language, which is known formally as kinesics. A perfect reference is the book *Body Language,* written in 1970 by Julius Fast.

In his book Dr. Fast outlines not only some of the hidden meanings of various body positions, movements and facial expressions, but most importantly concludes that body language in itself, and as a method of communication, is **not** an accurate indication of either obvious or hidden meaning. Rather, when body language is joined with the spoken communication, an observant (and trained) viewer and listener can get a clearer and even stronger meaning of the intention of what is actually being said, and meant.

A good example of conflicting languages, body versus spoken, would be the scene wherein a person is furiously angry and shouting at someone else, yet who is constantly smiling as he expresses his anger. Or, how about the person who is saying something very affirmatively, but at the same time shaking his head from side to side, which we all know means "no." Contrary and confusing signals which indicate that the person speaking is not all that convinced of the validity of their argument.

For the purposes of our Marriage Relationship discussion, non-verbal or body language communications can be observed and then understood within the context that they are delivered.

For example: A warm touch on the hand or arm would mean just what it says: "You are interesting. I would like to get closer and know you better." When someone moves nearer to another person and thereby moves inside the "boundaries" of that other person it means, "I would like to be with you." A brush by a person with his own body on another person's body is a sensual signal that might well be heeded and understood, and you don't need to be a rocket scientist to figure that one out.

Reverse or negative body language examples could include the beginning of a rather tense conversation with the arms of the person beginning the conversation folded across his chest in a defensive position, or with his legs crossed and perhaps with one leg swinging (kicking). Tense or exaggerated facial expressions can also be an indication of anxiety or frustration, and although the conversation might not have yet deteriorated to a critical or argumentative level, such negative body language expressions will almost always precede the angry or disappointed tenor of an upcoming discussion.

Anyone interested in a more exhaustive investigation into the fascinating subject of body language might read Dr. Fast's or Dr. Pease's books, which are listed in the bibliography. If you want to show closeness or affection, or perhaps simply friendship, a smile, a caress, a loving touch or a relaxed posture will prove to back up and reinforce your spoken words.

Symptom #2. Inability to normally display emotional response

Once again the childhood experiences of the individual will probably prevail. Very likely, as the parents displayed their emotions plus or minus in the original (nuclear) family in front of the children, so people, as they grow older, tend to display or not show their own emotions in the same manner. Subject to the following well-known generalizations:

General rule #1: It is not okay for males to ever display any emotions. Little boys, and especially big boys, don't cry.

General rule #2: It is absolutely okay and even expected that females will display their emotions. Sometimes a tad of crying can get girls, be they little or big, an awful lot of consideration.

So, females are allowed and even encouraged to openly display their emotions. Males, on the other hand, are trained to express their feelings in what is known as an "instrumental" manner. What this means is, that instead of actually having to say what it is they feel, your average male will do something, perform some act or deed which he thinks demonstrates how he feels and thereby escapes the risk of losing all his malehood by actually having to vocalize his feelings.

For example, if your typical man wants to show affection or gratitude to his wife he might wash her car. He thinks that his show of effort will be interpreted by her as evidence of his affection. Not so.

What happens is that the wife will

think, by washing her car, he is being critical of her for not keeping it clean. And thereby have her feelings hurt. Conversely, it also is possible for a male to display his anger or frustration in some sort of obvious and instrumental fashion.

Here's another male problem; many men are very insecure and uncertain of themselves and their abilities, and therefore very vulnerable to criticism. Most (all) men want (need) their wives to look up to and depend on them, which is why most males so often are afraid to reveal much, if anything, in an emotional manner. Please recall that men think (are taught) any display of emotions makes them feel or look weak or powerless in her eyes, and thereby take a chance of losing her respect.

How could a female ever hope to get her male to display any emotions? To actually say what he feels? Only by using the "I" method of communication, such as: "I feel so . . . when you . . . ," or "I love it when you . . . " With great and gentle persistence and endless determination, a woman might eventually convince her man that she liked it when he displayed some emotion and retired from the great-stone-faced crowd. There is always the chance (however slight it may be) that if the male finds out that he can make his wife happy by showing some emotional response, he may.

Have you ever heard this scenario? Woman complains that "You never tell me you love me." "Aw shucks," he says, "she knows I love her, so why do I have to tell her? After all, I washed her car just last week." Or this one: "Why do I have to tell her I love her? I told her that once forty two years ago; she knows."

Nobody said this would be an easy task, but perhaps just your knowing where males and the females are "coming from," will help with deficiencies in the display of honest emotional responses in your home. Gentle persuasion. Persistence.

Symptom #3. Inability or unwillingness to talk about problems

Again with reference to Dr. Gray's book about men being from Mars and women from Venus, this issue of how problems are treated is a very real mystery to most married couples, and a strain on many marriage relationships.

Basically here is the situation as it exists: Men do not talk about their problems with anyone. If a man has a problem he will go off into his "cave" as Dr. Gray puts it, and ponder the problem until he hits on a solution he likes, and once his solution is in hand he will emerge from his cave and then perhaps talk about the problem. Maybe! For a male to have to talk about his problem before arriving at a solution would be a sign of weakness, and we already have discovered that males will do almost anything to keep from looking weak or ineffectual, or dumb, and risk losing "face" or respect.

Women operate on an entirely different plane(t) than men. Women need and like to share feelings, and thereby gain intimacy with other females, and males, if they only would, by talking about their problems. If a woman has a problem she wants (needs) to talk about it, and once she has started talking, she may talk about all her problems in their entirety until she gets tired of talking. Males do not understand this method of operation and most men do not realize that while reciting her list of concerns she is NOT looking for solutions,

This is the tricky part for most men to understand: She isn't looking for him to come up with solutions. All she wants is to share her thought processes and talk about her problem(s) with him, as she sees them. Her solutions come later.

The male problem, as stated above, is that the average man thinks, when his wife starts talking about a problem, he is being put on the spot and he not only has to come up with a solution, but also it must be the right one. He finds out that if he offers a solution too quickly, she will reject it off-handedly because that is not what she wants. All she wants him to do is to listen. Just listen. Males have to learn how to say, "tsk tsk," "oh my," "wow," and other innocuously "sharing" phrases. Just empathize, sympathize, wrinkle the brow, look at her attentively and respectfully, and **KEEP QUIET !**

Once she is done with the recitation of her problem, maybe all her life problems, she will feel much better, perhaps even "validated," which means that her thoughts and feelings are considered important. She will then move the conversation to a brighter note and that particular episode will be history.

I've never been to a women's bridge-club meeting, but I've been told that it is not uncommon for the card game of bridge to never even occur at such a meeting. Rather, the entire time is spent by the ladies taking turns talking about their problems, and by sharing their own respective concerns and family "train wrecks," they feel closer to each other and leave fulfilled and "validated."

The fairly obvious solution to a perceived problem with free exchange of mutual concern over problems would be to:

a) simply accept the now-known fact that men and women handle problems and discussions about them in different manners;

b) if that isn't good enough, then perhaps the woman of the house could gently, over time, encourage her mate to be more open and to actually share with and tell her some of his concerns in life.

But attention must be given to the basic insecurity of the male human, and although, typically in any given circumstance, two heads are usually better than one, the fact remains that the male must not lose his bearings and sail out to sea on a course which would only reap, in his mind, disrespect and vulnerability.

One of the more popular myths existent with regard to the relationship known as marriage is that the marriage partners must be "best friends" and share all their thoughts, worries and hopes with each other. Doctor Arnold Lazerus wrote a splendid book titled *Marital Myths* in which he cites "Two Dozen Mistaken Beliefs That Can Ruin a Marriage (Or Make a Bad One Worse)."

Myth #1 is that husbands and wives should be "best friends."

Doctor Lazerus points out that sometimes the complete exposition of all one's woes and worries is not fair to the other marriage partner in that such a confession of concern about a problem may unduly upset the other partner.

The circumstance may certainly exist wherein the other marriage partner does not have a clear frame of reference or depth of understanding about the issue that is causing concern to the marriage partner.

For example: Man is worried about conditions at his workplace and is fearful of losing his job. No hard evidence exists that a layoff is certain, but nonetheless he has feelings of fear and insecurity. Doctor Lazerus rightly contends that it's probably grossly unfair to prematurely share (unload) with his wife his possibly unwarranted concern about losing his job. His point is, once she hears this news, she will begin to worry and have concern, perhaps needlessly, over her husband's perceived uncertainty of employment.

However, the principle also remains; the more each marriage partner can fairly share his inner thoughts and worlds, the greater the partners will enjoy mutual feelings of safety and trust.

Symptom #4. Triangulation

The habit, or trick, of always getting someone else immersed in the middle of a problem. Triangulation is an annoying ploy, frequently used by those persons who do not wish to, or cannot confront their own lives and cope with problems personally. Needless to say the poor soul who is always getting caught 'in the middle' and ends up taking sides, is the loser.

To the right is a small sketch of a typical third person triangle in which the issue the two people can't talk about or resolve is shown between them. At the top of the triangle is the third person who gets sucked in to the disagreement and ends up being the communication link between the disagreeing couple.

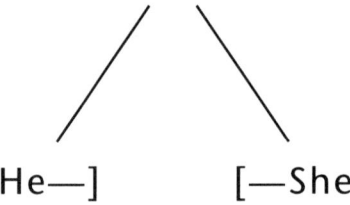

The usual upshot of a triangulation is confusion, uncertainty, failure to satisfactorily settle the dispute and damage to the third person, the poor pigeon who gets caught in the middle of the squabble.

Several possible solutions jump up to solve a problem of chronic triangulation: One is for the marriage partner who realizes this dysfunctional triangulation game is being played to simply refuse to participate in the triangle. Tell the other partner he can see what's happening, and simply announce that if the dispute is going to get settled, then "Let's do it ourselves and not always have someone else involved." Period.

Another course could be for the mate who knows about triangulation to tell the third person what is happening and strongly suggest that he should simply say "NO" when approached by the dysfunctional codependent marriage partner who is trying to start up another triangle, hoping to get his way in the dispute.

A continuing pattern of triangulation to solve family disputes is nearly always self-defeating, and some other solution short of abandoning all attempts to solve family problems must be found.

Symptom #5: Too high expectations and demands on others

The issue of expectations is covered under the first **E** in the word "relationship," and in that context expectations as a problem deals mainly with regard to whatever disappointments or misconceptions the partners expected would happen between them once they got married, and didn't.

However, when it comes to the subject of general codependence, the symptom of expectations generally shows up as too high levels of parental concern and ambition for achievement by the children.

We've all seen parents attempt to relive their own lives through the activities of their offspring and thereby hope (try) to escape or somehow diminish their own lifetime failures and disappointments. The antics and shabby behaviors of parents whose children are involved in youth athletic programs are legendary. Little League baseball is a classic example.

Hopefully both parents won't/don't come down with the same frantic fervor and wild desperation for the child(ren)'s success at the same time, and the non-or less-afflicted parent can talk some sense and reason with the maniacal parent who is pushing the child(ren) too hard.

As mentioned above, that other side of having too-high expectations can happen when one marriage partner expects too much from the other. But, any way you slice it anyone having too high expectations for others is trouble.

Symptom #6: Being too selfish or too unselfish

Of those two varieties of dysfunction, who would know which one is worse?

Someone who is totally selfish can be a pain beyond description. This disorder seems to occur to a good degree in those who live more or less in their own world, and have been "spoiled" by their parents and taught to think only of themselves. Often "only children" fit into this description, and their levels of selfishness can astound even a casual observer.

On the other hand, the person who is too unselfish will be seen to constantly short themselves physically and vocally to the un-asked-for perceived advantage of others.

For example, the mother who consistently takes the pieces of chicken she doesn't even like, such as the last part over the fence, so others may have what she sees as the better cuts, could be said to be demonstrating codependent unselfishness. Conversely, the selfish person will go through the dinner line first and thoughtlessly wipe out all the white meat, if that is what he prefers, leaving only drumsticks and fannies for those who follow.

Solutions to both ends of that spectrum would lie mostly in a course of persistent but gentle reminding of the person that his behavior, be it either way, is not only not necessary, but in fact, is quite detrimental to the family structure and certainly not a good example for youngsters to observe.

Extreme cases of either behavior, whether it be selfish or selfless, and unrelenting persistence of that behavior in spite of admonitions to the contrary, might possibly be symptoms of a variety of personality disorders. One could be the passive-aggressive disorder for the selfless or too unselfish person, and an anti-social personality disorder for the selfish person.

If, over time, friendly reminders to the person of his slightly off-center behavior doesn't result in some measure of adjustment, you might have to pay attention to the possible existence of one of those personality disorders which are treatable only by a trained professional therapist.

Needless to say, a person with either personality disorder would usually not limit the display of his behavioral dysfunctions to just his family, but would likely be having other interpersonal difficulties as well. But, nonetheless, someone being too selfish or unselfish is a well-known symptom of general codependence.

Symptom #7: Do as I say and not as I do.

This is one of the most confusing symptoms of general codependence and it exists in the circumstance wherein a person, usually an adult and parent, will, from time to time, deliver ultimatums or suggestions to others, like the children, which contradict his own obvious behaviors.

For instance, a man having a beer and smoking a cigarette telling his children to "just say NO" to drugs would be a clearcut example of this symptom. Needless to say, such obviously contradictory messages do not make a lot of sense to a young person who is just beginning to face life's challenges. Or to anyone else for that matter, since the exhibited behavior flies in the face of the advice being given.

People who come from a codependent background in which this sort of contradictory behavior has occurred are likely to repeat the pattern of confusion in their own later life, and even in their own marriage. As far as they are concerned, it's okay to warn others about certain behaviors, without regard to the apparent contradictions which may not be apparent to them.

Meanwhile they behave or misbehave and do about anything they may choose. In days of yore, like a long, long time ago, the ruling classes used to call this *noblesse oblige*. (Whatever the King says, goes, baby.)

Some spoken phrases are good clues to this form of codependence, and they would include "Don't EVER . . . !"or, "Watch out for . . . !" How about; "Don't end up like me . . . " or " I want you to do better for your own sake etc. etc. " And the old classic, "Everything I do is for you . . . " and so on and on ad sillium.

Solving this symptom is tricky and any hope for a solution would depend on the approach that might be taken. A possible avenue might be for a marriage partner to try to point out to the spouse how giving all this so-called "good advice" doesn't live up to and is contradictory to his own obvious behavior.

Be sure to deliver these observations and admonitions in private with only the confused advice-giver present. Do not embarrass the person who gives out all his contradictory messages by lashing out when the young(sters) or anyone else is present.

However, if a good fight isn't on the menu, then about all one can do is circle the wagons and slyly, over time, casually point out to the person(s) (kids) who are the recipients of all the "good advice" begin given, that while the suggestions are well-intentioned and perhaps even worthwhile, the message being delivered is indeed confusing and contradictory. Hopefully the kids had already had figured this out. Maybe, in due course, the person delivering the confusing advice will get the idea too, and cease the contradictory behavior, or practice keeping his big mouth shut.

It is held in many circles that a closed mouth gathers no foot.

Whenever you hear this "Do as I say and not as I do" routine you've got a really big clue that the person, who is verbally contradicting himself by his actions, is someone who has his own ton of problems with general codependence, and probably heard that same sort of confusing advice when he was a child.

Symptom #8: Don't enjoy yourself.

One dead giveaway of a person who was brought up in a codependent early family life is the individual who just can't ever seem to find anything or anyone to enjoy. In his view, to display pleasure or enjoyment is simply not good form.

People like this have been taught to think that one must remain humorless and deadly serious about all matters all of their life, because that's the way it was when they were kids Everything is a BIG DEAL and this sort of person is so negative and scared they either remain aloof and do not participate in any fun-type activities, or worse, they will tend to find fault and ridicule every possible source of enjoyment and sometimes even the individuals who are having a nice time and enjoying either the circumstances or the company.

And what to do with such a wet blanket? Realize that they have been "socialized," that is, taught as children to see things from the negative view that anything fun or funny is not good and/or perhaps even bad, and the way to be good and strong, is to not enjoy yourself. They have been taught that having fun and laughing is a sign of weakness and therefore not appropriate behavior. How's that for twisted logic?

Attempting to convince someone who cannot enjoy himself to relax and enjoy life would call for a stream of cool, calm and persistent conversation delivered over time. The discourse should be encouraging and positive in nature using only "I" statements, and never delivered in a critical manner, such as with "**You** never . . . " or You always . . . " statements. Stay away from the "you's," and be very careful not to attack the individual personally. Remember that nobody likes to be criticized. Especially males.

Author Kurt Vonnegut once told some graduates at a commencement address:

"Remember the
compliments you receive.
Forget the insults and criticism.
If you succeed in doing this,
please tell me how."

Of course the underlying problem is that the person who is so inclined to be a constant back-biter or fault-finder will grate on the nerves and sensitivities of his spouse, so while the problem might seem initially to be in, and with, the sour pessimist, the burden really exists in the mind of the marriage partner whose nerves are being continually tested by the negative attitudes of the complainer.

The seriousness of the situation depends on the mindset of the suffering spouse, for if the endless carping and meanness really annoys and makes him unhappy, then it is up to the aggrieved mate to find a solution, since at this point it is his problem.

Do you recall the earlier mention of a neat book penned by the famous psychologist Dr. Arnold Lazerus, titled *Marital Myths?* Well, Myth #21 is:

"Opposites attract and complement each other."

Without reciting Dr. Lazerus' entire text on this myth, it is fairly common knowledge that sometimes persons with completely opposite personalities are attracted to each other and, in the end, the very opposing traits or behaviors which caused the couple to be interested in each other in the first place, can end up being the cause of their eventual divorce.

Here's how it works: Say, for example, a vivacious outgoing lady meets a quiet, serious, stable, introverted man. She thinks he is exactly what she needs in her life to provide a calming and down-to-earth influence. Meanwhile, he thinks she is what he needs to provide more excitement and fun in what he realizes is his dull personality and life. Sounds good so far, right?

However, here comes the bad news: Once the honeymoon is over, the passion fades and life settles in, she begins to think that she has married the biggest male dud in the world, and he begins to think that he has married the biggest, dumbest, loudmouthed extroverted female in the world. Conflict pervades their marriage relationship, and as mentioned above, a divorce ensues with the usual casualties, the children, if there are any.

The lesson: The more two people can be alike in their backgrounds, likes and dislikes, outlooks, personalities, temperaments and characters, the better the chances will be that their marriage will succeed.

If you have trouble accepting that premise, go back and read the first chapter, Mirror, Mirror, again, which outlines the importance similarities play when choosing a mate. The companion book to this work, titled *Some of the Reasons We Behave the Way We Do,* contains extensive examination and explanation of the concepts of personality, temperament, and character. Your knowing about these personal traits will help you understand not only your mate, but yourself as well.

Symptom #9: Don't Ever Rock The Boat.

This is one of the most mysterious and baffling behaviors evident in general codependence. A normal person would think that anyone who is unhappy about something would take steps to ease his discomfort. Alas, such is not the case for anyone who is suffering from general codependence, for the thinking of such a person is that he is conditioned (accustomed) and can endlessly stand whatever miserable situation or circumstance is going on at the time, even though it may be pure hell.

The reason he thinks this is because he fears that if he changed anything, anything at all, the changes brought about may bring even worse conditions than the awful state he is living in at the time. Even if he tried to bring about a change in good faith with all sincerity and honesty on a short-term basis, he is still afraid the circumstances may worsen, and he isn't sure he can handle that.

I suggest you do not try to figure out this twisted pattern of logic, or better, non-logic, because understanding someone who is in substantial pain and who will do nothing to alleviate his discomfort is nigh onto impossible. But this behavior pattern does exist in some marriage relationships ,and many couples will live in interpersonal strife and disarray for years on end, all the while consistently and even stubbornly refusing to accept any form of help, or themselves trying to bring their lives under control and into a more happily peaceful condition.

From a therapeutic point of view, the "Don't Rock the Boat" syndrome is one of the most difficult of all the symptoms of general codependence to work with and is the stuff of the "battered women" and "battered men" syndrome. Any answers to such a personal psychic disability have to lie in a help-thyself and help-someone-else tangle much like an addictive codependence situation which will be covered a bit later.

But briefly, if help is to be found it must emanate from the following principles:

1) Everyone is responsible for his own life and happiness.
2) Nobody ever changed anybody else. A person can or will bring about changes in himself ONLY if he wants to. But, in the long run, there is really almost no chance at all that one marriage partner can get (force) their spouse to change behaviors.
3) If you believe you are in a "Don't Rock the Boat" circumstance, you can :
   a) either change yourself so you will be happy, or
   b) you can go ahead and try to change your marriage partner over time, but do not expect any help or guidance from your mate who refuses to rock the boat and make your marriage relationship better. Rather, you can expect reluctance, fear and resistance on his part to try even the smallest adjustment or shift in your relationship, or his behavior. To make matters worse (if that's possible) you can expect disdain and even anger at any attempt on your part to better your life. If you choose this course, plan on it being a long haul, but don't ever give up. In case you hadn't already guessed, giving up equals a divorce.

There then, are a few of the typical symptoms of this thing we are calling general codependence. You can work with them as you may, but, in case you have bumped up against one or more of these symptoms, you should also keep in mind the possibility that a more serious diagnosis might be applicable to the person with a persistently negative or warped attitude. He might have a genuine personality disorder.

If you think that might be the case, you ought to at least ask a psychologist about personality disorders and what can be done about them.

To briefly outline this business about personality disorders, reference is made to the excellent book written by the chief gurus of these dysfunctional behaviors, psychologists Dr. Theodore Millon and Dr. George Everly, titled *Personality And Its Disorders*, which is listed in the bibliography.

Doctors Millon and Everly list eight principal personality disorders in their book, and while space does not exist here to extensively outline each of the disorders, here is a list of them, along with a brief explanation of the symptoms of each disorder.

Happily, almost all forms of personality disorders are treatable by a competent therapist, because personality disorders are almost always behavioral in origin.

We aren't going to let you forget this:

Any behavior that is learned can be unlearned, and vice versa.

Only, of course, if the patient wants to be treated. The bottom line with regard to personality disorders is that if you think you might be up against one, just stop and think how unhappy the poor person is who suffers with the disorder. Try to get some help.

If you want to know more about personality disorders please refer to the fine Millon/Everly book which is listed in the bibliography.

Conclusions

1) Everybody, almost without exception, is generally codependent to some extent because everyone is brought up as a child in his original family with all the rules, rituals and traditions of the original family setting. They will never be forgotten. To further complicate matters, when you get married both of you will bring all of your own original codependent behaviors with you to your marriage. Once married, both partners will proceed to try merging (perhaps forcing) their original (nuclear) family dysfunctional codependency rules onto the other marriage partner with the net result that the two of you will come up with a new set of hopefully not too dysfunctional (screwed up) rules for your new family and marriage relationship. Of course the children of this new marriage will, when the time comes, have to go through the same merging/changing process their parents did.

2) Once you can detect that some, or at least part of your troubles comes from a condition of general codependence, at least you know what you are up against, and hopefully you can fix the problem yourself. If you cannot, the obvious alternative solution

Personality disorder:	Some symptoms of:
Anti-social	Fearless to reckless, sometimes "acts out." Can be antagonistic, belligerent and mean. Sees self as competitive and domineering. Differential (other) diagnoses could include: Schizophrenic paranoia—thinks everyone is watching and "after" him.
Histrionic	Very demonstrative and given to excessive statements such as "Oh, I'd die" etc.
Passive/aggressive	Gets own way by becoming sullen, quiet. Pouts. Enjoys "moods." Controlling.
Avoidant	The recluse—hermit. Won't go out in public. Sometimes "agoraphobics" fit this category.
Narcissistic	Constantly puts self down to get attention.
Dependent	Can't do a damn thing on their own.
Compulsive /obsessive	Impulsive, abrupt, gets an idea in their head and can't get it out. This disorder includes addicts of all sorts.
Schizotypal	Pre-schizophrenic. Can get confused about who, where and maybe what time period period they are in. Other forms of full-blown schizophrenia do exist too.
Multiple (MPD)	It is said the "nobody has just one addiction." It is also said that nobody has just one personality disorder. If a person has one, he may have several.

lies in your finding and utilizing the education and experience of a competent psychotherapist to help you straighten out the mess.

At this time in history there are out-patient as well as in-patient psychotherapy programs in various institutions. Psychotherapists often can do a good job with personality disorders. As a rule, after a few one-on-one sessions the client is referred to a "group-in-session," for perhaps a many as ten sessions. The value of group therapy cannot be overstated. "Group" is where it's at, therapeutically.

The cost of group therapy is usually

modest, but the results are frequently and typically stupendous. In addition, short of therapeutic referral, there are many support groups in almost every community in the country which cater to specific problems in life. For example, for alcoholics there is the famous Alcoholics Anonymous program (AA), and their counterparts, Al-anon.

Other support groups such as Alzheimer's and survivors or sufferer groups of various ailments and concerns are abundant. The list goes on and on. Look in the newspaper, or ask around to find, and use, a support group that might address your particular concern.

Well, that is what general codependence is all about. You might want to go back to page 126 and re-read the nine most common symptoms of general codependence. It is a pervasive problem, to some degree, in almost every marriage relationship. But once this condition is understood and admitted, almost any problem stemming from codependence can be solved. Granted that it might take time, but after a period of gentle, patient and loving communication and negotiation, success and peace surely will be found.

E

Stands For 'ENERGY'

This issue which I call energy is one of the most complained about and troublesome components embodied in my 20-issue consideration of marriage relationships. A good example of a failure of energy in a marriage is when wives are heard to complain of their husband's indifference, or even outright refusal to pitch in and help with the household chores.

In these days of two-income families, too often it falls to the female to not only work at a job all day, but then, after work she must come home and go to work again, preparing dinner, taking care of household duties and the children without any help at all from her male marriage partner. Such a failure of effort or outright indifference on the part of males, while perhaps not stereotypical, is nonetheless a troublesome behavioral defect, and therefore a problem.

Human beings are curious creatures. When in the courting mode and love is new, both males and females pay close attention to each other and expend energy on the intended mate, the target of their deep affection. While in the first stages of "getting to know you," it has even been known to occur that the couple might exchange compliments with each other. In addition to paying all this attention to each other, they give special care to their own dress, person and manners.

In the case of the male, he can be spotted opening the door for his lady to help her in and out of the car, and he may also courteously open other doors so she may precede him in gracious and queenly fashion. Not that she isn't capable of opening a door by herself, but he performs such minor tasks as a gesture of consideration and manifestation of the high esteem in which she is held. He wants to take care of her, which she thinks is really great because what she wants is to be taken care of. Generally speaking, at least in the early phase of their relationship, most males behave in a courteous and energetic manner.

By the way, if males are not considerate and caring during the courtship stage of the game, the female had better watch out, because if her man is thoughtless and perhaps rude before the marriage, such behavior most certainly predicts continued and perhaps even more grossly inconsiderate treatment after marriage.

In the same manner, ladies will spend huge amounts of time on their personal appearance and dress, and when in the company of their male companion, they conduct themselves in oh-so-gentle, demure and lady-like fashion. Sometimes you hear this conduct referred to as a "wile." "She's displaying her feminine wiles," they say. A wile is defined in my dictionary as a "crafty behavior, or subtle words meant to lure . . . etc." You do get the idea, don't you?

Consideration, paying attention and devoting energy to the other person are key elements in the courtship process. Then the couple gets married, and suddenly all those nice, kind, helpful, thoughtful and considerate little deeds and actions, and the close attention formerly displayed each to the other in the courtship stage go away. In absentia. Too often all those compliments and pleasantries are replaced with complaints and criticism.

Someone said, "I knew when we got married her/his name was Wright but I didn't know his/her first name was Always."

What happened and where did all the politeness and consideration go? Well, what happens is that it's too far around the car to help her get aboard, and it's too much bother to get dressed up for him when he comes home, and everybody just lets down on the energy level, and, as they say, "the honeymoon is over." Too bad.

True story: Mary is married to Don and, from all appearances, their relationship looks like just what could be described as a perfect marriage. They have a very nice home; he has a good job and brings home, by most standards, a very ample and comfortable income. They have three little girls who, in addition to being dressed like little dolls, are healthy and well-mannered. Mary and Don are evidently a happy couple. Mary is staying home taking care of the children and her beautiful home, having foregone her own career aspirations for the time being. They have nice cars to drive, and a fine circle of friends with whom to associate.

Don comes home every night right on schedule. He spends all his evenings and weekends at home playing with the girls and doing the "honey-do's" that come up. He works in the yard and fixes the house a little, and sometimes he putters around with a car. By almost anybody's standards, Don would be what one could call the perfect husband. And both of them in the perfect marriage.

Indeed, such is not the case, for Mary is so angry and upset that she almost can't stand it, and worse, she is thinking and talking about doing dire things to her marriage. Why? Because Don isn't paying any attention to **her** and what she wants in **her** life; then, on top of that he is not helping her at all with the daily household family chores without her directly requesting that he perform a certain task. Although he is spending a great deal of time at home, he is not putting any energy into their marriage relationship. As you will soon see, energy and time are two entirely different issues.

Here's worse news, she feels that he is taking her for granted. If there is one thing women don't like, and may not stand for, is being taken for granted. If

Don, or any other male who thinks he might be in this position doesn't show a little more concern, their relationship can and will hit the skids and the first thing he knows he'll be standing in front some "Family Law" judge who will "help" him out of his marriage, his car, most of his money, his furniture, his toys, his wife and children. All just because he didn't expend enough energy on his marriage relationship. Clue: better he should help out at home, without being badgered to do so.

The trouble with a loss of energy in a marriage relationship is that one critical default like taking someone else for granted all the time, can and will lead to a personal disappointment, and then to another and another, and the first thing you know, one can have a huge disaster on his hands. A simple thing like a lack of energy can be the beginning of latent or hidden anger and frustration which can develop. And worsen. To follow our usual problem analysis format, we begin with:

a) What is the problem? Well, one of the marriage partners, very often the female, feels she is carrying more than her share of the household tasks, is being taken for granted, and/or is not being treated fairly and with consideration.

b) Is this really a problem worthy of confrontation? That is a decision that has to be made by the person who is unhappy. A simple test to determine the existence or extent of a problem could be: If one of the marriage partners is unhappy, and thinking about a confrontation, then a problem does indeed exist. If the thought exists, then so does a problem.

c) Whose problem is it? Easy: The problem belongs to the person who is unhappy. The person being selfish or inconsiderate may well be completely oblivious of his partner's distress and probably is entirely happy with the way things are going in his life and marriage relationship. Why would he want to pitch in and change anything, or expend more effort without some motivation?

d) Who has to solve the problem? The person who is unhappy. Since the person unhappy typically is the wife who wants more help with the household chores, it follows then that she will not tell her marriage partner of her unhappiness because she thinks he should realize she needs more help. Recall the example in general codependence where the gal wanted to stop for a treat, but failed to directly request the stop be made? Remember? She said, "Do you (to her hubby) want to stop?" He thinks about it and says "no." She is hurt because she wants him to think about her wishes and wants. A problem with energy will fall into much the same category. She will think if she has to beg for help, he is putting her down, therefore, she may not even ask. Just smolder, silently.

An old Malayan proverb hits the nail on the head:

> "Just because the river is quiet does not mean the crocodiles are gone."

e) How many solutions are there to the problem? How many leaves on a tree? Solutions could range from tackling a minor annoyance to requesting major changes in the relationship. The best course for the person who is unhappy would be to initially decide just how much change she wants to achieve and will settle for, at least for the time being, and strike off on that course, using the techniques outlined later in the negotiation section.

f) Which solution seems best to try initially? Using both the communication and negotiation techniques, probably the best course would be to start out by striving for a minor adjustment of a less bothersome situation. To begin with a large and maybe even massive realignment of a number of duties and/or behaviors might be too much confrontation, and may not be well met.

g) When and how do you try for the desired modification? Once you figure out what changes you want and how much more help you need, simply follow the guidelines presented throughout this discourse. Be careful about when, in what setting, and how you discuss the request for changes with your spouse. Think "short term." That is, talk about the one change that is desired, to begin with, and try to seek agreement for just that one adjustment. If your spouse agrees to go along with your initial request for change, let it happen, and take a while to see if that amount of modification does indeed help ease your mental stress, or better, distress, before pressing on for more changes. Don't be afraid to speak up. Directly tell your marriage partner you are unhappy, to whatever extent, and exactly what it is that you are unhappy about.

h) What happens if you don't succeed the first time? Try again, on a different tack. Try for a different or lesser change other than the change sought in the initial effort. Give time a chance, too; that is, don't continually complain about the issue. Don't present irrelevant or perhaps inconsequential complaints. Stay calm, but don't quit and don't make any errors in logic like: "S/he won't help me with this problem, therefore s/he doesn't love me anymore."

If failure follows failure, don't hesitate to seek out a competent counselor, and have a couple sessions with him. Many times the inclusion of a professional and neutral third person such as a therapist or mediator into a stressful negotiation can be the difference between winning and losing.

They laugh about the "Couch Potato," but the message is, that for some reason probably stemming from a state of general codependence, a person who becomes so attached to his "Couch" and his own comfort, and exhibits a lack of energy and consideration in the Marriage Relationship concept stands a very real chance in due course of expending more energy than he wishes he had to expend, and it could well be in the divorce court.

A line by Zsa Zsa Gabor springs to mind. She said that she was always "a very good housekeeper." She always kept the house in the several divorces she had been through.

Rituals

A problem with a default in energy' might possibly be easily solved through the use of a ritual, or a series of rituals.

Up to this point, not a lot of mention has been made about what are known as rituals, which are defined as traditional or consistent behavioral patterns embodied within a family circle which can take on significance. Or, said another way, a ritual is defined as an act or series of actions performed in some regular, maybe symbolic, hopefully enjoyable, and possibly even useful manner, which become a part of the very essence of the relationship.

Maybe a ritual would be a certain type of family celebration observed for a special day or time. Perhaps a family has a more-or-less set type of Christmas-time get-together or celebration, or maybe a planned activity on a national holiday or birthdays. Maybe a ritual would be for the hubby to bring coffee and a sweet roll to the mommy on Sunday mornings. Or vice versa.

The number and types of family or even interpersonal rituals is almost endless. Rituals are an enrichment of family tradition and can be used to strengthen and identify relationships. Rituals are wonderful ways for marriage partners to share feelings in actions. Rituals could be described as positive general codependence.

Rituals are a good thing to start and keep going, no matter how insignificant or almost silly they may seem to be at the time they are thought up and re-enacted time and again.

Obviously one good way to display energy to your spouse would be to find some ritual or series of rituals, which would, over the long haul, develop meaning and closeness.

For example: Wife is tired of rushing home to fix dinner while hubby sits on couch watching TV, eating dinner with TV on, then the wife gets to do all the kitchen clean-up while hubby retires back to the couch and, guess what, more TV! A decent ritual to get started would be for wife to request, and perhaps even insist, that hubby come to kitchen to help with dinner preparations, talk to her during dinner without interruptions such as TV, then the two of them clean up the dinner dishes and retire to whatever joint or personal interests would occupy the rest of the evening. That would be a good type of ritual, a routine.

Another ritual might be for Mom and Dad to go out to dinner, or to do some other activity together they both enjoy, just the two of them, on a regular basis, like once a week. Such rituals as those mentioned, or others you might think up, would in any case be a very useful joint effort; enjoyable, shared, useful and, most importantly, done together.

How to start such a ritual? Unfortunately the task of coming up with and selling a ritual will fall upon the marriage partner who has the problem. If it's the lady of the house, then she should simply and **very clearly** point out to her man that what she wants is for "this" to happen: The "this" for example, being the getting-dinner-together with the children, if any, having an uninterrupted dinner together, cleaning up the dinner dishes, again together, then both retiring to the pre-bedtime evening rest period, whatever that might be. That's the request to be tried.

If the whole package won't sell, then start out with what will sell, and see if whatever part of the desired ritual will come to pass often enough to ease the tension existent in the mind of the unhappy person. Maybe, to begin with, the only thing that will stick to the ceiling is the cleaning up after dinner routine. A start is a start.

A brief word of caution here: please recall in the Communication section of the General Codependence category that women tend to use indirect communication when they want something. In this instance, the gal must directly tell her man just exactly what it is she wants to happen. No indirection. Plain talk.

Men, on the other hand, are inclined to display affection in an "instrumental" manner. Doing something rather than saying anything. But, males do understand clearly stated, direct and unambiguous requests.

So, gentlemen, now that you are off the couch, here's more news: helping out and/or expending energy in an instrumental fashion and thinking that you are showing all this consideration and affectionate caring by simply doing things for your spouse does not—repeat, does not—absolve you from the obligation to occasionally vocally express your feelings to your spouse in a loud and clear manner. Here are some examples:
"I Love you."
"I like the way you . . . "
"I sure appreciate your . . . "
"Boy, I'm glad you . . . "
"You sure look . . . (great etc.) . . . "

Studies have shown that the male who helps his wife with the housework is the male who has a happier wife. One of the biggest complaints women have is that their husbands do not help them enough with the housework, or with the children. Everyday humanistic logic tell us a grateful woman knows full well how to display her satisfaction and gratitude to her husband. So, boys, how big a brick wall do you need to fall on you?

A quote by a man named Franklin Jones seems appropriate:

> "Whoever thinks marriage is a 50-50 proposition doesn't know the half of it."

This author is not much into poetry but the other day I spotted a poem that rather tugged at me because the gist of the poem is just exactly what we are talking about here: the real possibility of the heartbreak which can attend a failure of energy in a marriage relationship. This poem, written by a Californian named Steve Kowit, appeared in a book of poetry titled *The Men of Our Time, An Anthology of Male Poetry in Contemporary America*, edited by Fred Moramarco and Al Zolynas.

How little is the cost of putting a little energy into a Marriage Relationship compared to the potential benefits.

The Rose

Home late, I eat dinner
and read the paper
without noticing
the rose in the yellow
glass on the dining room table—
not until
Mary shows it to me.
"Isn't it lovely?"
"Where'd you get it?"
"A fellow named Bill."
"Oh?"
"Just some guy who comes in
to the bar occasionally . . .
Isn't it lovely?"
"He gave it to you?"
I turn to the editorial page.
"Yes . . .
he just got out of the hospital."
She bends
and takes in its fragrance.
She is wearing that black negligee.
"The hospital?"
She straightens up and looks
at me and sighs.
"He's dying of cancer."
We stare at each other.
I want to embrace her,
tell her how much I love her,
how much I have always loved her.
But I don't.
I just sit there.
When she walks back into the
    bedroom
I see it at last,
glowing on the table,
leaning toward me
on its heartbroken stem.

"IF I TOLD YOU THAT MY BOSS NAMED HIS DOG 'DUMPY' AND NOW HE WANTS TO CALL ME 'DUMPY'.. WHAT WOULD YOU SAY?"

"HI 'DUMPY!'"

Joe Martin 1-2-94

Copyright ©1994 Neatly Chiseled Features

R

Stands For 'RESPECT'

Chapter five contained the initial explanation of the 20 components of the Marriage Relationship concept; now the issue of respect as a category of concern within a marriage relationship is defined in four dimensions thusly:

1) People need to feel that they are personally respected by others for the things they do, what they stand for, and who they are. Especially, everyone needs to feel appreciated, and not taken for granted. We all need a pat on the head from time to time. This form of respect is called "exterior respect."

2) Everyone needs and deserves his own measure of "interior self-respect," which includes the concepts of self-confidence and self-esteem. That is, everyone needs to think in his own mind and feel in his heart of hearts that he is okay just the way he is, whatever admitted personal shortcomings a person might have notwithstanding. Reality is, after all, reality. Nobody's perfect.

3) We must each have respect for the rights of all others to have and to hold their own ideas and viewpoints.

4) In order to have and enjoy a happy and successful marriage, both partners must have respect for their own relationship almost as if it is a separate entity, or a different person. And, as well, married couples need to have respect for the overall basic principles and goals of marriage as the primary social institution in our society.

To consider each category of respect on its own merit and as the need for respect exists within the marriage relationship we begin with:

#1 Exterior Respect: The Need To Be Respected By Others, Especially By Our Marriage Partner

Included in this arena of respect would be the simple fact of fair treatment and polite consideration exhibited by both marriage partners to each other. A failure of respect in a marriage relationship situation probably would indicate that the partner being disrespectful to his mate is suffering a loss of his own self-respect. In an attempt to drag the marriage partner down to what he perceives as his own low level of self-disrespect, he verbally or behaviorally abuses and puts down his spouse, thinking that such continued degradation of the mate will bolster his own lack of self-respect. Tearing someone else down builds him up. If you can understand that twisted manner of thinking you might need help yourself.

Whose problem is it? Obviously and unfortunately the problem initially belongs to the poor person who is suffering disrespect and abuse. But a serious secondary problem might exist in the mind of the partner who is demeaning and abusing his spouse in this manner, and we'll get to that consideration in a minute.

The existence of exhibited disrespect is actually a form of mental abuse, and should (must) not be tolerated by the person who is being abused, and demands immediate attention. If you need more encouragement for that call to action, go back and read under **A** stands for (mental) 'Abuse' section.

The obvious solutions to such situations of disrespect would almost certainly lie in direct confrontation. A show-down. Keeping in mind, all the while, the principles of good communication as we set out earlier in the general codependence section, and using effective negotiation techniques which will come along later when we get to the **N** in 'Relationship.'

If you decide to try the direct approach, you can probably expect the abuser to deny his bad behavior, or display one or several defense mechanisms. That sort of response would let you know that getting this problem solved will take some time and patience.

However, success will almost surely be gained eventually after time and persistence, and the person demeaning the other marriage partner will eventually get the idea that his behavior is not acceptable. Included in that period of time would be lots of encouragement, coaching and training, maybe even by a mental health professional, until the person consistently displays the appropriate respect for the marriage partner in public, and privately as well.

Another possibility at correcting the abusive behavior might be a try at "triangulation." Instead of a direct confrontation, maybe it would be possible to get someone else to talk to the abusive person about the way he is treating his mate, and relate the unhappiness of the abused spouse to the abuser. In the history of mankind, getting someone else to solve one's own problems has never proven to be a very successful plan, and this course, should you decide to try it, ought not to be counted on.

A difficult and unfortunate aspect of this form of disrespect lies in the consideration that continued bitter criticism of one marriage partner by the other spouse can lead to a condition mentioned earlier as one of the only three reasons for divorce: mental abuse. Mental abuse as defined earlier is abuse which is intended, over time, to destroy the self-respect and confidence of a person. Thus, a failure of respect of one marriage partner for the other, if not stopped dead in its tracks but allowed to continue over time, can get out of control and make the continuation of that marriage relationship a very doubtful possibility.

Attention to, and resolution of exhibited disrespect of one marriage partner for the other must be addressed with firmness and determination at the earliest time possible.

#2 Interior Respect: Having Self-Respect

Volumes and volumes have been written about this issue of a lack of self-respect and, as well, many fine articles, seminars and even taped self-help programs are available for those afflicted with a shortage of self-respect. In fact, so much information is available about this seemingly common human problem that, within this text, we shall do no more than try to summarize some of the more salient or obvious solutions. I will also cite some helpful attitudes or viewpoints which I hope will help solve a possible lack of self-esteem, or self-confidence.

The definition of personal or interior self-respect includes two concepts:

Self-Confidence—Performance

Simply defined, having self-confidence is knowing and trusting what it is we can and cannot do. When we are self-confident we trust ourselves. We have the personally held knowledge that we have the ability to do something, or to perform some behaviors or tasks. At the same time, a self-confident person will acknowledge and admit his own natural shortfalls without counting those limitations as a failures. Self-confident people will obviously perform better than those who have a shortage thereof because they know and trust what they can do. Those folks with a normal amount of self-confidence also will have more self-esteem.

It is a normal human condition for everyone to have some level of deficiency in self-confidence, and anyone who appears or tries to convince others, either through his appearance, perhaps with a frozen fixed smile, or through his words or deeds that he is always supremely self-confident, is masquerading and is a phony. We are all a mix of talents and limitations, successes and failures, and all the conditions that lie in between. For example, one might be fairly successful, or have not quite failed.

Because of the range of variations within the concepts of self-confidence and self-esteem, from very high to very low, it is interesting to note that one can have a relatively high level of self-confidence and at the same time honestly suffer a lower level of self-esteem.

Symptoms of a lack of self-confidence would include one's taking criticism too hard and in a personal manner. A brief comment about the difference between "criticism" and "feedback": Criticism is defined as a person's observations directed at another individual on a personal basis and at his very being or persona.

On the other hand, feedback is the impersonal comments by a person about the performance, or actions of someone else with the comments simply intended to be helpful. For example, when a coach tells an athlete how to perform, he is not being personally critical of or attacking the person; rather, he is simply attempting to offer feedback, aka instruction and advice, and trying to tell the athlete how he might better perform the action or feat he is trying to accomplish.

Unfortunately, occasionally someone will be critical and try to hide his criticism under the guise of feedback. Sometimes someone will try to offer feedback by virtue of a joke, and end up being critical. It pays to be careful.

Briefly stated, criticism, or critical remarks, are almost always begun with, "you . . . ("always" or "never", etc.)." Complaints and many feedback suggestions begin with "I . . . ("wish," "think," "hope," "feel," etc.). Or, "Why don't you try . . . ?" "Maybe if you would . . . instead of . . . then . . . "

Another symptom of a person's shortage of self-confidence would be the inability to accept compliments by saying, "Oh, they are just being polite," or "I was just lucky," or some other lame deflection of the intended compliment. A normally self-confident person when granted a compliment will simply say, "Thank you."

Self-Esteem—Personal Value Judgements of Our Own Self-Worth

The issue embodied in the concept of self-esteem has to do with what it is we think about ourselves. We each hold our own personal opinion of ourselves, which opinions are gathered from two sources. First is our own personal life experiences, and the other is our own perception or notion of what others think of us. Needless to say, our own judgement of what other people think of us could be entirely wrong.

Henry Wadsworth Longfellow wrote:

"We judge ourselves by what we feel capable of doing, while others judge us by what we have done."

From the point of view of life-experiences, children who are brought up in a family that is too severely critical of other members of the family often will suffer a shortage of self-esteem from their earliest days on earth. Please recall that earlier section called "general co-dependence" wherein it was cited that a seriously dysfunctional family situation can effectively prohibit the normal development of a child's self-esteem mechanisms.

Not uncommonly, "only children" are not allowed by their overly doting parents to be normal human beings. Even as children they are treated as "little adults" and are often saddled at their earliest ages by the parents' obsessive need for their only offspring to be a "perfect" person, which is, as we all know, quite impossible.

One's own ideas of self-worth could also be influenced by a person's focusing too firmly on past incidents that are perceived to be failures. For example, a classmate of mine was forced by his parents to be a clergyman. He tried, failed, and that setback never left his mind. He ended up being a pathetic, reclusive hermit. He died recently still in that sad state of self-perceived failure. He never did quit talking about how his mother wanted him to be a priest, but, since it was not to be, my friend believed he was a total failure. The way it turned out, he really was a huge and total failure. Another self-fulfilling prophecy made good.

Only-children who are taught to be perfectionists by their parents can develop an abnormal fear of failure, and this can eventually prove be a powerful deterrent to the development of normal behavior. Except for those poor souls who deliberately set out to sabotage themselves, almost no one ever sets out to fail, although we all apparently do, from time to time.

Almost never has it been known for a normal person to get up in the morning and say "Boy, am I going to screw up today."

Solutions to problems with self-confidence and self-esteem would most certainly include suggestions, such as:

- Don't be risk aversive. Take risks, and when you do take a risk, don't be afraid of failure. Some negative thinkers will obviously demonstrate their fear of failure by not trying to do anything, foolishly not realizing that to not try something is in itself a failure. Remember the children's story about the "little train that could," who kept saying, "I think I can, I think I can, I think I can." And it did. If you don't think you can, you won't.

- Don't sabotage yourself; think positively. One of the very best sources of positive-thinking training at this time are the wonderful books written by Iowa-born Dr. Robert Schuller who is the pastor of the Crystal Cathedral, Garden Grove, California.

Dr. Schuller might well be the most prominent "humanistic" psychologist of our times, and his Sunday morning "Hour of Power" television broadcasts are viewed world wide by millions of people.

By way of explanation, humanistic psychology is the concept which holds that we as humans can do whatever it is we want to do with our lives. "If you can dream it, you can do it," is Dr. Schuller's slogan. Reality check: Of course, a person who suffers from severe mental retardation cannot become a brain surgeon. However, the concept of humanistic psychology maintains that, given normal parameters of reality, people can become or do about whatever they want as long as they have faith in what they are trying to do, stay focused on the task or course, and follow through with the effort. That is, don't quit.

The "faith, focus and follow-through" by-words are Dr. Robert Schuller's, and are embodied in what he calls "possibility thinking," which could be simply defined as encouraging people to think positively, and to try to accomplish in their lives whatever dream it is that they might be able to think up. Positive thinking, according to Dr. Schuller can be both exciting and habit forming, as can his books, some of which are listed in the bibliography.

Thomas A. Edison is quoted: "Many of life's failures are people who did not realize how close they were to success when they gave up."

From another slightly differing point of view, the well-known behavioral concept in the science of psychology will tell you to imagine and to think about accomplishing frightening or challenging behaviors or deeds, before you try them. Then when you are actually up against attempting to perform some scary behavior or task, you will have already been through the procedure mentally. You have met the challenge in your mind's eye, and you will be more likely to succeed.

No guarantees, mind you, and if success eludes you, then try again, and try again until eventually some measure of success will be yours.

We shall get more into this subject when we come to the part about assertiveness training, which aims to teach individuals to be able to speak their minds unafraid. Meanwhile, don't be afraid to fantasize about your dreams, or challenges.

Don't forget that we are all imperfect human beings, doing the best we think we can do at the time. Failure, to whatever extent, is okay, and if you don't turn out to be famous or the world's best _____, who cares? At least you tried, you gave it a shot, and failure or disappointment does not mean that one is a bad person or is un-loved.

In the interests of improving self-respect on a self-help basis a good exercise is to take a piece of paper and head three columns thusly:

Then honestly fill in the appropriate responses. Self-appraisal, honest self-appraisal, is a wonderful thing. Once your own listing of qualities is accomplished, you can refer back to the schedule from time to time and then with perseverance, persist in your own continuing self-improvement program.

#3 Respect for the Rights and Opinions of Others

To focus solely on this issue of marriage relationship, we have to consider and grant the basic right of each of the partners in any relationship to exist as they are and to enjoy the basic fundamental privileges, duties, rights and obligations that each of us have as members of the human race.

We are who we are, and we are all born with whatever rights and innate human dignity we have, as we live out our lives within those entitlements. At the same time each of us is entitled to all the happiness and peace of mind that we can find or earn while on this old earth, along with the duty to observe the rights and dignity of all others.

Failure within a marriage relationship to carefully observe the inalienable right of the other marriage partner to have and to hold his own opinions and viewpoints is a grievous error. If a condition arises wherein one partner finds that his spouse is forcing

Qualities I have	Qualities I lack	Qualities I can develop

or bullying opinions upon him, the aggrieved person not only has the right but also the duty to advise the one who is being aggressively one-sided that he, as a human being, is entitled to his own opinions and attitudes, period. Should such advisement fail or fall short of the mark, then the obvious course of action would be to firmly identify and establish which subjects or issues are out-of-bounds for everyday conversational topics, and shall not ever be discussed in the interest of family harmony. Then don't discuss them.

You don't have to own the highest IQ in history to figure this one out: If, before marriage, one of the proposed marriage candidates holds very strong opinions on certain subjects, and is not able to keep from spouting off, and the other person then responds angrily and arguments ensue, maybe they both should rethink their marriage plans. Anyone who has been married knows that small skirmishes before marriage can turn into major conflicts with possibly serious consequences after the wedding ceremony is over.

#4 Respect for Your Marriage Relationship As a Separate Entity

As husband and wife, the marriage partners together join in bringing to life another whole entity, their marriage relationship, which possesses on its own all of the frailties and strengths that may be possessed by any individual.

A marriage may be happy or sad, prosper or fail, live or die. The success or failure of a marriage, as is the case in any other partnership, depends upon the behaviors of the people involved, and on their determination, intentions and desires.

Speaking of symbolism: In many marriage ceremonies a "unity" candle is lit during the celebration of the ceremony. Here's how this works in case you don't know: Two smaller lighted candles are placed on a small table, signifying the individual existence of each of the marriage partners. On that same table is a larger third candle which is lit later in the ceremony when the marriage participants each take their own candles and jointly light the larger candle.

The significance of this procedure is that while people retain their own identity by virtue of the continued burning of their individual candles, a new entity, a brand new relationship is being formed (born) and, like a child, depends for its livelihood and well-being on the care and attention of the principals.

As evidenced by soaring divorce rates, it seems that too often in these ultra liberal times marriage partners fail to realize or recognize the birth of this new relationship, and do not treat that which they have created with appropriate regard and concern.

Any measure of disrespect for the marriage relationship by either partner is a problem which belongs to both individuals jointly, although too frequently one person will think the other marriage partner is the one who must find the solution. If a state of disrespect for the relationship seems to be occurring, then that problem is worthy of and demands immediate attention and resolution by both of you.

Many solutions are available for problems between marriage partners with regard to this issue of respect, but almost all avenues to healing begin with frank and honest conversations about the state and condition of their relationship to each other, and to their marriage. Perhaps one partner feels the other person doesn't seem to care if they are married or not. Maybe one party feels some antagonism towards the other person for some condition or action which is upsetting, but he doesn't know how to begin to correct, or to even ask for adjustment of the other's behavior.

The worst-case scenario would be if one spouse foolishly looks at his own marriage as a short-term contract; that the children are, by and large, an accident and, like wild animals, when abandoned will be able to fend for themselves. This sort of greedy person thinks life holds more for him than he is presently getting out of the relationship.

Perhaps the key word in any examination of the issue of interpersonal respect is "Consideration." Have sincere consideration for each other, and have consideration for your marriage relationship. Talk about the issues in the prescribed manner and tone, and don't give up on your attempts to establish mutual respect for each other and for your marriage relationship even if the conversations don't seem to be going in the direction you wish they would go at the outset. Have persistence, understanding, and RESPECT.

No discussion about respect would be complete without reference again to the by-line of the comedian Rodney Dangerfield, who made an entire career out of saying, "I don't get no respect." He then launches into his comedy routines with one-liners such as:

> "My wife and I were perfectly
> happy for 25 years.
> Then we met."

Don't ever forget, as remote as the concept of respect might seem to be, a failure of respect can and will bring an end to your marriage relationship.

E

Stands For 'EXPECTATIONS'

Can't you hear it now?

"Gee, Honey, but I thought . . . "

We all assume that some things will happen in our lives, but one of the most surprising and perhaps disappointing events in life is when we really and truly expect too much of a relationship or situation and it just doesn't happen. Result: disappointment, frustration and maybe anger.

A young man once related to me that the most difficult time in his new marriage came in the earliest days when he discovered his wife was evidently not going to live or behave as he had expected. He therefore found that he had to adjust a good many of his pre-marital mental expectations to accept the reality of life, and how "it" was going to be from then on with his new wife in their new marriage relationship.

Of course, a good part of an error or disappointment, with regard to a failure of expectations in a new marriage, resides in the selection of the mate, and, as said before, maybe there wasn't sufficient preparation for marriage. Keep in mind that how the courtship period goes, even if it includes our foolish modern-day "living-in" (LI) period, not necessarily so goes the way a new spouse is going to behave after the marriage ceremony is over.

It's recognized that sometimes before marriage someone will "play the game" and behave in a manner he thinks will be most advantageous to serve his own purpose, which is to get married. Should such deception occur, needless to say, the seemingly sudden change in attitude or behavior by the marriage partner after the ceremony does little for the brand-new marriage relationship.

Short of an early collapse of the marriage at worst, about the best one can hope for when confronted with such an unexpected and disappointing situation, is to expect to have to go through a lot of adjustment and probably some plain and fancy mental gymnastics to get to a level where one can accommodate and live with the unexpected conditions or behaviors.

Of course, another part of missed expectations might well reside in a measure of immaturity, just plain innocence, or perhaps even ignorance on the part of the new marriage partners.

Males, ask yourself this: Did you honestly think she would always be cheery, pleasant and fun to be with, prettily dressed, and be oh-so-polite and agreeably accommodating? Didn't the thought ever occur to you that some days she wouldn't feel so good and would have to put her hair up in curlers and traipse around the house in pink mukluks, as females are occasionally wont to do? In that old robe you hate. And be grouchy? And picky? And argumentative?

It is held that the female always has the last word in any argument, and that anything a male says after that is the beginning of a new argument. "Bitchy" is the word some females use to describe such behavior.

Females: Did you honestly think the he would always appear well-dressed and show up promptly at the appointed time? And did you think that he would always keep on making you feel that you are the most important object of devotion in his life? Didn't you ever give a thought to the possibility that sometimes he might be a little, or a lot, late, and smell a little strongly of beer and sweat, and occasionally pass a little gas? And laugh. Did you never think for a minute that perhaps he might get a little lazy and self-centered and not really be possessed with and ready to pursue all those big dreams and plans that the two of you talked about when you were courting? And, by the way, don't you wonder who these curious "animals" are (his friends) who keep calling and coming around?

Do you think Edith Bunker actually knew what she was getting into when she married Archie?

Thus marks the end of the honeymoon: shattered expectations.

Brief reference was made immediately above concerning the modern present-day "live-in" co-habitation condition practiced by so many in these liberal times. Studies have indicated that the divorce rate for the live-in's is shown to be as much as 50% higher than the usual 50%, rate thus putting the "live-in" divorce rate at a surprising 75%, plus or minus a tad.

Ask then, how can that be? Didn't these people live together to get to know each other better, and to get to know what to expect after marriage so they wouldn't have to fall into the divorce trap?

Some possible answers to that question include:

1. No firm commitment = no Marriage Relationship.
2. Someone might have been on his best behavior.
3. Someone might have foolishly thought that after marriage he would be able to change the new partner to be more like himself and therefore perfect.

She related with tears in her eyes and anger and desperation in her voice that the very memorable day they got married and said the words, the vows of commitment to each other, when they got to their honeymoon cottage, to her complete surprise, the very first thing he did upon entering the room was to slam her up against the wall and say, "Bitch, now you're going to do exactly as I say!" Needless to say, their marriage didn't last very long.

Was she disappointed? Angry? You bet; all of that and more because she most certainly didn't expect to be treated that way. Who would?

In reality almost every married person can acknowledge with total honesty, that no one really never knows his intended mate, or what to expect when entering into a marriage relationship, until after they are married. About all anyone of us can do is fervently hope and pray that our own judgement and intuition are pretty close to being right, love notwithstanding, and that the person with whom we have entered into a contract of marriage has enough personal integrity to stand by and continue to display the same values, behaviors and attitudes that he displayed before the marriage—consistency, in other words.

"People are too hard on each other," were about the last words a dear older friend of mine uttered just prior to his death. He had spent his entire lifetime in the clergy where he most certainly had the opportunity to view this issue of expectations at first hand on a daily basis.

People have too many expectations. People are too hard on each other, and, by the way, whatever happened to the age-old "live and let live" concept? If you are living with someone who is happy, isn't that reason enough for you to be happy too, with them?

A disappointment with regard to expectations becomes the problem of the person who is disappointed and thinks he is unhappy. Then comes the question: Is the problem an actual error in expectations, or the inability of the person who is disappointed to accept the fact the person he married is, after all is said and done, just an ordinary person with the typical load of foibles and screw-ups. Not Superman or, Wonderwoman.

The situation may well be that the new marriage partner won't change or doesn't want to change just to accommodate the whims and wishes of the new spouse. People don't want to change because they like themselves just as they are. On top of that, if they have to come up with some big change or behavior modification every time the spouse comes down with a whim and says "jump," where does that end? Does a person always have to ask, "How high?"

This has been said before, and will be said again: It is written:

A woman marries a man expecting
he will change . . . but he doesn't.
A man marries a woman expecting
she won't change . . . but she does.

You can only ask yourself, is this a problem? Is this really a problem, or can I live with the situation as it exists, and hope, in due course, to learn to accept and appreciate the new marriage partner for what he is. It can happen that over time, through loving persuasion and persistent encouragement, you may be able to somewhat alter the other person's behavior or shift the conditions that are upsetting. However, the only reason a person would change behavior would be that he wishes to please the mate. How many times has it been said that nobody ever changes someone else.

Change, if it is to come about, must be the desire and intention of the person in whom change is sought.

Controlling someone, or forcing someone, to change to fit one's own wishes can be a dicey and even dangerous thing to try to do. Look at it this way: If you think that you have to control your marriage partner, then evidently either you married the wrong person, or have the wrong idea about the concept of personal responsibility and the right that every person has to live his life in the manner of his own preference—assuming compliance with societal norms. And, by the way, don't forget that his bothersome behavior and traits very likely came down through the years from earlier or nuclear family general codependence factors.

Controlling someone and having a person "out of control" are two different conditions. Anyone who is "out of control" needs help, and anybody who thinks he has to control someone else needs help themselves. We are each our own person with our own traits, personalities, temperaments and characters. What you get is what you got.

Just because someone is silly enough to have gone into a marriage relationship with incorrect expectations, which can't, or won't be fulfilled, doesn't necessarily mean that they he has entered into a bad marriage. What's needed is whatever measure of accommodation it takes for the two marriage partners to adjust over time to the real-life personal situations as they may exist.

Again a brief mention of a common error in this category I call expectations: parents who attempt to relive their own earlier lives in the efforts and activities of their children. Please recall that one of the many symptoms of the condition known as general codependence is having, too high expectations. I mentioned earlier stories of poor parental behavior with regard to little league baseball and other generally extra-curricular activities, such as sports and music.

Without belaboring the point, one cannot succeed, himself, in someone else's success. Oh sure, a parent can and should be proud and relish the success of another person, a child for example, but again, we are what we are and who we are. That's just the way life is.

Not that parents can't hope for and encourage good performance by their children, for to not do so would be almost negligent, but placing too high a level of emphasis on another person's performance, whether they be a child or a mate, denies the very reality of life.

To bring the subject into focus, try considering this: Maybe you think that your parents and your grandparents, and even their parents' parents didn't have high expectations for each other to fulfill when they got married? Do you think that their marriages worked out exactly as each of them planned and hoped for? Of course not.

Here's another twist: If you think you are disappointed in your expectations of how your spouse acts or thinks, how do you think your spouse has coped with what his expectations were of you that didn't pan out the way he thought they would? Did he tell you of his disappointments? Did you change to suit his whims or wishes?

As a rule, people work through their lives on what's called the "best efforts" basis, which means we all do the best that we can. Of course, since we all are human, sometimes our best isn't too good, or not nearly good enough; then, of course, we not only disappoint ourselves, but also someone else as well. But as the saying goes, that's life. You win a few, you lose a few.

The bottom line is to realize we must all live our own lives to the very best level we can, and that's about all there is to it. If you or anyone else starts making plans or establishing behavioral standards for someone else to live up to, and then expects him to live up to your dreamy goals, you really are asking for more disappointment.

The rules of logic tell us that one can never say "all" or "never" about something, but in the case of this issue of expectations, as the years go by, wouldn't it be fair to say that all marriage partners have experienced some amount of disappointment with regard to their **expected** marriage relationship?'

The way to solve a shortfall in expected behavior is simply to negotiate and communicate, then work things out so they are acceptable to everybody, and above all, be realistic and understanding.

It is written:

To be happy with a man, you must understand him a lot and love him a little.

To be happy with a woman, you must love her a lot and not try to understand her.

Most rational marriage partners will want, and honestly try, to please their mate, so why not just enjoy your life and your spouse for what they are. And relish who they are.

L

Stands For 'LIVING'

Living, as a category of concern within the Marriage Relationship concept, is a very serious subject, and, as such, if poorly handled or allowed to deteriorate too far, a default or serious problem in living, as defined herein, can be a very destructive issue in a marriage.

Living deals with several different aspects of the actual physical existence of the marriage partners.

The first section of our consideration of living deals with the adjusting to the day-in, day-out routines, and personal issues which include individual procedures and habits, and the health of the marriage partners. As we all know from firsthand experience, people certainly can turn up with curious rituals and behaviors. A discussion concerning what is known as assertiveness training is included in this section.

The second part relates to the actual physical conditions, situations and circumstances that one might find himself having to live with or endure.

The third part of the "living" category deals with the subject of stress and how to cope with being stressed as a result of the acute frustration suffered while trying to live with someone who displays some aggravating behaviors. Stress is also a by-product of living in unsatisfactory conditions or circumstances.

Personal Issues

Not infrequently, unusual personal habits or routines will occur in more intimate areas of living behavior, and in personal areas that would not be generally observed in the courtship stage, if a conventional dating-to-engagement-to-marriage routine was followed. Obviously, if the dating-to-marriage path was strictly followed, one really never would get to know just how the other person lives, since the marriage partners could have their "better side" showing before they get married.

Because of this possibility, there is a chance that no stress-causing personal quirks of behavior or attitude would ever appear. Surprise! Or, if such undesirable traits or characteristics did appear, there is always the chance the beholders of the curious or annoying behavior could have kidded themselves into thinking that, without a doubt, they would be able to either, a) change the new marriage partner and modify or eliminate the undesirable behaviors, or, b) think that they themselves would learn and be able to live with the annoying behavior.

That last part is the old, "I can handle it, I can handle it, I can handle it, I CAN'T HANDLE IT" disaster scenario.

Once again, with regard to changing someone, and to restate the general rules, keep in mind that nobody ever succeeds in changing someone else. It is true that, with encouragement and persuasion, also known as positive reinforcement, another person can be brought to the point where he would change or adjust his behavior(s) to please someone else. But the cold fact is, any change must and only comes from the person who will accept changing himself.

Occasionally someone will attempt to force another person to change by using threats, negative reinforcement, or punishment. Even though, at the time, it might seem that the application of force brought about the desired modification, the bad news is, perhaps he exchanged his overt behavior for a smoldering resentment that will show up later in other areas of the relationship.

An explanation of these three terms is appropriate:

Positive reinforcement (R+) is the gaining of a change in behavior by providing a reward for the modification. A cookie for a puppy. A carrot for a rabbit. A jump for a Mexican Jumping Bean. Boston Cream Pie for lovers thereof.

Negative reinforcement (R-) is gaining a change in behavior by withholding some treat or pleasurable event to encourage the desired change. Example: Mom says, "If you kids don't clean up your room, you can't watch TV." Or, Mom says, "Since we didn't get to go to the concert, I have a headache."

Punishment is probably painfully familiar to everybody and should not need a great deal of explanation. By the way, too much, or excessive punishment, could possibly qualify as abuse.

Good examples of the existence of difficulties in living can be seen almost daily in local newspapers wherein letters do appear from a wife who complains, for example, that her husband doesn't bathe often enough to suit her, or he may display some other undesirable personal behavior(s).

Whose problem is such behavior? The problem belongs to the person who is unhappy. There is always the possibility that the person performing the unsettling behavior may be completely unaware that he is annoying his mate. Or, if he is aware, because he's been told about a hundred times, and he still persists, there are about only two conclusions one can come to:

a) He isn't interested in changing anything to suit someone else,
b) He is deliberately trying to be aggravating.

Of course, if the latter reason is the case, that marriage relationship really has problems.

Bill doesn't ever hang up an article of

clothing, make a bed, put anything away, or finish a project. This behavior drives Sue nearly crazy. If she is going to find some measure of relief she will, over time, either have to gently encourage Bill to perform some of the tasks that she thinks he should, or resign herself, pick up his clothes, and make all the beds. If he starts a project that is destined to never be finished, she will likely have to either complete it herself, or hire professional help. This sort of behavior is not gender specific, which means both males and females can be messy, and not finish a project.

The question then would be, is Bill's perceived errant behavior a big enough problem to cause a serious confrontation? Probably not, but that's not to say that some measure of correction in Bill's behavior can't be achieved over time through a process of negotiation. Negotiation as a category of concern in the marriage relationship format comes along a bit later.

The companion book to this work, titled *Some of the Reasons We Behave the Way We Do*, covers the "right brain, left brain" concept, which states that people who are what they call right-brain-dominant are sometimes inclined to be messier and less inclined to finish what they start than left-brain-dominant folks. Experience tells anyone who has fought this battle that there is absolutely no point in whining or nagging at the offender. Indeed there is clear evidence, as you will see, these brain-dominance concepts **do** carry some meaning.

On the plus side there certainly are several really good reasons for someone to want to change or adjust his personal behaviors, rituals or living status to make the husband or wife happier, and they could include:

a) Simply wanting to make the spouse happy. After all, what's the matter with putting out some effort out to please your mate? On top of that, simple logic would indicate that if you can make your marriage partner a happy camper, doesn't it follow then that you stand a chance of being made happier, too?

b) Perhaps, from a selfish point of view, maybe the offending marriage partner should consider making the small behavioral changes requested just to cut the noise level down to a deafening roar, and thereby get along a little better. If some disagreeable behavior is being committed, maybe the offender ought to be smart enough to see if he doesn't get his act together, their marriage relationship might be in jeopardy. People can stand only just so much aggravation, you know.

c) How about a trade off? What's wrong with making a deal, having a negotiation, and if partner A wants _____, and partner B wants _____, then through direct communication, make the desired adjustments between the two marriage partners and everybody wins.

But the bottom line with regard to this or any consideration of personal behaviors that might be annoying to a spouse, is that any changes to be made must be willingly self-accomplished. One can encourage, suggest, cajole, whine, persuade, harangue, plot, threaten, cry, whimper, throw things and give good examples, but if any modification in behavior is to come about, that change must occur through the actions of the individual himself.

It was Ben Franklin who wrote:

"Before marriage keep your eyes wide open. After, half shut."

Danger zone: What if the person requesting change is a perfectionist for whatever reason people are perfectionists. Does the spouse have to comply with the erratic thought process of the perfectionist mate? Is this not the "opposites attract" syndrome?

She cried bitter tears of anger and frustration as she told how her "perfect" husband had not requested, but had demanded that she hand-iron all the laundry, including his underwear and socks, and that this ironing was to be accomplished in a perfect manner. At the end of the day when he returned home from work, the laundry was to be laid out in an exact manner and at a precise location for his close inspection. She cried, not because she had done his silly bidding, but because she didn't have the nerve or personal courage to tell her "perfect" husband just what her own feelings were with regard to his idiotic laundry demands.

This lady didn't know how to tell her tiresome perfectionist husband that if his underwear had to be ironed in a most precise manner, then he should grab the iron and do it himself because she simply was not going to comply with such a stupid request. She was absolutely right, but she did not know how to assert and defend herself, which brings us to the next concept:

Assertiveness Training

In the area of practical psychology, under the category of behavior modification there exists a treatment program for bringing about a personal change designed for those who find it difficult or even impossible to stand up for their own rights and wishes, and who can end up being trampled upon mentally and physically. This program is known as assertiveness training, and is a process that warrants close examination and explanation.

Assertiveness training as a therapeutic process is usually quite economical and rather quickly accomplished in a group setting such as a seminar or classroom. Obviously, behavior modification training can also be accomplished in the more expensive and time-consuming one-on-one therapist/client basis. Assertiveness training programs are also available in self-help programs using prepared printed or taped programs, and although the do-it-yourself process can work, a successful outcome is less assured and not as likely to provide the desired results as the group approach to the problem. Groups are great, because the members have the opportunity to talk themselves through their problems and actually practice the confrontation in the process known as "role playing," or "behavioral rehearsal."

Role playing as a therapeutic process was begun some years ago by a Dr. James Moreno, who reasoned that if someone practiced what it was he wanted to say with other members of the group before he had to face the antagonist, then when he came to the actual confrontation to assert himself, the chances of success were enhanced because the individual had already been through the conversation several times, albeit theatrically. It has been proven that the role playing experience is worth the effort, and because of the rehearsal, a person is more likely going to be able to successfully assert himself.

No one ever should feel that his own failure or inability to assert himself, to be able to speak right up and say what it is he feels or wants, is an isolated defect or social disability, because it is not. The reluctance to assert one's self is a very common human problem, especially for gals, and proof of this generalized mental discomfort is evidenced by the typically large female attendance at the many assertiveness-training sessions offered.

Briefly stated, assertiveness training in the group setting initially involves a period of self-examination with the participants asking themselves the question:

Why can I not, or, why do I not assert myself?

The answer usually is simply one's being afraid of the consequences of speaking up and/or a generous dose of general codependence, which dictates that the person has not been brought up or reared in his original family in a manner which will allow him to assert himself. He has been taught that to speak up and tell what it is one wants is bad form and can sometimes result in a really big fight, and maybe even punishment.

Although not entirely gender specific, it seems women have more trouble vocally asserting themselves than men.

Once the basic question has been asked as to why the person can't or doesn't assert himself, the next step is to figure out in what areas of concern it is that the person is not able to assert himself. Example: In a group setting, once the area or areas of conflict are identified, the group helps to figure out what would be an appropriate rejoinder for the person to make to assert himself adequately, and then to "model" or rehearse the planned response or complaint, so that when the time comes for the confrontation he's ready.

Another good thing about the group therapy is that, in the modeling process, actual experience will be gained by some other group person who pretends to be the other party who performs the objectionable behavior. The person learning to assert himself will, out loud, in front of God and all the other group members, actually practice, and learn to assert what it is that he wants to convey to the offending party.

In addition, the group as a whole in a feedback session will try to suggest just when and how might be the best time to begin being assertive. As the seminar continues, the group leader and the other members will help and encourage the person who is attempting to overcome his lack of assertiveness.

Once the ground work has been accomplished, the group then settles down to a practice, practice, practice, routine until all the group members have not only a good grasp of the techniques and the methods required to be able to assert themselves when they need to, but also they may learn a great deal by playing the role of the person who is oppressing the one trying to learn the technique of self-assertion. That's a neat double-edged advantage.

If a person does not care to use a group

therapy setting, then assertiveness training can be done on your own. In the language of psychology this is known as a "covert" process. Covert in this case means that you must do all the necessary preparation, education and practice on your own—self-help, do-it-yourself, in other words.

For example, to follow the same pattern as a group session, first figure out what it is you want (need?) to be assertive about. Then plan what you want to say and how you are going to say it. Try to know what your goal or goals are, and engage in lots and lots of practice of the routine all by yourself by actually saying out loud, what it is that you wish (need?) to be assertive about.

Note two conditions: One is that the covert or self-help practice sessions must be done out loud so when the time actually comes for the confrontation and the assertiveness to pour out, you will have gotten up all your courage, the spoken words will have been heard by yourself over and over in previous practice sessions and they won't be such a shock when you hear them. The trouble is, if the practice statements are not spoken out loud, when the time comes for you to actually hear yourself speaking up, the sound of your own voice can be upsetting and disconcerting. "Holy cow, did I really say that?" you will wonder. One cannot effectively practice assertiveness-training entirely in his head.

The other condition is to practice the assertive speech not only out loud, but also in front of a mirror! By using a mirror you will not only hear what you are saying, but at the same time be able to observe and practice your own delivery and posture. To insure the best possible outcome, you need to use as many advantages as are available.

The above brief outline of the psychological training technique known as assertiveness training is not intended to be complete, which it obviously isn't, nor is it meant to be a therapy-guide. I've included it in this text to give the reader some idea of the existence of assertiveness training programs, and to offer encouragement to anyone who might feel he has a problem, to seek out and attend an assertiveness training class or seminar.

Bad news dept: Simply being able to assert one's self does not guarantee success or a happy outcome. But if you do assert your feelings or wishes, you have a chance of succeeding. Whereas, if you never speak up and you never assert your self, you have almost no chance of ever gaining the changes you seek.

A word of caution: The idea of being assertive and the concept of aggression are two different things and must not be confused.

Being assertive means realizing that everyone has the right to speak one's mind, to hold and to express one's feelings and ideas, and to convey one's wishes to others, as the need may be.

Being aggressive on the other hand is a whole different concept, and someone who is aggressive is apt to force his wishes or attitudes on others.

Be assertive, not aggressive.

Health Concerns

" . . . in sickness and in health, until . . . " is one of the phrases commonly included in the recitation of the marriage ceremony vows.

The physical and mental condition of

each of the marriage partners is a prime concern not only of each individual, as far as his own health is concerned, but also each person has an obligation to watch over and attend to the well-being of the other partner, to the best of his ability.

When life is going along swimmingly, with no problems, the issue of health can seem to be remote, with the exception of concern over some known personally destructive behaviors such as smoking, being overweight, the excessive intake of alcohol or other chemicals, and/or other detrimental personal habits or practices.

Obviously, we all should try to live in as healthy a manner as we can.

However, since we all are mortal, and death is a certainty for each of us, health concerns can and do become more critical when one of the marriage partners suffers an illness, or comes down with a life-threatening or terminal disease. As life goes on, and the inevitable aging process continues, the overall well-being of the two marriage partners can be expected to falter or fail, and special attention to each other's physical as well as mental stability, becomes much more important.

I mentioned earlier an actual case wherein the man of the house in his later married life became vocally abusive to his wife, and, as you may recall, the underlying disorder was a case of yet-to-be diagnosed cancer, which unfortunately was terminal. The message told there is that a fairly substantial change in a person's overall outlook, or a shift into unusual behaviors might just possibly signal a subtle change going on in his physical or mental health.

Living Conditions

Curious or personally weird behaviors apart, there is still another more difficult area in this issue of living which can cause trouble between marriage partners. That is the actual living site and the situation or condition of life which may not be what one of the marriage partners desires, is accustomed to, or can even tolerate, for that matter.

Say that one of the marriage partners grew up in a "Country Club" area, and the other one perhaps in a location in the city or town which might be thought of as a less prestigious. Messiness or tidiness aside now, I'm just talking geography, street address, location and public and personal perceptions.

Once again, a problem in the category of living which concerns location and/or conditions is the problem of the person who is unhappy, for whatever reason. The chances are that the other marriage partner may be either accustomed to the situation as it exists, or he may be a person to whom such considerations are not all that important and he just isn't thinking about this issue as a problem. The solution to such a problem would almost always have to be a joint effort by both marriage partners, but the impetus or driving force would necessarily have to come from the spouse who seeks change, to satisfy his/her standards and placate his attitude towards the living quarters.

Many solutions are available to solve such a problem, and included might be simply a change in the attitude of the unhappy marriage partner. Granted that such an shift of opinion might not be easy to accomplish, but, nonetheless, a change in viewpoint is possible, and an option. Baseball coach Tommy Lasorda is quoted as saying, "The difference between the impossible and the possible lies in a person's determination."

Another option might be a needed change in the family economic status. Perhaps if the income of the family breadwinner (usually, although not always the male) is quite fixed and is not able to accommodate the increased expense of different housing, maybe what is needed is a second income from the efforts of the other partner. Occasionally a solution, perhaps temporary, could fall into the area of a family move to an interim location.

For example, if the cost of real estate and the accompanying expenses, such as real estate taxes, are too high in one location what about another area? How about moving to an acreage in the countryside and becoming a "gentleman farmer" or a rancher? In our community some of the younger people are moving to the less expensive surrounding small towns for the many obvious advantages found there. Maybe renting or buying an income-producing duplex or fourplex for a while would be a viable solution.

The moral of the solution-story is that if neither end of the spectrum is really what both marriage partners want or are comfortable with, find a compromise. Work together and not against each other's ideas and attitudes.

They tell the story of the smart lady who, before the marriage ceremony, decided that in her married life she would overlook the five worst habits and living traits of her new spouse during their married life, no matter what they might be. She didn't actually write down a list of those five to-be-forgiven habits or traits, but then, as their marriage went on through the years, every time he would do something that would really annoy her, she would say to herself, "Well, he's lucky that's one of the five things on the list that I'm going to overlook," and their marriage relationship went on. Smart Lady.

When dealing with a problem in living, make a firm pledge to yourself to keep cool, try to understand what the problem is, and realize that finding the solution might take some time. Use the skills briefly outlined in the Communication section of General Codependence. Pay attention to the How to Negotiate section, and while you are at it, look inside your own mind and see just how flexible you are. Always wonder: Does your mate have some hidden complaints that he is not telling you about, too? The above assortment of conclusions brings us to the end result of difficulties and problems in the category of living, and it's known as:

Stress

Stress as a human emotional or psychological reaction should not need much definition, but stress in the world of psychology is defined as the development of a state of tension or anxiety either in a person's mind, or between individuals, over some issue or groups of issues. A great deal of information is available in magazines, television and other media sources concerning the management of stress. "Stress Busting," and "Stress Management," they sometimes call the process.

Since so much information is available

in other sources, I shall, within the context of this work, confine the discussion to and focus mainly on the procedure known as "Stress Inoculation Training." This treatment plan for handling stress was devised primarily by the famous psychologist, Dr. Donald Meichenbaum, whose "ABC" format for a person's ability to handle stress, and which was mentioned earlier, provides a basic roadmap or guide for an individual to be better able to cope with stress.

Before we get to Meichenbaum's process, let's consider and use the same problem-solving pattern that we have been using in each category. First we must pay attention to the question which asks, what is the problem in the relationship causing the stress.

Then ask, is the issue really and truly a problem, and how much struggle and confrontation is the problem worth? Maybe the perceived stressful behavior or condition is simply a case of the failure of one of the marriage partners to accomplish the changes that s/he foolishly thought could be brought about once they were married. Whether or not the desired changes are valid can be moot. Sometimes a change can be sought as a whim, a wish, or a bad childhood memory. For example, if the parent of one of the marriage partners had a drinking problem, this symptom of general codependency could be carried forward with a vengeance into a later marriage relationship.

Whose problem is the stress? The problem primarily belongs to the person who is stressed and upset. Whatever problem exists, it is his problem. And within some boundaries, he and he alone will have to find the solution or solutions to ease the stress.

Too often in these times people will simply think that if they divorce the person who is stressing them they will forevermore be free of stress, and, of course, how foolish that thought is. No matter who it is one is involved with in a marriage relationship, there will always be behaviors or circumstances which will cause stress. Therefore, stress is not only inevitable but can actually prove to be a good thing. The marriage partners, by working through their problems together, can become emotionally closer than they were before they confronted the various issues.

The obvious first solution would be to resolve to overlook the conditions which cause stress, and say, "Well, okay, if that's the way it is then that's the way it is," then forget about it. This is a lot easier said than done.

Secondary solutions would fall into the communication and negotiation arenas wherein the person feeling stressed would communicate his concern and distress to his marriage partner in the correct and appropriate manner as set out earlier, and then enter into a negotiation phase.

Unless hubby, as an example, is told by his wife that she is upset about something, how can he ever realize some changes in his behavior or shift in a certain condition is needed? Then, what can or will said hubby do to lessen the stress on his spouse? If anything. In a spirit of compromise, how much change or modification of behavior, condition or situation will be enough to lessen the anxiety to a more acceptable level in the mind of the poor person who is upset about something which is, in his view, a potential train wreck.

Another method for you to cope with your own stress would be, again, to use the three steps in "Don Meichenbaum's 'ABC' Stress Inoculation Training" idea which was be mentioned earlier in the Reversal section. But the concept is important enough to summarize briefly. Here are examples of the basic coping statements which are the elements of this proven and often-used psychologically therapeutic process:

A—The Action

A stands for the action or event which will occur (again) and upset you. Figure out exactly what it is that upsets you, without letting a whole bunch of "presenting" thoughts get in the way. Think about what you can do to cope with **your** problem, and **your** stress.

Do not think negatively, and don't worry or dread being stressed. Don't spend a lot of time blaming your marriage partner for the situation, because, after all, you are the one who has a problem, and s/he could be going along thinking things are swell.

Again, probably easier said than done, but keep in mind that if you let the stress run and maybe ruin your life, then you will lose. Maybe what you think is your own anxiety over an annoying situation or behavior is only your own eagerness to confront your marriage partner over some other issue. Remember that "presenting" is a defense mechanism people use to deflect attention away from their real problem. "Presented" excuses or complaints are often true to some extent, but usually not the whole problem.

B—Behavior

This category refers to your behavior and how you respond to the stressing event. To begin with, 'psyche' yourself by telling your brain that you can handle the stressful challenge. Be cool. Convince yourself that you are not going to be distressed, or let your Marriage Relationship be messed up by this situation. Make a serious effort to reason your anxiety away. Remember that the behavior or situation you hate has been expected to reappear, and somewhere in here put a little mental note to move on to category "C".

C—Coping

When the event, behavior or circumstance that stresses you happens, pause, and plan to **think** rather than to react. Consciously try to relax, and keep focused on the here and now. Never forget that you are in complete control of your own life and thoughts. Figure out and plan ahead what it is, if anything, that you have to do in response to what is happening. Don't forget the "Dance of Anger" mentioned earlier in the **A** Stands for 'Anger' chapter. Maybe you don't have to do anything but sit back, relax and smile.

THINK: Put a measuring level on your stress from 0 to 10 and see where you are on the scale. You can expect your levels of anxiety to vary from time to time. The reason for this exercise is to help you get your brain working and override your typical and/or usual emotional response.

THINK: Don't expect or ever kid yourself into thinking you will ever be able to completely handle whatever it is that upsets you. You may not. But even if you get some relief from the agony, the bad news is that very likely you will always live with some amount of concern that the situation or event may reappear.

THINK: Don't expect or hope that your spouse will ever be able to completely remove the behavior that stresses you from his inventory of personal quirks. He can probably do better, but then, can't we all?

THINK: Tell yourself, over and over if you have to, that all you want is to get YOURSELF out of a snit, and reduce your anxiety level to a more manageable level.

THINK: Learn how and plan to give yourself compliments and congratulating statement when you have weathered a stressful situation. Tell yourself you have won, and that you managed to control your own emotions. Plan and tell yourself you'll do as good or maybe even better the next time the situation comes up.

THINK: It wouldn't hurt to remind yourself that you might be making more of the situation than it is worth, and that things aren't as bad as they seem. Be pleased with any scrap of progress you make and go forward. Nobody ever "promised you a rose garden," as the song says.

Thus is the essence of the so-called cognitive behavior therapy system; a self-treating, self-help, anti-stress program. As mentioned at the beginning of the section, anyone can achieve some amount of relief from stress through self-instruction programs, but if the pain is just too much to bear and you find yourself considering drastic steps, you should seek out more help by finding and using the services of a professional counselor.

Stress busting is not that difficult thing to accomplish, and living endlessly with severe stress is more than most folks can tolerate for long, and they don't because they get DEPRESSED!

Depression

We can't leave the issue of living without a few lines about a very common problem in relationships, and life, known as depression. For the record, depression is the seed-bed of suicide.

Everybody, and that means everybody, at some time in life goes through some form or depth of depression. It doesn't make any difference if the depressive episode begins as a "downer" from some stressful situation, or a roaring crash-and-burn five-alarm blaze. The result, known as a depression, is the same depending on the depth of the episode. Depression is very tough on strong relationships, and can even destroy the weaker ones.

What happens in a depressive episode is that the person disconnects himself from people. Even the fundamental elements of life such as eating, sleeping, working and playing, move from the easy-to-do natural behaviors to almost impossible-to-do tasks.

At the end of the day, because of all the energy used up struggling with the depression, a person so afflicted is tired beyond belief, but still cannot find escape in sleep.

The American Psychiatric Association, in its book titled *Diagnostic and Statistical Manual IV* (DSMIV) sets out a series of symptoms of depression which include feeling sad, unwarranted anxiety, loss of interest in ordinary activities such as work and play. Some people have trouble thinking or making decisions, and they complain about aches and pains that can't be treated. They say they feel worthless, hopeless and guilty. Pessimism and indifference, along with the loss of contact with friends and family, as well as fear of crowds, are other possible symptoms.

Obviously, depression in whatever level it occurs in a marriage relationship can be a train wreck. Later on, we come to another "I" which stands for intimacy and we will see then how depression can take its toll on the essence of a marriage. In this case, misery does NOT love company, and the non-depressed partner, at best, has his own ringside seat at a painful lesson in futility.

What to do about an episode of deep depression? Begin by acknowledging that some level of depression does exist, and most importantly, **seek help!**

The sources of help vary, and without going into a long detailed explanation, let's just hit the nail on the head and say that the **best** course to achieve relief and healing from a deep depressive episode, according to almost all responsible and competent mental health professionals, is a combination of physician- or psychiatrist-prescribed medication, and psychotherapy.

Anti-depressant medicines, which must be monitored and can be prescribed only by a physician, are usually effective in relieving the near-term symptoms of depression. Care and attention must be paid not only by the patient, but also by his family as well to check for possible adverse side-effects of an anti-depressant drug. Sometimes side-effects resulting from anti-depressant medications can cause a whole set of new problems.

With regard to the need for psychotherapy, specific models have been developed for the treatment of depression, and the value of adding therapy with medication is that drugs can help people through the short-term discomfort of depression, but the psychotherapy will teach them to identify the sources of stress which cause or contribute to their depression. Hopefully then, they can learn how to avoid those sources of stress, and thus dodge recurrent depressive episodes.

Typically when one consults a psychotherapist about a depressive episode, he will have two or three one-on-one session and then be referred to a group session. As I mentioned earlier, group therapy is very efficient and cost effective. Usually ten once-a-week sessions will not only solve the immediate distress, but also prepare the person to resume his life, show him how to avoid falling back into another deep depression.

Depressed people often think about their funeral and spend time drawing or changing their wills. One of the worst symptoms of depression is persistent thoughts about death, dying and, most dangerous of all, suicide. Many suicides are the direct result of a major depressive episode.

Suicide

When talking about stress and depression, great care must be taken to help anyone who is in a severe depression.

An attempt at suicide might not be far behind.

These few words cannot list all the statistics of suicide, nor the sad consequences to family and friends of those who do themselves in. But, if one is alert and informed, there will be clues given which can indicate a possibility or inclination of a person to kill himself.

Clues? Most suicidal persons feel high levels of inner conflict and disarray, and they usually give out signs or hints about their serious troubles in a call for help one way or the other. Following is a small sampling of what the clues may include:

Verbal: Direct—"I'm going to do it—kill myself."

Indirect—"I'm no good for anyone (or anything) any more."

Behavioral: For example, slashing one's wrists in a non-fatal "attempt," or a drug overdose with a last-minute phone call to someone telling what he has done. Perhaps a bad car "accident," or "accidental" shotgun firing.

Situation: The "setting of the scene"—something happened to trigger the depression such as a death, divorce, bankruptcy, onset of serious or terminal illness, the anniversary of a loved one, or any other drastic change in that person's life.

Syndromatic: Which means a combination of conditions listed above along with severe depression, and feelings of hopelessness, loneliness, worthlessness, etc., etc.

Some clues are buried in myths. For example, it is said that talking about suicide will drive the person further down that road. Not so! Talking with a depressed about suicide might be just what is needed for that person to get some relief from the black and white point of view they are stuck in. People who are suicidal are not able to see any options other than the taking of their own life to stop the mental pain. Talking with them might give them a feeling that they have more time, that you care about them, and there's always the chance they might be able to gain control of their lives. BONUS! Your getting them talking **gives YOU more time to get help!**

Another myth: Those who threaten suicide and may even have some failed attempts will never actually do it. Again NOT TRUE! Some who have attempted suicide, failed, and subsequently got some theraputic help to learn the appropriate responses and controls, clearly say that if left alone and without help, they would have eventually succeeded. Go back and look at the previous column with regard to verbal clues.

Another myth: Once suicidal, always suicidal. Again NOT TRUE! Those who have attempted suicide, failed and got help, can live long and productive lives. The secret they learned is how to control their thoughts and responses.

Final disclaimer: The purpose of these few paragraphs is not to provide an all-encompassing source of information about suicide, but only to alert people to the danger of suicide as a by-product or a deep depressive episode brought about by some stressfull situation.

IF YOU THINK FOR EVEN A MINUTE YOU ARE UP AGAINST A SUICIDE GET HELP ! IMMEDIATELY !

After all that, a conclusion that floats to the top of the churn is that this business of living is all about stress and how we handle it. See how much trouble stress can cause?

Living is a huge category of concern in any marriage relationship, and sometimes the best ally one can have is just simply, TIME.

A

Stands For 'ADDICTION'

The issue of addiction is difficult to discuss because of the large number of things that people can and do become addicted to. The list includes sex, alcohol, gambling, drugs, eating disorders and God-only-knows how many other substances and behaviors. Also add the bad-news fact that an addiction can appear at almost any time in a person's life. Then, if a bona fide addiction appears, what in the world do you do, from either the addict's or codependent's point of view. The most inclusive formal definition of addiction is probably this one proposed by D. Donovan in his 1988 book, *Assessment of Addictive Behaviors,* which says:

> Addiction is seen as a complex, progressive behavior pattern having biological, psychological, sociological and behavioral components . . . wherein the individual's pattern of behavior is marked by an overwhelmingly pathological involvement in or attachment to the addictive behavior and subjective compulsion to continue it [the addiction] and reduced ability to exert personal control over it.

That sure is a mouthful of semi-technical jargon, but still a pretty complete explanation and definition of addiction. Most everyone knows what an addiction looks like because almost everybody has witnessed some sort of addiction occurring to someone in his lifetime.

Some addictions are life-threatening. Some are criminal in nature, and some are ruinous to person, family and finances. As we all know, many of the chemical and eating-disorder addictions can result in the death of the addict. A chemical overdose can outright kill a person. People addicted to eating disorders on either end of the pendulum, overeating ("OE") or starvation (anorexia), and bulimia (throwing up food), can abuse their bodies so badly they may eventually die. A sad example of such a tragedy is the death of Karen Carpenter of the musical group The Carpenters, who suffered from anorexia.

By way of further explanation, "anorectics" who starve themselves can be identified because they are usually so terribly thin. Folks with bulimia might look normal as far as body weight is concerned, but they maintain that weight by vomiting almost all they eat. Both conditions are mental problems (syndromes), carry heavy psychological as well as physical consequences, and each diagnosis desperately needs immediate treatment by a mental health professional.

Individuals who commit illicit sexual contact with children are pedophiles, and conviction in a court of law for a crime of pedophilia can result in the offender going to jail. Where they richly deserve to be. For a long, long time. Pedophilia is considered to be a type of addictive behavior, and recovery from this awful syndrome is quite rare.

Those who are addicted to gambling can end up losing everything—family, as well as finances.

Debate continues over the causes of addiction, with blame being placed on genetics or inherited tendencies. Some contend that addictions come from early "socialization" or childhood influences of the behaviors of parents; and others hold that dependencies can stem from association with persons who are using some drug or alcohol, and blame their own loss of control on what they call peer pressure. Other times, pathology or illness is blamed as the root cause. Once in a while you can hear a person who is addicted to a drug or behavior accused of not having any character because he doesn't behave like everyone else in society.

From the point of view of our basic discussion about marriage relationships, what difference does it make where an addiction comes from? Once a person develops a dependency, there is grief enough to go around; not only is the addicted person in trouble, but also the other members of the family. The whole family, marriage partner and children as well, are all then said to be codependent'on the behavior of the addict. The entire family life-structure can, and often becomes quite limited, confusing and painful.

The issue of codependence, addictive as well as general was covered in **G** stands for 'general codependence.'

Three issues come up once one begins to study the subject of addiction, and we shall consider some solutions, and they are:

1) Diagnosis of a possible addiction.
2) Treatment possibilities available for addicts and codependents.
3) The impact of an addictive circumstance on a marriage relationship.

1. Diagnosis of Addiction

Accurate diagnosis of any addiction is not as easy to accomplish as it might seem, because there are so many shades or levels of involvement with various substances and/or behaviors that can be addictive. For example, not all alcoholics lie in the gutter in the classical form. Many people could qualify as bona fide alcoholics who do have some control over their drinking patterns. Some might not start drinking until after dinner, but then, once they have begun they do not, or cannot stop until they are either completely blotto and go to bed, or pass out, or all of the above. Some stop at a bar on the way home, arrive at the stiff-as-a-plank state, then drive home.

Other alcoholics could qualify as "binge" drinkers, in that they might not have a drop of alcohol for days or weeks on end, until all of a sudden they "fall off the wagon" and enter into a period of furious drinking which is continued sometimes for days, until they are blind drunk, or at best very sick.

Some alcoholics drink a little alcohol all the time, all day, every day, resulting in their never being obviously drunk in the classically tipsy form. Their constant daily consumption of booze results in their being always slightly "high," so no one ever sees them completely sober, therefore a casual observer has no offsetting normal behavioral patterns to compare with their everyday slightly inebriated state.

One morning while I was in a liquor store in a large eastern city making purchases for an upcoming business cocktail party, I noticed, after I had made my selections, that there was a long line of people who were waiting to get checked out. Keep in mind that this event occurred in the morning.

Here was a line of about 15 persons waiting patiently in line to buy a pint of vodka. A pint of vodka in the morning? Anyone who buys alcohol and is of a slightly thrifty bent will tell you that a pint of vodka costs about half as much as a bottle four or five times larger, so why buy the smaller and therefore far less economical quantity?

When I got up to the cashier I asked her how come all those people were in the store that early in the morning and each buying just a pint of vodka for $4 when they could have bought almost five times the amount of vodka in the larger 1.75 liter (5 pints) bottle for only twice the money, $8 or $9? Such apparent wastefulness didn't seem to make sense.

Her matter of fact answer: In order to get their hearts started and therefore sustain their addictions, these poor souls had to down at least a pint of alcohol before they went to work, and some bought two pints. Once they had downed the pint or two they could then easily throw away the evidence, the small empty bottle, and go to work. Isn't that sad? She then commented that the same people came in every morning to make their purchase.

When I left the store I went around to the side of the building, looked in the dumpster and, sure enough, it was crammed nearly full with empty pint bottles. These folks all went to work slightly stiff and none of their co-workers probably ever had any idea that they were under the influence of alcohol because they never had the occasion to see them completely sober. They were half-stiff all the time.

This author has seen friends die who were raving drunks, true alcoholics, and who chose this "passive suicide" course. "Active suicide" is when one jumps off the bridge, puts the gun to the head, or hangs one's self. Passive suicide is the indirect route to death by using or doing something that in itself might not be life threatening when used to moderation. but when used to excess results in the person's demise. W. C. Fields is quoted as saying, "Moderation is okay, as long as you don't use it to excess."

The point is, a diagnosis of any addictive behavior is much easier talked about than accomplished, and there is no way of telling with any sort of accuracy how many people are addicted to alcohol, or any other chemical or errant behavior. Some experts estimate as high as 10% of the populace are addicted to alcohol. Because of the secretive nature of most addictions, there is no way to accurately cite any number or percentage figure of the general population who are afflicted with any addiction. There are "closet" drinkers, sex addicts, gamblers, drug addicts, and every other form of addictive behavior.

Sometimes in therapy or in a clinical setting, someone suspected or thought—or maybe "accused" would be better—to be addicted to something will be given a test to take which is supposed to help the therapist discover if there's a possibility of an addiction to some drug or behavior. Any competent therapist will view this test, or any series of tests simply as clues to possible errant behavior or addiction. The final and accurate diagnosis of addiction is possible only by the admission of the individual that he has lost control over that facet of his life, and needs help to regain his ability to deal with the chemical substance or errant behavior that has upset his life balance.

Please note the use of the word competent preceding the word therapist because anyone who knows anything about testing knows that any test that is given or administered is nothing more than a single clue to the person's innate behavioral inclinations. Tests are given for almost every possible human trait, including a person's IQ, personality, addictions, aptitudes or whatever reason for which the subject is being tested. But in the end, a test, any test, is just one clue. Three tests are three clues. Never, never, is one test conclusive evidence of the presence of an addiction, any errant behavior, or almost anything else for that matter.

A large number of tests, called a "battery of tests," might be a stronger indication of the possible existence of a problem, but the fact remains that, while the clues might be important and indicative, the final diagnosis of an addiction of any type can be made only by the admission of the person suffering the addiction.

Too frequently, ill-trained or self-serving therapists who call themselves "addiction specialists," whose only credential is having been the town drunk, will whip out and administer a test with the results pronounced by the incompetent test-giver to be absolutely conclusive. A final diagnosis of an addiction is officially declared, and the poor person who took the slanted test is then subjected to a barrage of frantic efforts to get the him into an expensive "rehabilitation" hospital. Whether or not these self-serving "specialists," or incompetent therapists do this shoddy work without remuneration, or fee, is a subject hidden deep in the bowels of the movement.

Sometimes one can see one of these tests in the newspaper, often concerning alcoholism, with the results of that one test being acclaimed as valid and true, and if the person taking the test answers one or two of the dozen or so slanted, ambiguous questions in the wrong manner, they are proclaimed as having an "indication of having a possible problem with ____." Fill in your own label. And the pressure to enter "treatment" begins.

Another big problem with diagnosis of addiction is that, as a general rule, before anybody is ever ready to admit to his addiction, he lives in a state of what is known as denial, and how in the world does one ever get someone who is deeply imbedded in denial to admit and come to grips with his own dependency? Only by and until the addicted persons themselves have "hit bottom," as they say, and are in so much trouble they cannot continue their lives in the same chaotic pattern, do they finally realize they need help. A possible avenue to keep the person from having to "hit bottom" could be a strong intervention process, which will be explained in the next section.

Three main courses lie open for diagnostic confirmation of any addictive behavior; they are, self-admission, evaluation, and intervention, and we shall briefly look at each possibility.

Self-Admission

Many of today's recovering alcoholics simply woke up very ill one morning and finally admitted to themselves that they were hooked on alcohol, they had endured enough of the cruel torture of their addiction, their life was out of control and being wasted or ruined, and death was surely in the cards if they continued on the present course. They knew, then and there, help was needed to beat their addiction. Many of today's recovering alcoholics stopped their addictive behavior in this "cold turkey" manner, with no outside treatment, no preparation, no help whatsoever; they then endured a great deal of mental as well as physical pain. These "cold turkey" recovering alcoholics managed to escape from their addiction only by dint of guts and fierce determination.

Other alcoholics, when they woke up so sick they couldn't believe it, finally admitted their addiction and called someone they know to be active in the famous Alcoholics Anonymous (AA) movement for help. The Alcoholics Anonymous movement is popularly known among alcoholics as the "Program," and the decades old AA "twelve-step" treatment program is the recovery model for many other addiction-recovery efforts.

The Alcoholics Anonymous program revolves around four basic building blocks, which are:

Meetings, which are held daily in virtually every town and city in the country;

The personal support of the sponsor, who is either an individual assigned to the newcomer by a local AA chapter, or perhaps a friend who is already in the program, and chosen by the addict to provide the aid and support the new recovering alcoholic so desperately needs in his attempt to get his dependency under control and into remission;

Faithful adherence to the "12 step" program for the specific addiction. Both the essence of the program, the concept of the importance of meetings, and the 12-step concept will be explained here in due course. And, most importantly:

Strict abstinence from the chemical or addictive behavior.

In the opinion of many observers it appears that the self-treated or "bootstrap" recovering alcoholics don't seem to be as happy or as well-adjusted later in their recovery as those who achieved initial control over their addiction with the help of a treatment center. In fact, sometimes the self-treated recovering alcoholic will, at some later date, go to a treatment center to achieve greater balance in his life, and to develop a more thorough understanding of the disease. The "treatment center" aspect of addiction treatment possibilities will be mentioned shortly.

As you see then, the accurate diagnosis of any addiction by anyone other than the addict is a difficult if not impossible task to achieve, which brings us to the second consideration, known as:

Evaluation

Sometimes a person suspected or accused of being addicted to some chemical substance or errant behavior is encouraged to go to a person or persons who are considered to be specialists in the area of diagnosis of a particular addiction. We just considered the area of testing above, so there is no reason to review those ideas. Depending on the training and approach of the evaluator(s), a diagnosis is ultimately made by the specialist with regard to the possibility of an existing addiction. Not infrequently, the evaluator(s) are employees of an institution which will stand to prosper (profit) if the client is adjudged addicted, and of course the expensive process of addiction therapy is to begin at their institution.

Three quick thoughts pop into mind; 1) never ask a barber if you need a haircut, 2) a tire salesman if you need a new set of tires, or, 3) an "addiction specialist" if you need treatment.

Problems can arise in any evaluation procedure when, after interviews and 'testing', the evaluator pronounces the existence of an addiction and the suspected addict, being already deeply embedded in denial, not surprisingly disagrees, sometimes vehemently, resulting in a stalemate unless the evaluator can somehow get the client to admit to the addiction and ask for help.

Other problem areas with regard to evaluation can appear when the suspected or accused addiction might lie in the mind of someone else, an accuser, and the perceived addiction could be part of a power play and struggle for control, rather than a real addiction. As you would guess from your knowledge of codependence, the accuser in such a case could very possibly be the badly damaged offspring of a truly addicted parent.

Thus, the evaluation of someone by a self-pronounced specialist may not be a reliable diagnosis. Which brings us to the third method of evaluation or diagnosis that is neither an evaluation nor diagnosis, and is known as intervention.

Intervention

The technique known as intervention involves the surprise landing on the doorstep of the one considered to be addicted, usually by a team of persons who are concerned about the health and/or condition of the alleged addict. The team doing the surprise intervention would typically include the addict's employer, family members, children, fellow workers, clergy people, friends, some of whom have been down the road so to speak, and are members of AA. The obvious goal of the intervention team is, by the fact of sheer surprise, to shakeup, stun, or simply overwhelm the suspected addict out of the denial he is thought to be in, and get the individual to agree to some immediate action about his perceived or real addiction. The action sought can include, among other things, immediate admission to a treatment center, his joining the AA, or perhaps just his simply stopping the addictive behavior on his own.

Intervention as a diagnostic technique, which it really might not be, has mixed results and is sometimes not accomplished very fairly. This brief description is the essence of what the process of intervention is all about. Needless to say, a critical member of the intervention process is the inclusion on the team of the codependent spouse, and often the children too.

Hopefully, after all that descriptive effort, you've come away with the notion that completely accurate diagnosis of an addiction is not an easy thing to accomplish without the sincere consent and/or admission of addiction by the person.

2. Treatment of Addiction

We will list both sides of the treatment spectrum, initially with regard to treatment of the person who is addicted, and then offer some suggested avenues of treatment, or maybe better said, aid and comfort for those who are, as codependents, in the position of having to live with someone who is suffering with an addiction.

As far as treatment of the addict is concerned there are basically three treatment courses available to attempt resolution of a person's addiction, one of which is the previously mentioned self-help, gut-it-out, cold-turkey, do-it-yourself method. While this very difficult process can work, it does work reportedly only with great difficulty and struggle on the part of the addict.

Obviously there are no statistics available on the success of this method of controlling an addiction because, who knows how many poor souls are attempting to treat themselves, and without that information, how would anyone ever know how a do-it-yourself treatment program ever came out? Self-help recovery from an addiction is certainly a possibility, and any success and escape from the dependency by an individual on his own is solely due to that person's sheer grit and determination.

The second process for addictive rehabilitation involves the addict reaching out in his hour of desperate need to someone in one of the appropriate self-help addiction recovery plans. For example, a person having trouble controlling his behavior with regard to the consumption of alcohol would contact the local AA office. A person with drug addiction problems would contact Narcotic's Anonymous (NA) group. Someone with eating disorder problems would contact the Overeaters Anonymous (OE) program. Anyone addicted to gambling would get in touch with the Gambler's Anonymous (GA) people, and so on for each type of addiction. In many Sunday newspapers a complete list can be found of all the active support groups active in your area.

To explain a typical recovery process, using alcoholism as the addiction, a person who feels he is addicted to alcohol could seek help by contacting someone in AA, as mentioned above. The AA person who was contacted would either respond to the call himself, or if he was personally unable for some reason or the other, then another recovering alcoholic would be sent in answer to the cry for help. This response process is the "Twelfth Step" of the famous 12-step recovery program(s). An explanation of the AA 12-step program will be along in a minute. Once the call for help is received, the newly admitted addict is taken under the wing of the individual who is himself a successful recovering alcoholic, and who is then known as the sponsor of the person seeking help.

From that time on, the sponsor is the personal guardian angel of the newly self-declared addict. Sponsors offer support, counsel and strength 24 hours a day, seven days a week to the newcomer in the program.

As mentioned earlier, of the four key elements to the AA treatment plan for overcoming the disease of alcoholism (sponsor, meetings, adherence to the 12-steps and total abstinence) the first step is the acquisition of a sponsor, who begins by taking the newcomer to a meeting. Meetings are held every day and at all hours of the day and night in almost every community in the United States. And, in fact, around the world.

A brief explanation of a meeting, as related by a recovering alcoholic: The meetings, which are usually about an hour long, provide the support, resolve and diversion that the recovering alcoholic desperately needs to stay sober. That is not to say that the role of the sponsor isn't critical to the attempt to achieve and maintain sobriety, but ultimately the responsibility for sobriety rests solely on the shoulders of the addict alone, and it is up to the them to get to meetings if that is the only way they can stay sober.

Decades later, after achieving sobriety, many recovering alcoholics still regularly attend meetings. Some attend several meetings a week, others hurt so badly they attend two or three meetings a day! This desperation should show anybody who wonders just how terribly difficult recovery from alcoholic addiction is, even after a long period of time. That's why they call themselves recovering alcoholics, in that they never fully recover, but are always in a recovery process, never to be "cured."

Actually, anyone at all familiar with the concept of group counseling will immediately recognize the function of the AA meeting concept as a self-help group therapy session with no structured leadership, as opposed to the strict or more rigid therapist/client format used in a typical psychological group.

The meetings are opened by the moderator, and the program is either someone who has volunteered to share his life with the others at the meeting, or what they call a "step" meeting, during which one of the 12 steps is discussed in open forum. The meeting where one of the recovering alcoholics tells his life experiences with regard to alcohol is called a "drunk-a-logue," and is frequently very entertaining, as well as quite sad. As one could guess, recovering alcoholics as a group are generally wonderfully fun people, very out-going and interesting. Many of the recovering alcoholics easily could be stand-up comics they are so humorous, poised and organized.

The third cornerstone of the AA movement is the famous "12-step" program, which was formulated over 50 years ago by two men who were themselves battling alcoholism. These 12 steps have been generally adopted by almost all addiction-recovery programs, with appropriate changes in the words defining which addiction is being addressed. The meanings embodied in the various steps, and the addict's strict adherence to the basic principles are critical to anyone's successful recovery from an addiction. You might be interested to see for yourself what the 12-steps actually say, so following is listed, with exact quotation, the famous AA 12 steps. You can insert the word describing whatever addiction with which you might be concerned where the word "alcohol" appears, in Step 1, and Step 12.

The Alcoholics Anonymous 12-Step Program

Step 1. "We admitted we are powerless over alcohol and that our lives have become unmanageable."

Step 2. "We came to believe that a Power greater than ourselves can restore us to sanity."

Step 3. "We made a decision to turn our will and our lives over to the care of God, as We understand Him."

Step 4. "We made a searching and fearless moral inventory of ourselves."

Step 5. "We admitted to God, to ourselves, and to another human being the exact nature of our wrongs. "

Step 6. "We were entirely ready to have God remove all these defects of ours."

Step 7. "We humbly asked Him (God) to remove our shortcomings."

Step 8. "We made a list of all the persons we have harmed and became willing to make amends to them all."

Step 9. "We made direct amends to such people wherever possible except when to do so would injure them or others."

Step 10. "We continued to take personal inventory and when we are wrong we promptly admit it."

Step 11. "We sought through prayer and meditation to improve our conscious contact with God as we understand Him, praying only for knowledge of His will for us, and the power to carry that out."

Step 12. "Having had a spiritual awakening as a result of these steps, we try to carry this message to alcoholics and to practice these principles in all our affairs."

As said earlier and before listing the 12

steps, this philosophy of life as set out and embodied in this text has existed and endured without change for the past several decades, and this format has served thousands upon thousands of sufferers very well. Those active in the AA program point with pride to the fact that the cure rate in AA is 100% for any person who fully and faithfully follows the program'without deviation.

The final requirement for success in the AA program or any other "12-step" recovery program, is total abstinence from the addictive behavior or substance for the rest of the addict's life.

Two final thoughts to close this brief description of the good work of Alcoholics Anonymous: If you watch for them, you can see two bumper stickers which appear on the rear bumpers of a lot of cars, one of which says "One day at a time," and the other, "Take it easy." Both of these thoughts are critical and essential to the success of anyone's attempt to escape the disease of alcoholism or any other addiction. We can only live but for today since yesterday is gone, tomorrow isn't here yet and may never come, so just pay attention to and get through today. The other saying simply tells people to take it easy. Be calm, determined and persistent; take your time, and success surely will be found.

Treatment Centers

The third possibility for treatment of an addiction is the treatment center approach, which began only a few decades ago, and has developed into a huge industry. These centers abound across this country for treatment of all types of addictive behaviors, both on an in-patient as well as out-patient basis. It is not uncommon to see national advertising on television by one or the other of the large treatment centers.

Unfortunately, the statistical cure-rate for clients of the treatment centers, especially the alcoholism centers, seems to hover in the disappointing less-than-25% range, unless the patient enrolls and follows the AA program. So you can see, even with the aid of intense short-term professional help (30 to 90 days), overcoming an addiction is at its screaming best a very difficult and painful process.

I would have no business attempting in this text to set out exactly what the treatment procedure is in any particular treatment center. Exact information with regard to the typical 30 to 90 day treatment process would be available either from the center, or from someone who has attended, or graduated, if you will, from that facility.

Caveat emptor—buyer beware: Before anyone goes to or attends a treatment center the rules of "informed consent" must apply. Informed consent means that the patient, and the patients family, must know exactly what the treatment process will be, the status of living conditions, an estimated time frame for completion of the treatment, a range of cost estimates, and an explanation of some of the typical after-effects, if any, of the program. References should be gotten and verified although this might be hard to do since the center will probably claim it cannot divulge names in the interest of patient confidentiality. If that's the way it works out, then work backwards, find someone who has "graduated" from a center and ask them what happened while they were in treatment, and how they fared upon graduation. They will tell you.

A word of warning; sometimes folks are so thrilled in their recovery, they become over-enthusiastic about the treatment process and wind up sending all the rest of the members of the family including the dog, to treatment. Whether they need it or not. People who do not have an addiction do not prosper when put through the often severe process of addiction treatment.

Once a person has graduated from a formal in-patient, or outpatient addiction treatment process there are several courses of action available to the now-recovering addict, and this may be the reason that the cure rate for whose who complete only the course of treatment in a center is so low; they pick the wrong option.

Option #1. Some "graduates" are allowed to immediately return to their homes, families and jobs, hoping against hope that the addicts won't return to their addictive behavior. This plan doesn't work very well because all the pressures or influences that caused—or maybe better said—precipitated the addiction in the first place will all still be in existence, and the odds are very good that the person will return to the bad behavior.

Option #2. Some "graduates" do not return to their homes right away, but enter what they call a "halfway house," which is just that, a bridge between the treatment center and the real world. While living full-time in the halfway house, the recovering addict is assigned a sponsor and is introduced to the program. Into AA, for example, if that's the case.

The patient is slowly reintroduced to his work, and his family. Not his friends. Those who are "recovering" anything cannot re-associate themselves with those persons with whom they were friendly while in the grip of the addiction. The making of new friends is a critical part of the recovery process. After a while, when the patient seems to be coming along okay, the addict returns home, but only under the continuation of his involvement in the program, which means, he maintains close contact with his sponsor as long as needed, go to meetings regularly, abides faithfully by the 12 steps, and absolutely maintains total abstinence from the addictive substance or behavior. The cure rate for this addiction recovery plan is very good.

Option #3. The third possibility for the addict's return to normal life is a compromise of the above two levels of re-entry, in that the recovering addict goes home, but immediately and devotedly enters into the total AA program; sponsor, meetings, total abstinence and adherence to the 12 steps. This course of action for the addict and the addict's family, as well, involves many substantial lifestyle changes, including the addict's acquiring a whole new set of friends as mentioned above, and the requirement for the entire family's cooperation and support as the recovering addict makes his way through the dark halls of recovery. This option can work quite well, and the addict can return to work at once.

Two quick notes: on two occasions the issue of friends was just mentioned, and this is a crucial point. The addict must not resume running with the same people he ran with before treatment. This change is usually not a huge problem because the former drinking buddies often won't have anything to do with the newly recovering addict. Their thinking; if the friendship was resumed they would be under pressure to not drink any more, too, which is about the last thing that interests any confirmed boozer.

Point two is that all the other family members MUST not drink alcoholic beverages in front of the recovering addict. At least for quite a long time. Recovering alcoholics simply cannot stand to watch others drink beer, wine, or cocktails while they sit with their coke or cup of coffee. After decades of sobriety, almost all recovering alcoholics are not able to be in a setting where drinking hooch in any form is the order of the day.

Research in recent years has shown that the best chance for recovery from addiction lies somewhere in the combination treatment center AA approach. Needless to say, more research is called for to most accurately pin-point the best courses of action to assure success after treatment.

One trouble spot: many insurance plans will pay for the in-or out-patient care; other insurance companies seem to be reluctant to pay for the halfway-house interlude, which throws the financial burden on the addict and his family. As if they didn't have enough trouble. The family members not only had to suffer through the difficult pre-treatment time, but then they also have to endure the period of confinement. Which bring us to the treatment for codependents.

Treatment for Codependent Spouses and Children

The codependent family members are considered to be as sick and upset as the addict himself, and help is available from the various groups affiliated with each addiction type. For example, the group dealing with those who are codependent to alcoholism is called Al-anon. The purpose of this group is to provide support and education to the codependent spouses and their children about the disease of alcoholism which has entered the family.

Codependents of other addictions might also possibly attend the Al-anon meetings if the addiction they are struggling with does not have its own active codependent support group. However, before attending the alcoholism Al-anon meeting it is a good and polite procedure to ask someone who is attending those Al-anon meetings if it would be okay for you to attend. Most surely the answer would be "yes," but sometimes the Al-anon group might be having what they call a closed meeting, for only the specific members of the group. Beyond a doubt, a later Al-Anon group would be available, or you might be able to locate a support group which applies specifically to the addiction in question.

A quick look in the phone book would likely show a phone number for an Al-anon group, but if you cannot find a listing, then a call to the local AA office asking for the name of someone in Al-anon that you could talk to. If all other courses fail, call a clergy person or two, for very often they know of church members who are in the AA, or in Al-anon.

One of the reasons you know you will find someone who will help is that the Al-anon members subscribe to, live by, and endorse the 12 steps of the "AA", and if you recall, the 12th step is a promise to help anyone trapped in an addictive circumstance, who asks for guidance or support.

We are told that the crux of the "Al-_____" movement is to not only provide support and education to the codependents, as we mentioned, but also to enlighten the codependent spouse and the children to the fact that the addiction being endured by another member in the family is really nothing that they can do anything about. They didn't cause the person's addiction, and they should NOT "enable" the addict's behavior. All they can do is to sit tight and hope against hope that the addict will regain his balance before he crashes, dies, or goes broke.

"Enabling" as a process is what people do when they mistakenly prolong and nourish the bad behavior of an addict by helping the addiction continue, sometimes by virtue of misguided good intentions. For example, if a husband brings whiskey home to his already inebriated wife, he is "enabling" her drunkenness. It is held in a court of law, and in the court of life, that people who "enable" other's poor behavior be it criminal or addictive are guilty of conspiracy, aiding and abetting, facilitating, depraved indifference and being an accessory to the bad behavior, and are as guilty as the person who committed the crime, or in the case of an addiction, are responsible for the continuation of the addiction.

Thou Shalt Not Be an Enabler!

The basic premise of the Al-anon movement can be embodied in the following question and answer:

Q. Who is the most important person in your life?
A. You are the most important person in your life.

Therefore, the spouse and any children who find themselves living in a state of codependence with an addicted spouse, offspring, or parent must look out primarily for their own welfare, and attend to their own health and sanity.

In recent years a new group has appeared called the Adult Children of Alcoholics (ACOA), whose goal is to address the trauma that the addiction of a parent to alcohol causes to the codependent children later in their adult lives. It has been found that children living in a codependent addiction-ridden family might not suffer damage until they are grown adults. It is the mission of the ACOA to address this late-blooming distress, and to help the adult children of alcoholics come to terms with their own lives, and hopefully not their own addictions. Tracking down an ACOA chapter would involve the same steps outlined above.

The Impact of an Addictive Circumstance on a Marriage Relationship

Of course, the impact could be disastrous if the behavior of the addict caused any one or a combination of the three reasons to get a divorce: infidelity that can't be stopped or tolerated; abuse; or if an awful situation went on too long and a state of total incompatibility developed which made continuing to live in the marriage relationship unbearable.

There is really not too much that can be said past that point. An addiction, any addiction, in itself, is not a cause or reason to divorce. If an addiction is an illness, a disease, as experts contend the addiction of alcoholism really is, then did you not say that day, "in sickness and in health?" Ask the question: If your spouse came down with cancer or heart disease would that be good and sufficient reason to divorce them, just because they were sick? Some people do, but is that right?

In conclusion, an addiction to some behavior or chemical by a marriage partner is an unfortunate circumstance. There is not too much that any marriage partner can do with an addicted spouse except to try to get him help, or treatment. But the fact remains that each marriage partner must look out for his own life and health, as well as the lives and well-being of the other members of the family, especially the children.

Sometimes married people forget that very often the "better" comes along quite a while after the "worse." But, if you think you've got an addiction problem, GET HELP! FIND OUT!

T

Stands For 'TIME'

"This time like all times is a very good one if we but know what to do with it." R.W. Emerson. Time, as the essential part of human existence, can have a great deal to do with the success or failure of anybody's marriage relationship from several points of view, including:

1) The amount or QUANTITY of time spent in the relationship.
2) The value or QUALITY of time spent in the marriage.
3) Personal attitudes towards time.
4) Learning how to look at and use time as an ally, not as a weapon. Giving time a chance in other words.

Time As a Quantity

To begin with, let's take a look at the quantitative factors regarding time that could affect your marriage, and take into consideration the amount of time that needs to be spent on the relationship.

From an occupational point of view, all one has to do to see the impact of a shortage of time being given to a marriage relationship is to take a look at certain high-divorce-rate occupations such as airline pilots, medical care-givers, and over-the-road truck drivers. These three occupations rate sky-high on the list of professions with high divorce rates for the obvious reason: The airline pilots, the medical persons and truck drivers, are simply not at home enough for their relationship to achieve stability and survivability.

The only way a marriage might survive in any of these occupational instances, or in any case where either of the marriage partners simply does not spend enough time at home because of an over-interest in work, hobby, or avocation, would be if the left-at-home marriage partner:

a) Had been reared in a family in which his own parent(s) were never at home because either they were workaholics, or had very time-consuming outside interests. The person was accustomed to not having that family member be at home, even at critical times.
b) Have the circumstance wherein the at-home partners have an extremely strong local support system (family)

to aid them through the many holidays, weekends, times of family crisis and other periods during which their mate is absent.

c) Happen to be a person who possesses great and unusual personal mental strength and endurance so he will be able to handle the absences on his own. Not very many people exist who are so strong and have such single-minded determination and purpose.

d) All of the above.

Picture this: two days before Christmas Eve s/he goes out the door to go to work and doesn't show up again until a couple days after Christmas, only to leave again a day or so before New Year's Eve with return set for January 3rd or 4th at best. Now wouldn't that be a fun holiday season for a woman or man at home with a child or two, or three or more?

Obviously, the message is that both mates' occupations or numbers of jobs, if that's the case, are critical factors to be considered before one enters into a marriage relationship. If you are considering entering into marriage with someone who is engaged in an occupation that requires a lot of time to be spent away from home, don't kid yourself by thinking that you will be able to: a) get them to change occupations, for you may not; b) think that, beyond the shadow of a doubt, you can handle the mate's absence. What happens later on if you find you can NOT handle his being gone all the time?

The apparent solution to possible problems with time would come in two sections:

A) Before entering into a marriage, the two partners endeavor to arrive at some point of accommodation and understanding with regard to time. The agreement should be fair, reasonable, realistic and preferably not have an expiration time or end-date. The agreement should be considered as the basic carved-in-granite rule for their lifelong relationship.

But, that is not the way the old world turns.

While on one hand, people need to know what to count on and what to expect to the best of their ability, on the other hand, as in any relationship, things can happen to change one's mind-set, or circumstances can change. An agreement that once looked sound and workable, goes sour. The agreement becomes a foundation for disagreement.

For example, what if a lady married an MD, which seemed like a whippy "catch" to her at the time. Then later she got tired of his always being at the hospital or seeing patients. Can she ask him to abandon his medical profession? Is this not the old, "I can handle it," "I can handle it," "I can handle it," "I CAN'T handle it!" routine? Which brings us to:

B) Having another agreement to sit down and talk over the situation again if one of the marriage partners gets into trouble over time. For example, in the field of mediation, very often an escape clause is inserted into the final "Memorandum of Understanding" between the conflicting parties which requires that, if anything changes and the agreement becomes onerous or burdensome, the parties agree to return to mediation again before running off to an attorney.

In like manner, in your marriage, have an agreement which binds you both to a "let's sit down and talk this over" requirement before anything serious is said or threatened. In the unhappy event that a person's occupation, hobby, or outside interest starts taking up too much time, then one can only resort to the communication and negotiation techniques as set out in this text to resolve the problem, unless there's something else wrong.

For example: What if the circumstance occurs that one of the marriage partners just isn't spending enough time at home to make the marriage relationship work, and he is not involved in a really high time-consuming occupation, or engrossing hobby or interest? Then the question is: What is the reason for the absence? Has this absent person become a workaholic? Has he fallen victim to some addiction? Has he become involved in another relationship? Could it be that he is so very unhappy and dissatisfied, he thinks the only way he can survive in their poor marriage is to be absent?

Without going into a lot of discussion about whether or not a workaholic might well have personality disorders, let's just generously grant the possibility might exist that your everyday garden-variety workaholic is simply suffering from a bad case of mis-aligned priorities (see under **P**), likely coupled with a more than ample dose of downside general codependence, (**G**) or, as Daddy or Mommy did, so do I.

In talking with my friend "Phil" one day, I asked him, "What is most important in a person's life, one's family or business/occupation?" He stunned me when he said that obviously the most important of the two considerations was the business or career because, as he put it, if the business or occupation wasn't going along well then the family wouldn't either. He was saying that money, or the family standard of living, as provided by the occupation, is the most important factor in a person's life. An obvious case of poor logic, and badly confused priorities.

Hopefully, most folks think that just the reverse is true and that one's marriage relationship and family are the most important factors in anyone's life. Please recall that always the most important person in anyone's life is himself, but in the list of priorities (**P**), as used in our consideration of the Marriage Relationship format, the family should top the list. Granted that the need for money is of real importance, because therein lies the basis of living standards and conditions and, to some extent, family accomplishments.

All parents want to do as well as they can financially to sustain their family and lifestyle in a manner to which they would like to become accustomed, acknowledging whatever various limitations might exist. But isn't it interesting that such directly opposing views can exist on such a critical issue by two males who are in relatively similar life-circumstances?

By the way, the term "family" as used within this text and with reference to the Marriage Relationship concept is defined as primarily the spouses, and then the children, if there are any. In that order. Extended family relationships and the "Family Systems" theories are a separate consideration, even though some measure of overlap does obviously exist between the basic relationship and the rest of the family, which might include step-children and other relatives who may be living within the nuclear family.

Who knows how much time is enough time to be spent within the relationship? Nobody. The amount of time needed to be spent is the amount of time that is acceptable to the other spouse, with consideration being given to whatever conditions might exist in lives and minds of the partners at that particular moment.

Time requirements can and do vary widely from spouse to spouse because some people simply need and demand more time and attention. On the other hand, some people need more of their own personal time and space as they like to call it. We are all very different people, so a substantial variance exists in the amount of time needed to be given to a marriage relationship., It all depends on the partners' actual needs.

It is possible that extenuating or unusual circumstances can enter into anybody's marriage relationship on a temporary basis. For example, maybe for some reason there are too many bills to be paid with existing income(s), a college student or two develop, or elderly parents need a hand, and both partners find themselves working very hard at too many jobs just to stay afloat. But, as with the few examples given, all of the reasons for time shortages would be short-term efforts; sooner or later whatever situation occurred that was causing the money strain would either solve itself, or eventually be realized as simply being just too much to cope with, and the extra effort brought to an end. We are back to the **M** (money) issue—thou shalt not work too many jobs!

Again, how much time is enough time? If the wheel squeaks, oil it. If one of the marriage partners is unhappy and complains about the short amount of time being spent in and on their relationship then there is a problem, and the obvious solution is to simply work it out. Communicate with each other and negotiate an arrangement which will provide enough time so that the squeaker, the marriage partner who is unhappy over the time issue, will be satisfied or at least content for the time being.

Quality Time

The second part of the time discussion involves what I call "quality time." Quality time is the time spent together closer to the "Intimacy" issue, which comes along a bit later. But, quality time involves paying close or closer attention to your marriage partner, his wishes, his wants and, in fact, sharing in his life.

Janice is really very angry at David, although he comes home every evening right on time, stays at home on weekends and plays with their two little girls and takes them places. No matter. Janice feels that David is not paying enough, or any, attention at all to her. This is a true story, although the names have been changed to protect the guilty. Conclusion: Janice sued David for a divorce with the "presenting" complaint that he didn't know how to handle money.

By now we know better than to pay very much attention to "presenting" complaints, don't we? The cold fact is that she just wasn't being fulfilled or validated or whatever other type of descriptive word might be given to such an unfortunate family situation and he, David, simply wasn't spending enough quality time with his wife even though he was more than fulfilling any quantitative or total amount of time with her and with their children. Simply spending time-at-home doesn't always count when it comes to whether or not the time spent is of the quality variety as far as your relationship is concerned.

But what about the two little girls? How are they going to come out? As usual, the children are the real losers, and this silly divorce should have been avoided by these two fine people, by their sitting down and working out an arrangement regarding quality time that would have redirected David's efforts to a degree which would have satisfied Janice's need for more close attention and intimacy.

Here in Iowa, a semi-enlightened judicial system has decreed that both parties involved in a divorce proceeding must attend a series of lectures (given by an attorney) to "help parents understand what children go through during (and after) their parent's divorce." (Source: *The Sioux City Journal*, Thursday, February 3rd, 1994.) This is progress in the judicial sector. Think about the children.

How much is enough quality time? Again, quality time is that amount of close intimate, one-on-one, togetherness, sharing, husband-and-wife time that will satisfy, reassure, validate, and reinforce both marriage partners in their relationship to whatever extent they feel needed, wanted and therefore appreciated in their life. It's just that easy.

How to do quality time? Equally easy: Take a weekend trip, from time to time, just the two of you, or go out to supper on some scheduled basis, like once a week or every other week, or pursue any other activity that the two of you can do together and that you both enjoy. Notice the "both enjoy" part. Some guys' idea of quality time is taking her fishing, to a car race, or bowling. Some gals' idea of quality time is dragging him to a concert, play, or museum. Quality time is when you two do something you both enjoy, without offspring or anyone else present.

A local professional man related his answer to the need for quality time in his marriage in this simple manner: Every evening he goes home at about the same time, and he and his wife have this arrangement where they sit down, just the two of them, children not allowed, and for 20 or 30 minutes they have a cocktail, a cup of coffee or glass of wine and share each other's lives. Then when the period is over, once again the family is involved, their family life is strengthened, and continues. He says that now that this ritual of sharing time in the shank of the day has been established, they both agree this period together is the most important part of the day to the two of them, and the small interlude is rigorously observed. Thus is quality time.

If I make it sound like it's an easy thing to work out this issue of quality time, let me hasten to recant; such is not necessarily the case. Too often the partner who feels he is being shorted in the quality time department won't say a thing about it because he feels so hurt about being left out, taken for granted, not appreciated, or ignored. He thinks that his partner should care enough about him to know that he needs more quality time, more sharing and more attention.

Like, what are we, mind readers? We must have the resolve and courage to assert and communicate our wishes and needs to our marriage partner. Please refer to the communication section in the **G** for 'general codependence' category if you need to be re-enlightened or have your memory refreshed. If you feel you have a "quality time" problem in your marriage relationship, you must start talking and negotiating with your marriage partner to find a solution. You actually owe your mate the benefit of your insight and feelings about this issue which you feel is a problem before it's too late. Don't forget, your spouse may not be even slightly aware that a problem exists! Be fair. Communicate.

Personal Attitudes Towards Time

The third aspect earning some limited measure of consideration about this wondrous thing called time, is the matter of personal attitudes towards time which people can assume, and which can be another source of aggravation in a marriage.

For example, if a person has trouble arriving on schedule, or keeping track of time, this behavioral short-fall can really be annoying to the other partner who might be the punctual type. As has been pointed out, opposites do attract, you know.

Some people can show up an hour late for an appointment or a social engagement and never even say "I'm sorry." The reasons for a disregard for time can come in several shades, including a good dose of familial general codependence, ("monkey see, monkey do"), a bad case of right brain dominance direct from the right brain/ left brain concept, personal disorganization, phonyism, or maybe just a selfish lack of regard or consideration for other's feelings and convenience.

In the last analysis, who cares what the reason might be that someone is customarily late, or has troubles with time? If a person has trouble with time, and being on time, then that's the way he is, so get used to it.

However, if one marriage partner feels he is having trouble regarding time and that this annoyance or inconvenience is problem in their relationship, then a problem exists. You could have to negotiate with the person who is persistently inclined to be late to be more timely by using the communication techniques set out earlier. These include mostly "I" statements such as, "I hope we can . . ," "I am so embarrassed when . . . " "I just hate to be late . . . " and so forth. All the while keeping in mind that the one who is always tardy might be so badly "right-brained" he cannot help himself, and you might have to gently help him.

Usually with a little negotiation and some game-playing, a "later" can be adjusted around to where he is more prompt. Not totally prompt, mind you, but just more prompt. One never gets all of anything.

Giving Time a Chance

The fourth issue and certainly an important aspect of this subject of time has to do with learning to use time as an ally and a positive force in your marriage relationship, and to not use time either to another's disadvantage, or as a weapon. Why? Because almost always it will simply take time and patience to work out the problems and the conflicts that will inevitably come up in every marriage.

Sad to say, in recent years writers, commentators and even psychologists have preached that self-perceived personal growth is more important than marital stability, and of course here we are in these later days of soaring divorce rates, and all of us paying the too-high price for these selfish ideas.

A man named Carl Lewis once wrote: "Life is about timing," and that thought could well have continued in a paraphrase which stated that a marriage relationship is about timing, too.

How unfortunate that the typical wedding vow says, "for better and for worse." Better it should say either "for better and for worse and for better and for worse and for better, and for worse," over and over and over. Seems like there's always a worse after a better, and a better after a worse.

In every marriage relationship there is the exciting initial getting-to-know-you stage, which takes some time. Then there's the "having children and seeing to their education" period, which takes a lot of time. And during all that time there's the time needed for one's career and life-work, whether it be in the workplace or at home, all of which effort takes its own toll.

Then finally when the last child is ready to leave home and the nest is empty, marriage partners very frequently find out that they are virtually back at the point of starting completely over with each other. They've been so busy through the years with all those other elements and events that were going on in their lives, they didn't have, or maybe better said, didn't take time for each other.

This time in a marriage, when the last chick leaves the nest, is known in counseling as the "empty nest syndrome," (ENS) and can be a time of great stress and danger for many marriages. Divorces by middle-aged folks which occur at this juncture are silly and needless, because all they have to do is sit tight, get to know each other again, learn how to have some fun together, and give time a chance. If they will do these things, frequently they will "re-fall in love" with even more intensity and meaning than the first time around.

Add to the ENS predicament the undeniable fact that we all continually change through our lives, so the person you married way back then most surely is not the same person you are presently trying to live with 25 years later. You have both individually changed so very much over the passing years, all according to the predictable processes of human development. Everybody changes, all the time.

> It is written: Change is inevitable, growth is optional.

Time is the glue that holds people and therefore families together through the years. A brick wall is made up of a quantity of bricks held together with mortar (glue), and a marriage relationship is not much different, except that, instead of bricks, the structure of a marriage relationship is comprised of a whole lifetime of memories, events, rituals, children and other relationships that have happened. The whole wall, the entire structure of marriage, is held together by the glue of time.

While there is, generally speaking, some overall pattern of what a marriage relationship goes through as it endures the years, there is no firm pattern for couples to expect because everybody's life is different. Most certainly there is a lot of commonality in the things that happen to people in the course of their marriage, but there is no question that we individually handle times, good and bad, in a myriad of different manners because of the many variances in our individual personalities, temperaments and characters. Please recall that the issue of good times or bad times are covered earlier under Reversals.

How to Use Time as an Ally

Realize that time is probably on your side, and that almost always when troubles and difficulties rear their ugly heads, if you'll just ride out the storm, eventually things will calm down. Then you can look back and see what you might have done to a) either have possibly avoided the storm or, b) perhaps be able to see how the storm could have been handled in a different manner so that the waves of pain, anger and dismay which came crashing down on you would not have hurt so much. How could you have ridden out the storm in a better fashion?

What if the two of you were in a small boat out on the big "lake of life" when all of sudden a big wind came up and, being too far from shore, there is nothing to do but either a) ride out the storm the best you can together, or b) throw in the towel and both drown. Let's assume that the two of you have the innate intelligence and courage to fight for your survival and ride out the bad weather; once the storm had passed you were safe again and you won. Both alive and well. Badly scared, hopefully smarter, but alive.

Compare the boat-in-the-storm scenario to a serious conflict in a marriage relationship. If you give up and quit, sooner or later you will drown in your own sea of anger, loss, strife, bitterness and all the other awful negative things that happen to people who divorce. But if you will just hang in there and fight for your marriage, victory will be yours. Quit and lose. Fight and win. It's just that easy.

Let's talk about why one got caught out in a lake in a boat and didn't see the storm clouds gathering on the horizon? Let's talk about why wouldn't it be possible for you to see the trouble brewing well before the deluge hit so you could have done something to avoid even the possibility of serious and irrevocable loss?

Possibly the most dangerous mental attitude having to do with time within a marriage relationship is that frame of mind a person can get into which says, "I must do something now! I must take some action NOW!" When this imperative "now" frame of mind appears, couples and individuals start making mistakes, and not only can the errors they make be incredibly huge, but also can carry staggering costs and penalties as payment for impatience and perhaps selfishness.

It's been stated by people who are

involved in the divorce business, including attorneys and psychologists, that in their opinion, from a low of 50% to a staggering high of 90% of divorces didn't need to happen if only the people involved would have calmed down and given themselves some time to solve or adjust to whatever stressor(s) were causing the deadly strain in their marriage. If only they would have stopped being selfish and thinking only about themselves and how they feel, and would have given consideration to their family members and friends, and especially to the children, if any, who are the real losers and the casualties of divorce.

As well, thought should have been given to all the other down-side ramifications that will surely come to pass as a result of a stupid, ill-advised divorce; including but not limited to all those other awful side-effects listed earlier in Chapter Two, titled The Wages Of Divorce. A divorce is never a picnic. A divorce is a hard, bitter, angry, divisive event, and don't let anybody tell you otherwise.

Joan Kerr once wrote: "Being divorced is like being hit by a Mack truck. If you live through it, you start looking very carefully to the right and to the left."

If only people were more patient and flexible, and spent more time working things out instead of spending all their time being angry and/or consulting with some attorney whose very business is getting rich by destroying marriages, at the terrible expense of the children.

How to get the time to work things out within yourself? Initially, if the disagreement is one of moderate severity, then you need only follow the rules of communication and negotiation to resolve the conflict on a fair and equitable basis. On the other hand, if the dispute is too intense and too much anger and frustration are present, then two courses of action seem apparent.

One thing to try is for the two of you to agree to just "cool it" for a period of time, by simply avoiding the troublesome issue. Later on, when your heads have cleared and everybody is calmed down, talk it over and see if some agreement cannot be reached or compromise achieved to resolve the difficulty. Be sure to pay attention to the Negotiation section later on in the text.

In a more extreme conflict, a brief separation accomplished one way or the other might be in order. In a period of separation both parties have a chance to assess their thoughts, examine their responsibilities, see how it feels to be apart from the mate and learn a little bit about how things are going to be once a divorce is final if that is a course under consideration.

Two ladies, Ronna Romney, whose father is the late George Romney of manufacturing and governmental fame, and Beppie Harrison, wrote a fine book titled, *Giving Time a Chance: The Secret of a Lasting Marriage,* which may be of great help to people having serious troubles with time and coping in their marriage.

The authors re-state many of the principles of a marriage relationship listed in this guide, but their book's real value lies in the extensive research of well-known couples who have been married for a long time. They relate the methods used by these famous couples to get along with each other, even after decades of marriage.

One very interesting comment made in

the book that the authors especially noted, with regard to couples married 50 years or longer, is that those couples quickly agreed, that they were both still working on their marriage relationship day after day. After 50 years!

The basic theme of their fine book is that any married couple, in order for the marriage relationship to last, must have total and unending commitment to their marriage, and "nobody walks," as they say. Both marriage partners must have patience and understanding, and above all, give time a chance to heal.

Nothing lasts forever, not even your troubles.

Clara Winston is quoted: "Time, for all its smuggling in of new problems, conspicuously cancels others."

Hang in there.

I

Stands For 'INTRUSIONS'

An intrusion as defined earlier in the definitions section has to do with the entrance of some outside, extraneous new idea, interest or activity that is intrusive or time consuming, and by its very nature or presence can alter the existing balance in a marriage relationship.

An intrusion can be a new uninvited and unexpected event or interest, or perhaps a new involvement or activity eagerly sought after by one of the marriage partners. An intrusion might be a wonderfully refreshing variance in a marriage or it may be an unwelcome and a very upsetting influence. Obviously, a negative or detrimental intrusion could deliver a devastating and final fatal blow to an already teetering relationship.

Who knows where intrusions come from? The person who falls prey to, or gets involved in, a new interest which might be called an intrusion, either already has the open time in his mind or life to accommodate the new time-consuming activity, or he might be using the intrusion as a defense mechanism intended to keep him from facing up to a problem. Maybe a new intrusion, be it good or bad, is allowed to fill some vacant spot or need in the life of the person.

What do you do when your life and your marriage relationship are interrupted or disrupted by your spouse's sudden and consuming interest in this other new activity or interest? Quite obviously if a problem exists, it belongs to the person who is unhappy about the new interest entering the life of their marriage. The innocent bystander, if you will.

If and when an intrusion appears, the first question to ask is whether the newly arrived interest is a serious negative influence, and therefore a problem. Just because something is new and different does not make it a negative influence. Then comes the question, how much confrontation and/or concern is this new development really worth?

Could it be that the intrusion might turn out to be an even greater bonding involvement for the your marriage than if it had not appeared? Is the new interest or activity something that both marriage partners might enjoy doing together?

Granted that the non-intruded-upon partner might have to extend or expand himself to join in and participate, but then, what's wrong with that? Maybe if both marriage partners joined in, the new activity or interest could prove to be of good value to their relationship in the long run.

Add to that question the next inquiry: Is the intrusion likely to be long-lasting, or just a fleeting interest or activity which will run its course in the near term? After all, isn't it good for all of us to try new and different ideas and activities from time to time? Anyone sitting in the same place doing the same things year after year can find his life not only very boring and depressing, but also deadly. There is such a thing as a good intrusion.

Some people, by their very natures, are inclined to develop rather intense interests in various new endeavors and activities from time to time throughout their lives. That is just the way their minds are put together. As luck and life would have it, some of these new interests and activities are good, some may not be so good. Some will fall between the cracks and be just sort of pesky little activities or concerns which need explanation and definition, something you'll to have to live with. Good intrusions are wonderful little gifts, albeit rare. But what if the intrusion seems to be dangerously destructive to the marriage relationship, and causes great concern and consternation?

Then what does a person do?

First of all, the non-intruded-upon marriage partner should not initially take the arrival of the new intrusion personally. The new interest or activity might be something that your partner needs in order to maintain his mental balance and cope with the stress of a transitional period in his life.

In my companion book, *Some of the Reasons We Behave the Way We Do,* specific note is made of the predictable mental and physical developmental changes that occur in each of us as we go through our lives. An additional great source of information about the aging process can be found in Gail Sheehy's famous book titled *Passages,* which is listed in the bibliography.

The management of stress has been mentioned earlier. But, here is one thing that none of us can ever forget: Each person in a marriage has to run his own life and thought processes, and sometimes things can get a little mixed up in anybody's mind and require some diversion. Crossed wires can be uncrossed. Sometimes it takes effort, and sometimes all it takes is time.

The possibility always exists that an intrusion might simply be the fulfillment of a long held dream or dreams. Jim had two goals that he wanted to achieve before he was age 50; one of them was to own and fly a hot-air balloon, and the other was to get his "ham" or amateur radio license. As things turned out, Jim did manage to achieve both goals before his fiftieth birthday, but, after all that effort and time, he found out, after falling about 30 feet to the ground, he didn't much care for hot-air balloons. Not only a lot of work, but also extremely dangerous to fly. Nor did he care for the amateur radio scene which he found to be boring. Alas, so much for dreams.

You can just bet his wife thought he was completely nuts, as he was spending all that time and money frantically trying to accomplish both goals. She was probably right, except that good old Jim seemed to need to try to accomplish both those activities at that time in his life. But, you know what? Jim's wife never said a word, bless her, not a single word, and in quite short order both the hot air balloon and the amateur radio hobby were history.

An attitude which could be of value for the marriage partner who is not involved in the new activity, would be to look at the intrusion for what it is: simply another interest in that person's life. The activity really doesn't have any bearing whatsoever on their marriage relationship. The case might well exist that if the non-involved spouse voiced a lot of concern and complaints about a new intrusion, these objections could simply be an extension of an ongoing power struggle, and a continuation of the need or attempt of one marriage partner to exercise more control over the other person than he probably should.

However, if one feels that the intrusion is not a plus in their marriage and has good solid and plausible reasons to feel that the intrusion is a problem, then the intelligent approach would be for the two partners to sit down and enter into a communication process with the focus on the intrusion as the "bad guy." Be careful not to get mixed up and label your marriage partner as being a bad guy, trying to wreck your marriage. "You don't love me any more," etc. etc. Ad irreleventium.

The possibility can exist in the minds of the people seeking or involved with the new intrusion, that they see no connection at all between their new interest and the marriage relationship. So, the course to pursue, via the communication and negotiation channels suggested, is to arrive at some level of compromise with regard to the marriage partner's involvement with the new intrusion. Maybe he could change the time of day he works on the project or activity, agree to spend less time with it, or perhaps go out of his way to get you somehow involved, if possible.

One of the more interesting exercises in the practice of counseling therapy is to bring a step-ladder to the session and have the complaining clients actually climb up a few rungs, and "take a look at life from the top of the ladder." As they talk from that high perch about their complaints and the events in their life they don't like, sometimes matters are seen from a slightly different and more objectively detached viewpoint. A variation of that dialogue is to have the complainant climb up the ladder and have someone else "model" (role play) his position in the dispute. Watching others discuss your own problems while you are eavesdropping from on high can work well too. Objectivity can be a wonderful tool to enable understanding.

Becoming angry at the marriage partner is not the answer, nor is thinking you are the victim or the target of the intrusion. If you do, and then set out to wage war over the intrusion, you could be in for some really tough sledding.

How many ways could a problem with an intrusion be solved? Any number of solutions are possible and include:

- Ignore the intrusion.

- Rejoice and be proud of the fact that

your marriage partner has a new interest or hobby.

- Join in the new activity or interest, if that is a possible and acceptable course.

- Enter into a skillfully planned negotiation session, with the goal being to diminish the perceived impact on your marriage relationship.

For example, there are lots and lots of gals who go out and play golf with their husbands maybe not hating every minute, but certainly not relishing the experience. However, they are smart enough to know that if golf is the soup de jour, at least for the time being, then that's the way the cracker crumbles, and since they as wives are also here to stay, too, then, "Fore"!

In like manner, there are lots and lots of men who go to concerts and other assorted cultural events, hating every second, but if that's the way she wants things to be, then that's the way they will be.

The assumption made in those two brief sentences is that the intrusion, as it may exist, is not specifically gender-related like sewing would be for females, or hunting as a male activity. Nobody reasonably expects a male to join a sewing circle, or for a gal to get up before dawn, go out and sit in a cold blind waiting for some dumb duck to fly by so she could try to murder it.

Most certainly in the history of humanity, cross-gender activities have been happily engaged in by members of the opposite sex. There's a retired old-timer in our town who does the most beautiful needlepoint, and he is so proud of his handiwork.

An important viewpoint which certainly needs to be repeated: if your marriage partner is afflicted with an intrusion, you should not immediately assume the attitude or position that this new interest of his is a lessening or deflection of his interest in you and your marriage, unless and until you have hard evidence that indeed, such is the case.

A brief word in an inward direction: If you are the one who has been smitten with this new activity, or involvement, which could be identified as an intrusion, then please have all the patience and understanding you can muster to help your partner get through any concern he might have about this new interest of yours. His quick or full acceptance of your new interest or activity may not be all that easy for him to handle at the time. Realize that he may take your preoccupation in whatever this new intrusion might happen to be, as a lessening of your interest in him.

If your mate tells you he sees the intrusion as competition for your attention and affection, then, for crying-out-loud, take every opportunity and make every effort to reassure him of your unwavering love and interest. Constantly assure him that your interest in this new activity is just something that you would like to try, and the activity has nothing at all to do with him, or your relationship.

If, as mentioned above, it is you who have developed a new interest or activity, then, as the one who is newly involved, the only fair thing to do is to give your marriage partner ample time to adjust, and if he simply won't or doesn't want to go along with the intrusion, you may have to decide for yourself really just how important this new-found intrusion is to you. You could have to come to grips with the question which asks: Is your continued involvement with the intrusion worth risking the very existence of your marriage and family?

If the answer to that query is not a quick "NO!" go back and take another look at Chapter Two, The Wages of Divorce, which outlines very clearly many of the terrible consequences which happen to people who stupidly divorce. A very real chance exists that keeping the intrusion simply would not be the wise course, or anywhere near worth the cost.

The final letter in the word relationship is that **P** which stands for 'priorities', which is a detailed consideration of what is really important in a person's life. Before you give a moment's thought about dumping your marriage and family to pursue some new intrusion, you better read about the subject of priorities first.

Intrusions as such can and do cause a lot of troubles for marriages, since new ideas, new desires and changing interests seem to be an inevitable part of our ever-developing lives. So, if an intrusion shows up, as it probably will, hang tough with your marriage partner, your marriage relationship and your family. Communicate, negotiate, be flexible and above all, be patient.

O

Stands for 'OUTSIDERS'

As set out earlier in the definitions section, an outsider is a person who either assumes or is somehow given permission to enter very closely into another's life and/or marriage, and who then proceeds to engage in copious meddling in all sorts of affairs that aren't his own. This definition also applies to a small group of people.

The chapter that immediately preceded this "outsider" section dealt with intrusions, which are defined as some new idea, hobby, activity, or other involvement which can enter into people's lives and also turn out to be a source of stress in a marriage relationship. Outsiders are people. Intrusions are ideas and activities.

We are going to consider this issue of outsiders, with regard to four different categories of involvement:

1) Your pure outsider type.
2) Friends as outsiders.
3) Psychological counselors as outsiders, and finally,
4) Attorneys, who are the ultimate outsiders.

The Pure Outsider

Pure outsiders, in the rawest form, are those individuals who are experts on and know everything that there is to be known about whatever subject is under consideration. The "W.F.E.O.E." again. (World's Foremost Expert On Everything.) Outsiders sometimes appear as "kitchen lawyers." Anyone who has ever been in the military services will probably recall the loudmouth know-it-all's who were known as "barracks attorneys." Same breed.

Outsiders are people who freely and without encouragement set out to inflict their own value systems and ideas, and present opinions and solutions pertaining to any problem or situation that might exist. They give abundant advice concerning any and all possible aspects of every problem. It's the old "lets-you-and-them-fight" trick, because the outsiders don't have a thing at stake. It's not their life, marriage relationship, or family that is in jeopardy. Outsiders stand to lose nothing and, having given forth all their free "expert" advice and counsel, stroll off into the sunset with no personal consequences whatsoever. See ya.

Liz, a newcomer to town, was invited to join a bridge club, and unfortunately it came to pass that six of the eight gals in that card-playing group were divorced. So, guess what, the bad influence and critical comments by the other members only added to Liz's already high level of marital stress, dissatisfaction, confusion and frustration. Eventually Liz also went the way of the rest of them, and got her divorce.

You say she was silly to be so influenced? You say she should have run her own ship and that she should not have paid any attention to the carping and whining of the other ladies and not have let them influence her? You are right, of course. But, one must quickly admit that even before she entered the circle of divorced ladies, our Liz suffered with what she felt were already serious faults and insurmountable problems in her marriage. The whining and complaining of the other ladies threw more fuel on the already burning fire. The message is: Never underestimate the power or impact of the impressions gained, and the potential influence that can be exerted by associations with others.

One of the key early topics in John Gray's book has to do with this very subject: the greater possibility of adverse impact by outsiders on women because of the feminine trait gals have to want and need to talk about their problems. With almost anybody, but usually other females.

Males, on the other hand, as Dr. Gray points out, are noted for refusing to talk about their problems. Therefore, there is less chance that an outsider can influence a male. He just won't talk about it. With anybody.

If an old saying would ever be applicable, this might be the time, and the saying is: "Forewarned is forearmed," and since you herewith have been duly warned about outsiders, then the thing to, do is to not only keep the danger of outsider influence in mind, but also, if you are already in some mental pain over your marriage relationship, be careful who you talk to, and avoid anyone who comes forth or who turns out to be an outsider with his know-it-all advice.

Let's face it, no outsider can ever have a complete understanding or grasp of the entire complex nature of any problem over which you might be suffering at the time.

There is an old saying which holds that if it walks like a duck, quacks like a duck, lays duck eggs and poops duck poop, it's most likely a duck. If the part of the saying holds that you can tell them by their speech (quacking), here could be some common examples of suggestions typically offered by outsiders:

"If I were you, I'd_____."
"Don't let _____ do _____ etc."
"If I was in your shoes I'd_____>"
"When ____ did that to me I_____."
"Never ____," or, "I would never___."
"What you should do is _____."

As you can easily guess, all their offered suggestions about what you should do are in the drastic-to-catastrophic "Let's you and him/her fight," status.

Watch out for outsiders.

Friends as Outsiders

A friend, a good friend, if you are lucky enough to have one to talk to, is not necessarily an outsider. A good friend will listen to your discussion and explanation of your marital problems or any other problem you may have, but will not offer suggestions to solve the problem, or give advice. One can tell a true friend almost anything, and simply in the telling find a measure of relief from the burden of the problem.

Meanwhile, and here's the good part, whatever intimate thoughts, fears, or disclosures you made to your friend do not directly affect your friend's life. When the conversation with the friend is over and you are through "unloading," your friend can then just get up and go on his way, unaffected. That's not to say that he might not feel badly that you are having distress in your life, nor that he might not have bitten his tongue to keep from giving advice, but as far as life is concerned, your problems are your problems and they just simply don't affect his family, life, or marriage relationship.

Andrew Mason wrote, "Sainthood emerges when you can listen to someone's tale of woe and not respond with a description of your own."

Needless to say, a true friend will not ever tell a soul of your conversation, or anything of your concerns and pain. Any breech of confidentiality would be most disappointing and probably constitute the end of what you thought was a close friendship.

What sort of background training or experience could possibly allow outsiders to be so boldly arrogant that they would even attempt to solve another person's problems? That question brings us to a consideration of the people who are educated and trained in the fine art of counseling people to help solve their problems.

Are Counselors Outsiders?

Counselors are not outsiders, for several reasons; one is that persons who are established as counselors have not only been through the educational process of at least the master's level degree in Psychological Counseling, or a medical degree with a specialty in psychiatry, but also they have had to spend considerable time in counseling practice under the supervision of an experienced and licensed counseling person.

If counselors are licensed, be they psychologists or psychiatrists, you know they have jumped through all the hoops, passed all the tests, spent time getting experience, and have finally managed to achieve licensed status, which is indeed no small accomplishment. It must be mentioned too that psychiatrists should also be board certified by their specialty.

But why isn't a counselor an outsider? Because a good counselor will NEVER, EVER give a client direct advice or tell anyone what they "should do"!

The underlying belief and philosophy of counseling is that clients already have the answers they need to their problems stored in their brains, and the only reason they cannot execute their lives and solve their own problems is that they cannot face up to, or accept, the underlying and buried problem or situation.

People, clients, in such a state are said to be in conflict with themselves, and it is this personal internal struggle which makes them incapable of solving the problem, or a set of problems, They are said to be "stuck." The task of a counselor is to help clients cope with their inability to solve the problem(s) by skillfully asking questions which will, in due course, bring the clients to the point where they can admit and resolve their own deep-seated conflicts. Getting clients "un-stuck" and thereby able to solve the problem(s) by using one of their own already-imbedded solutions is the goal of psychotherapy.

Counselors get paid, and some of them very handsomely, to perform their services, but the beauty of the counselor/client relationship is that at the end of the session or series of sessions, if such is the case, the client gets up, leaves, and goes about his life. That is absolutely the end of the contact with the counselor by the client.

Here are some ethical guidelines that are not commonly known about the counseling profession: One is that it is very bad form and, in fact, completely unethical for a counselor to have any later relationship with a client outside of their counseling sessions. The counseling educational process spends a lot of time and energy constantly advising and reminding student counselors about what is known as a dual relationship, the essence of which is the principle that it is ethically unacceptable for a therapist to have any relationship with a client more than as his counselor.

If a potential client and a counselor are already friends, and that person approaches the counselor for help, the client must be referred to another psychotherapist for help.

Because of this dual relationship prohibition (unless you have found a bad and unethical counselor), there should be no chance that you will have any further relationship with your counselor. If there is any suggestion or hint by the counselor that s/he would like to have some other closer or continuing relationship with you, the first thing for you to do is leave the therapist's office, and then follow these guidelines.

If the counselor is a psychologist, contact the State Licensing Board in the state in which you live, and advise them of the unethical advances by the counselor who is obviously a foul ball. If it happens that the state in which you live does not have a counselor licensing board, call some other counselor listed in the yellow pages of a phone book, and advise them of this poor conduct. In states which do not yet have licensing or regulation, the counseling profession tries very hard to police its own ranks and protect the public. If you have little luck with this course, contact the county or state attorney's office and tell them the story. Especially if the counselor's advances seem to be sexual in nature, and thereby possibly a criminal offense.

If the counselor is a psychiatrist, contact your local or state medical association. All of the above conditions and warnings apply to psychiatrists too.

Which brings us to the sad conclusion that not all counselors are created equal. Some counselors are really great and gifted, others are just plain lousy. On top of that, if you get involved with a therapist and you just don't like him personally, get up and leave; above all, don't go back to see him again.

If a counselor starts telling you what you should do, get up and leave because you've run into a bum counselor, and, as mentioned above, they do exist. Not wholesale, mind you, but there are some really incompetent therapists out there, and many would be out of their depth in a parking-lot puddle.

As was set out in the Introduction, the entire purpose of the book is to provide folks with a in-home self-help marriage counseling guide, but if this guide just won't be enough to help you solve the problems in your marriage, then seriously consider seeking out some help from a counselor.

A bit of rather bad news: Marriage counseling has a mediocre to poor success rate in conflict resolution for several reasons.

One is, too often by the time a troubled couple gets to the counselor, their marriage has deteriorated to extreme levels, and no help in the world could ever bring it back to life (aka total incompatibility).

Another is, except for one approach, the counseling profession just does not know what to do other than ask, "What seems to be the trouble?" and, here come the endless "presenting" complaints.

Still another is, almost always, ONE of the marriage partners has already made up his mind to divorce, and is going through the counseling charade to make himself "look good" later on. He can always say, "We tried going to marriage counseling, but it didn't work, etc. etc."

After the warning above about watching out for an incompetent counselor, here are some guidelines to follow which will help you find someone who is known as a good and capable psychotherapist.

1) Ask around and see if a friend knows of anyone in the counseling profession with a good reputation as a marriage counselor, and who has had some success solving marital problems.

2) When you do find someone whose reputation seems favorable, check on his credentials to be sure he has had the educational background and training it takes to be a counselor. Having a grouping of letters such as M.A., M.S., L.S.W., Ph.D. or M.D. or any other variety of alphabet soup behind a person's name does not necessarily infer, or confer, competency.

3) Do not be afraid to ask, before you begin with the counselor, exactly what his hourly rate is, or fee per session. Check and see if your health insurance will provide payment as what they call "third party payors." Some will, some won't. Find out what the counselor expects or requires for the payment of his fees. Do you have to pay each time or can you make payments over time? What is the charge when and if you are moved into group sessions? Ask, if need be, whether they have sliding fee scales which adjust themselves to your income level. Examples of these sorts of practices would be in the county, city, or state mental health agencies, and other private groups such as the Lutheran Social Services, and the Catholic Charities.

4) Be sure you have what is known as "informed consent," which means

that you both understand to the best of your ability just exactly what direction, procedure, or technique is going to be used (if they know) and how the counseling process is going to affect the two of you and your family. If you don't agree with, or like what they say, settle up and leave the premises at once, then find someone else to help you. Some counseling procedures are not exactly user friendly. The "if they know" is included above because sometimes a therapist will have to change techniques in the middle of a series of therapy sessions, but you should be so advised if this happens.

5) Don't ask the counselor if he could guess how many sessions it may take to work to a solution. The number of sessions depends entirely on you and your spouse, how much anger exists, and the depth and complexities of the problems. However, it is only fair for you to advise the counselor of your financial situation, and if such is the case, that you won't be able to afford to return for expensive session after session to fine tune your marriage relationship. Once the counselor gets you to a basic understanding, you should be able to fine tune your marriage with the aid of this marriage counseling guide, or if needed, find a marriage support group.

Attorneys: The Ultimate Outsiders

Toward the end of Shakespeare's *Henry VI, Part Two,* Dick the Butcher, one of the rebels against the king, utters the secret wish of so many folks throughout history. When they get power, Dick says, "The first thing we do, let's kill all the lawyers."

Divorce attorneys, those lawyers who practice what they facetiously call "family law," and other attorneys who dabble in whatever divorce proceedings they are lucky enough to get their claws into, are the ultimate outsiders. The way these attorneys make their living is by giving advice and manipulating events in people's lives to destroy their families. Family law? Better it should be called "Anti-family Law"!

Q. What is brown and black and looks good on a lawyer?
A. A Doberman.

How tragically amusing to see two "family law" attorneys working on opposite sides of the same divorce case. Their method of operation involves the attorneys lobbing grenades of hate, anger, frustration, accusation, suspicion, insinuation, greed and selfishness at each other and therefore at the divorcing couple, to accomplish one goal—to be sure that the divorce action will continue and be prolonged for as long as it can be, so they can both make the most money possible, each from their own clients.

Q. How cold was it?
A. It was so cold, I saw a lawyer with his hands in his own pockets.

The concept of what attorneys call "client control" means the attorney(s) must keep the two divorcing parties from any attempt to try to effect a reconciliation. "Don't talk to _____" was the order given by an attorney to his client. The foolish client obeyed her attorney which kept the case alive, maintained his fee-ability, ultimately destroyed her family, and the greedy attorney made a ton of money.

The concept of fee-ability isn't too hard to verify if you consider this idea: Say that you already have an attorney hired to pursue a divorce action, you called him and said, "Let's call the whole thing off; my wife or husband and I are going to get together and work things out." Obviously, at that instant, the attorney cannot charge you another nickel. His fee-ability has ended. He has lost client-control, and, the case.

Q. Why won't sharks attack lawyers?
A. Professional courtesy.

In one notable instance of gullibility, one of the divorcing couple said he would like to suspend the legal proceedings and see about a reconciliation. The attorney told his client that a reconciliation wouldn't be a good idea, or be at all necessary at the time, because the law firm always put a "reconciliation clause" in the final divorce decree, and 95% of their divorces ended up reconciled. Now really, how dumb does someone have to be to believe that lie for a half a second? Lie, cheat, steal, do anything to maintain fee-ability is the lawyer's way.

In the course of one tragic divorce case, the defendant was hauled in to a court hearing 14 times in 15 months. Why? Because the plaintiff's attorney, like most attorneys, charges twice as much for court time as they do for office time, and through all his needless courtroom shenanigans the attorney greatly enhanced his total fee. In fact, he enhanced his fee so enthusiastically the plaintiff got stripped of almost all the money she had.

An interesting sidelight in the practice of divorce litigation is the current trend in family law education which includes providing attorneys with training on how to put a newly-divorced client into bankruptcy along with the divorce. Does this tell you anything about what a terrible shellacking one almost always takes while getting his divorce? Bankruptcy equals more fees.

From *Forbes Magazine*: "Thoughts"—"I've learned that in a divorce, only the attorneys come out ahead."—37 year-old's discovery. (May 6, 1996. Page 160)

Case in point: One night not too long ago, a national television network devoted a complete news program to the issue of the financial losses experienced by divorcing couples. The larger part of the program contained interviews of women who had been totally fleeced and left virtually penniless by their attorneys while they were in the needlessly messy and expensive process of divorcing.

Q. How did the attorneys ever get so greedy and so powerful?
A. Easy, there are too many of them.

Consider this set of comparative facts:

Country	Population	Attorneys
Japan	125 million	30,000
U.S.A.	260 million	866,000 + (in 1995)

The obvious point is, the population of Japan is roughly one-half of the U.S. population, and with fewer than a total of 30,000 attorneys in the entire country!

Here is a comparison of the per capita ratio of attorneys:

Japan: roughly 1 attorney for each 4,000 people.

U.S.A.: roughly 1 attorney for each 250 people!

In 1950 when America's population was about 150 million, about 200,000 (98% males) practiced law, or about 1 attorney for every 750 people. Between 1950 and 1970 the attorney/population ratio didn't change. But between 1970 and 1980, when the American population increased by only 20 million people, the number of attorneys doubled to the 400,000 range. In 1995, only 15 years later, there were more than 866,000 lawyers in the United States. Statistics for 1999 are not available at this time, but at the rate of 35,000 new lawyers added to the bar every year, the total now in the USA must be right at one million.

In Japan, only 700 new lawyers are admitted to practice law annually! That's why there are only some 30,000 attorneys in Japan! (Note: See bibliography listing—*American Almanac of Jobs and Salaries.*) The math works out.

Is the over-supply of lawyers in the U.S.A. going to diminish? Not likely. Law practice is a very lucrative profession, and on average, is ranked as 12% higher than a medical doctor's income (general practice).

If, tragically, you are living in one of the three reasons to divorce (abuse, infidelity, total incompatibility), there are two new developments you need to know about. Look at this:

Bombshell!

You don't need an attorney to get a divorce!

If you must divorce, in most states divorcing couples can do their own legal work, and get their own divorce on what is known as a "pro se" (pronounced "pro-say"—*pro*=for, *se*=self) basis without an attorney!

Here's how a pure "pro se" divorce could work:

- Type your own legal paper work—the petition, and file it in the County Clerk's office.

- Come to complete agreements on all issues.

- Prepare a document containing all the agreements and file it in the county court house.

- Appear in court at the prescribed time. That's it.

Realistically speaking, probably not too many folks can or would be able to do a complete "pro se" divorce. But there is a new and exciting alternative process emerging to help folks who must divorce, and it is:

Divorce Mediation

Mediation in general is anything but new as a dispute or conflict resolution process. Through the centuries, many cultures have used mediation to resolve conflicts, and only recently is the practice of mediation once again gaining the respect and attention it so richly deserves.

Briefly stated, there are two types of mediation process, one being in the civil/commercial and environmental fields, the other in divorce proceedings.

Q. Why do you think there are so few attorneys in Japan?
A. Because the Japanese are smart enough to use mediation to resolve their disputes. What do you think all those students do who are not admitted to practice law? Mediation.

A mediator is a person trained in the process of mediation, and serves, as a neutral disinterested third party, to help disputing parties come to an understanding and hopefully a resolution of their conflict. Mediators never make a decision or ruling. But through skillful questioning, and with benefit of his training and life experience, he guides the disputants to their solution(s).

Conversely, an arbitrator typically renders a binding decision in a dispute.

Briefly stated, a trained divorce mediator will accomplish the following tasks in the "pro se" divorce process:

1) To provide for the care and feeding of children, if any, so that both parents can continue to be the caring and loving parents they would want to be.
2) To effect a fair and equitable property settlement.
3) To provide for the future economic well-being of both partners.
4) To provide for other family members, for example grandparents, and any other unusual situations as they may exist.
5) And finally, once all the arrangements are completed and agreed upon, to write the "Memorandum of Agreement" document which contains all of the details and is submitted to the court.

Once the memorandum of agreement (MOA) is complete, signed, and delivered to the divorcing parties, they may then take the MOA to the court themselves on the appointed day, or for a couple hundred dollars or so, they can get an attorney to do all the legal paperwork, and go with them to court.

Depending on the complexities and competition (anger), most divorce mediation processes take from two to four or five two-hour sessions, and the total cost, again depending on the complexities, should range from $500 to $1200 or so. Excluding possible legal help as mentioned in the previous paragraph. The first session is typically free.

At this time, do-it-yourself "divorce kits" are easily available at stationers, bookstores, and on the internet, which will greatly facilitate divorcing couples who wish to use the "pro se" approach. A check on the internet under divorce forms shows over 900,000 sites available!

Conventional wisdom, on the other hand, would predicate that if you are in the extremely unfortunate position of having to go through a divorce for one of the only three reasons for a divorce to ever happen, you can't get your thumb out of the legal mouth, and think you need an attorney, for heaven's sake, ask the lawyer how much he is going to charge before you get too far into the process. Then, above all, hold him to that amount. Don't let him run the fee up as most attorneys surely will do, if you don't keep your eyes open, and be steadfast. Attorneys are not above what is known as fee-splitting, which means if one lawyer is gouging his client and the other attorney isn't doing too good, they'll divvy up the larger fee between them. Totally unethical, but then, look at who you are dealing with; attorneys.

There is an old business saying which pertains here:

"Don't take your eyes off
the cash register!"

The syndicated columnist L. M. Boyd frequently includes a squib in one of his daily newspaper columns from his "love and war" man, and this one is too good to not include:

"Item no. 898C in our Love and War man's file on divorce is the observation of Barbara Ehrenreich, the literary social activist: 'For women, divorce can be the gateway to destitution. For men, it is more likely to be the golden parachute to freedom.'"

Children As Casualties

Previously mention has been made that the real casualties of a divorce are the children. In Chapter Two, titled: The Wages of Divorce, extensive listing of irreparable damage to offspring is set out.

Here is more evidence.

Doctor Judith Wallerstein, who co-authored the book titled *The Good Marriage* with a Ms. S. Blakeslee, has spent the lion's share of her professional life dealing with families and broken marriages. She has just published a 25-year study which sets out a most disturbing series of facts:

Offspring of any age are traumatized by their parents' divorce. (We already knew that.)

The negative effects of the divorce on the offspring are long-lasting, profound and cumulative. (Ditto.)

The children of divorce are more likely to have trouble with drugs, alcohol and sex, as they grow up. Some begin their struggle as early as age 14.

A direct ratio exists between the amount of damage to offspring, and the level of conflict that occurred during the divorce proceedings. That is, a bitterly contested and hard fought divorce, especially with regard to custody issues, causes more damage to the children.

That last finding, concerning the ratio of damage to conflict, should be enough to cause any divorcing couple to at least find out about "low-conflict" divorce mediation.

If anyone needs a reason to avoid a

divorce, Judith Wallerstein's research and book will easily provide that excuse.

A final admonition: If you think or know that your spouse is being influenced by an outsider, realize that the problem is yours to solve, and begin resolution and negation of the outsider influence by starting your own campaign to work out solutions and acceptable compromises to whatever problems exist.

Please note that I didn't say that you will be able to get rid of, or solve all the problems in your marriage, because that's not the way life works. All you can do is try, to the best of your ability, to search for and find common ground with your spouse so everyone can live in peace and dignity.

Learn to be flexible.

The only thing carved in granite is your tombstone with your name on it.

Don't forget to use the techniques of communication, and learn how to negotiate, which is the very next issue.

N

Stands for 'NEGOTIATION'

Perhaps the most fascinating and worthwhile issue in the entire Marriage Relationship concept, next to communication, is this subject of negotiation. One thing that can truly be difficult to do in this life is to try to negotiate a solution to a problem or situation, real or perceived, that is really bothersome to one of the marriage partners. Especially when the person with whom are trying to negotiate is somebody you love or really care for.

So what is a negotiation process anyhow?

A negotiation occurs when one person or group of people try to get some other person or group of people to modify or change a certain facet of their behavior or position on an issue or issues. While at the same time adjusting their own thinking or attitude to such a degree, that, when the negotiation is completed, everybody is satisfied and can live with the end results, at least for the time being.

Getting (forcing) someone to completely conform or give in to your wishes, is not a negotiation but simply a one-sided power play. While a brute-force power play might seem to work for a while, the chances are very good that in the long run, either the original situation or condition will return in all its fury, or be replaced by a new and different, perhaps even more onerous status or behavior than the original bone of contention happened to be.

Before I begin to explain the basic components of a negotiation process, first a quick review of a earlier stated concept; understanding the difference between the terms "criticism" and "feedback."

Everyone probably knows more than they wish they knew about criticism and what it's like to be criticized, which is no fun at all. Criticism can be, and frequently is, harsh, and as a rule is begun with "You always . . . ," or "You never . . . " statements aimed in someone's direction in anger or in a spiteful manner, intended to hurt the feelings or belittle the one being criticized. Criticism is almost always painful and injurious to the self-esteem of the recipient.

Severe or persistent criticism can frequently be the cause of damage to a relationship. Continued criticism of a person over a long period of time could actually turn out to be mental abuse which was covered earlier under **A** Stands for 'Abuse.'

Feedback, on the other hand, is meant to be constructive in nature, and, simply stated, is nothing more than a communication intended to give assistance or aid about a specific subject or action, delivered in a calm, friendly and hopefully informative manner.

Huge differences exist between criticism and feedback and you really need to understand the distinction between the two concepts, because comprehending these terms and how they work can make all the difference in the world in how successful you will be when attempting to negotiate an issue with someone.

To put the concept into a real-life situation, let's say that you and your spouse are having a calm discussion about some topic which you would like to get changed to make life a little more pleasant. Face it, there is always a chance your marriage partner may not even be aware that something he is doing, or not doing, is bothering you. The danger always exists that when you do tell him of your desire for some change, if it affects him directly, he may not be initially interested in bringing about much, if any, modification in his life or behavior. Like, why should he? What does it get him? He thinks, "picky, picky, picky."

On top of that, unless marriage partners have been through this material in the Marriage Relationship format very likely they don't know a thing about the difference between criticism vs. feedback as a means of conveying constructive suggestions. Until they understand the idea of feedback, they will almost certainly view any attempt to bring about some level of change in their own behavior or attitude only as an attack upon themselves, and feel they are being criticized, probably unfairly.

The challenge is to acquaint and educate the other marriage partner about this concept of feedback vs. criticism so you'll be able to talk with him about a problem without his taking your comments and suggestions in a totally personal manner and as criticism. By using the tools of persuasion, you will be able to convince him, in a pleasant manner, that the changes you seek are fair and reasonable.

Earlier in the communication section located under **G** for "general codependence," some time and space was devoted to the concept of how to word requests to your marriage partner so that such requests do not directly attack him, but reflect how YOU feel. For example:

"I feel so ____ when you ____," and not, "You always____."

Some phrases can be used to soften initial attempts to give feedback to someone like this:

"Gee, I wish . . . ," or,

"I feel that it would be swell if . . . ," or,

"I guess I wonder if you could . . . ," or, "It would please me no end if you . . . "

Here's another possibility: Begin the conversation by talking about criticism and feedback. You could say, "Look, I'm not being critical of you, look at this as feedback, but . . . " etc.etc. Sometimes simply changing the focus from the **issue** to the **process** of negotiation, and criticism vs. feedback, can turn the trick.

Which brings up the next consideration which is the range of four outcomes of any negotiation, which are:

"Win/Win" is the best possible result from any negotiation because when folks in dispute arrive at this conclusion after a session or series of sessions, everybody is pretty happy with the results of the process and the way the whole thing worked out. All parties can feel they won to some extent; at least they didn't get slaughtered, and nobody lost face.

"Win/Lose" is a possible result of a negotiation, and in this configuration what happened is that you totally won and the other party completely lost. They got whopped. It doesn't take much of a social scientist to figure out that this result, while seeming to be a total victory, in addition to possibly being unfair, might well prove to be a bad bargain in the long run when the other party figures how they can get even for the defeat. The profound words of the late, great, philosopher W.C. Fields leap to mind:

"Never carry a grudge. As soon as
you get even with the sonovabitch,
try to forget it."

This win/lose result is no better than the next one, except that the circumstances reverse. "Lose/Win" result means that you lost, and they won. Losing is no fun for anybody, and of course losing can cause hard feelings and often deep and long-lasting resentments.

Then logically the worst and least satisfactory solution to or result of, any negotiation is the: "Lose/lose." This is the end result of a negotiation wherein everybody loses. The best example of a failed negotiation process would be your typical divorce, wherein everybody loses. Except the attorneys. Elaboration about the lose/lose end-result shouldn't be necessary.

Before anyone heads off into the mysterious fields of negotiation, you need to have a basic understanding of the three elements of any negotiation if you hope to have success.

Author Herb Cohen wrote a fine book entitled *You Can Negotiate Anything*, in which he breaks down very effectively and in a clear and understandable manner the three elements of any negotiation process, which are: POWER, TIME, and INFORMATION.

Cohen's book does not specifically deal with marriage relationships; he talks about all other types of possible situations in which a negotiation might be appropriate. He talks about dickering over the purchase of a lawn mower, an automobile, and even about the check-out time at a hotel. It is his contention that everything is negotiable, all you have to do is try.

His principles of negotiation are easily applicable to marriage. Here is a quick run-down of the negotiation process, as applied to a marriage relationship, using his three elements.

Power

Power is defined as having the ability to gain control over, or to achieve a desired outcome by having the ability to force a settlement or conclusion over the person with whom you are supposedly in the process of negotiation. Using power is **not** negotiating, and might produce a hollow victory especially if the **method** of winning wasn't fair-play either.

If you are married, here's an example that in all likelihood you know all about: He and she are not in agreement over an issue, and neither will budge an inch, so someone throws in a power move like, "Okay for you _____, you are herewith shut off." Most married people will quickly understand the connotation embodied in that statement. Such a move or power play in addition to being quite unfair and beside the point, has the potential to cause even deeper damage to the relationship than the original disagreement trying to be negotiated.

How does one get into a position of having power over others? The psychology books spend a lot of time and space examining this concept, and they list the following methods by which one can have power over others:

ASSUMED POWER is gained when someone just simply stands up and says, "I am in power," and that is the end of the story, if indeed they are allowed to get away with the power grab. The person who assumes power that way may not deserve, or know how to handle the newly assumed power. Power can be lost in a marriage relationship when one of the marriage partners either fails to maintain his own identity and/or is not able to assert himself and retain his own position of equality in the marriage.

DELEGATED POWER comes to pass when, by agreement, or consent, power is assigned to someone. Power can be assigned by an individual or a group, and the power delegated carries the responsibility of performing whatever duties and obligations are embodied in the agreement. An obvious example of delegated power in a marriage relationship would be if the two partners were to agree between them that, okay I'll take care of _____, and you take care of _____.

Each marriage partner then has his own area of mutually (agreed upon) delegated power, and they also have the responsibility to perform whatever task(s) the agreement carries with it. Assignments of power must be made in a marriage relationship so that both partners not only know and agree as to who has to do what, but also so they each also realize that they have the responsibility to complete the task or tasks in a competent and timely a manner, and without hassle. Delegated power, however gained, needs to exist within every marriage relationship, and frequently comes about as the result of a negotiation process.

AUTHORITATIVE POWER is gained through a legal process, like in a civic election when someone is elected sheriff. Sheriffs have considerable authority in maintaining observance of the laws of their jurisdiction, and at the same time they could have serious and even possible criminal liability if they misperform or are derelict in their duties. Authoritative power can enter a marriage relationship when a divorce decree mandates one of the partners must or can undertake certain responsibilities. Failure to perform according to the decree, while probably not criminal in nature, could certainly upset a divorce arrangement, and might even end up with a contempt-of-Court citation.

CONSENSUS POWER occurs when two or more people, within the framework of their group or organization, agree to give someone or several people certain power(s). Consensus power can be gained either by getting the most votes, which is called a majority, or by getting more votes than any other person which is called a plurality. A perfect example of the granting of consensus power by a plurality vote would be the presidential election of 1992 when the winner achieved victory by virtue of a 43% plurality.

One final type that needs to be included in any discussion about power is the "principle of least interest," which really isn't a real manner of power, but a perceived or imagined strength which simply says that:

> "Persons who think they have the least to lose, have the most power."

The key word in the definition of the principle of least interest is, "thinks" because so often people will mistakenly think they have nothing, or very little, to lose by destroying their marriage relationship in a divorce, only to find out later that their losses are indeed intense, extensive, bitter, long-lasting, and expensive.

The principle of least interest is alive and well in the marriage relationship arena because of the foolishly arrogant and romantic idea so many people have in these very liberal times that they can simply dump their mate, go find the truly perfect person, and live happily ever after. Of course, not only is such a selfish assumption unrealistic, but also highly unlikely to ever come to fruition. But then, anyone who's caught up in the principle of least interest isn't too bright anyhow.

Remember the old contradiction, dump the mate and keep the problem? Rather, the answer is to keep the mate and dump the problem.

So, that's what power is all about and how one gets power, and the next issue in any negotiation is that of time.

Time

Time as an elemental part of a negotiation has several faces, including the basic suggestion set out earlier which states that WHEN one tries to do a bargaining session is very important and even critical to the possible success of any negotiation process. For example, never begin, or continue a negotiation session at bedtime, or when the person with whom you wish to negotiate with is busy, tired, drinking, and/or preoccupied with other serious matters on his mind. Like hockey, or football.

Pick a time, arrange a time, or even make an appointment with your marriage partner to discuss whatever issue needs to be negotiated, so that the few minutes devoted to the session will be as free from distractions and interruptions as is possible. Agree to set some sort of a time limit on the negotiation period. Twenty minutes or a half-hour ought to be sufficient time for a single-issue discussion. But, you say, "What if we can't come to a conclusion, we can't arrive at a satisfactory conclusion in that short time?"

Here are two "thumb rules" you can count on:

1) Don't expect to have much success with any negotiation process on the first attempt or few attempts to arrive at a solution to a perceived problem. People involved in sales work know that 90% of the first-time sales are made after the 10th sales call. Pleasant persistence and determination are the key elements of any successful negotiation (sales) process. Face it: A negotiation is a sales effort. You are trying to "sell" an idea to your mate.

2) Realize that you may never achieve total success in your grand negotiation process. Perhaps you will be able to gain some small considerations, and then run into a wall. If that happens, and you are done with the process, or feel you have gone as far as you can go, feel satisfied with whatever achievement you accomplished. Later on, if you feel you need still more accommodation and change, you are faced with renewed and additional negotiation efforts to build on the success you have already achieved. Once you have gained some degree of accomplishment, then "give time a chance," which is still another facet of this subject within the framework of a negotiation process.

"Giving time a chance" is a great idea covered earlier in the section where "**T**" stands for time. If within the context of a negotiation process, you are trying to work on a problem and the conversation isn't going well, stop the discussion and plan for a later date when you might have better success.

Not too much happens very quickly, it seems, and you probably aren't going to solve a knotty problem within your marriage relationship in a day, or a week, or maybe even a month. Realistically speaking, however, you can expect to eventually succeed, to some extent, but the chances are pretty good it may take you a while.

An unseen advantage to calling a halt to a negotiation that isn't moving very well, or has simply gone sour and now closely resembles an argument, can be that the marriage partner with whom one is negotiating may have to take time ("time out") to think about what is being asked of him. Sometimes, while he is off ("in his cave") contemplating the issue, he may come to his own conclusion about the request for change. Where initially he might have been very firm and disinterested, maybe later on, after thinking about it, he will see a reason why it might be in his own interest to be more compliant and accommodating. The need for a "time out" might be more applicable to male rather than female behavior.

With reference again to Dr. John Gray's book, *Men Are From Mars etc.*, Dr. Gray correctly points out that men are inclined to go into their "cave," as he tells it, to solve their problems. If the lady of the house brings up a negotiation, she can probably expect her suggested changes to not only fall on deaf ears and not solve her problem, but also she could expect her marriage partner to "go into his cave" to figure out for himself what he thinks about the request. Then, later on, once he has arrived at his conclusion in male fashion, he will emerge (from his "cave") and hopefully be ready to negotiate. Or accommodate. You never know, but maybe just letting a little time pass will bring forth at least a part of the hoped-for result.

Information

Information is the third and final element of a negotiation process and is defined as that circumstance where one of the parties happens to know something important, either about the other party, or about the issue under consideration, and that information could possibly affect the outcome of the negotiation.

An example of someone possessing information in the negotiation of a business deal would be in the case of a home purchase if the buyer knew the sellers must sell their house by a certain date. Without question, if a buyer knew this fact he would have a huge advantage, in that he could wait until the last minute before submitting a low bid, knowing the sellers would be under pressure to accept his offer because time for them to sell the house was running out.

Information as a bargaining chip isn't that easy to come by in a marriage relationship because both parties already pretty much know all there is to know about each other and the issues in their relationship. But that is not to say that having information, as it may exist, is not of value.

For example, let's say that he really likes Boston Cream Pie. That's a bit of information, isn't it? So, if in the course of the negotiation she remembers his fondness for Boston Cream Pie, perhaps she can somehow work that delicacy into a break in the negotiation, and maybe have a little better chance of achieving a bit of success. Any port in a storm.

Here is another possible example of how information might enter into a marriage relationship negotiation: Say she knows he would like to go on a fishing trip with the boys, meanwhile, she wants something like a new carpet, or whatever, for her home. Here is an example of a negotiated trade-off if there ever was one, and best of all, a perfect example of a "win/win" solution to two desires. He gets to go fishing, and she gets the new carpet. As a couple they both won and their marriage won as well because they worked out and negotiated the settlement.

Warning: Never use information in a negative manner or as a threat. Should one possess some detrimental or adverse information about his mate, it could be very dangerous and possibly even grossly unfair to hold this negative piece of information over his head as a threat or weapon to achieve success in any later negotiation process.

The Negotiation Process

So you want to negotiate some issue or issues in your marriage relationship, then how do you go about the negotiation?

PLAN your approach. Try to know what it is you hope to gain in the negotiation, and estimate how much success you really need to achieve to feel satisfied. Examine your own conscience and see how much "give" you have in the negotiation.

Remember: The concept of negotiation involves both parties giving up some ground, while at the same time gaining some advantage, or at least not coming out with the short end of the stick. PLAN how you are going to stage the negotiation.

For example:

a) When and where would be a good time to have a negotiation session without interruptions or distractions?

b) Plan that the negotiation session will be conducted in a calm reasonable and polite manner, in a quiet setting, and for as short a period of time as possible.

c) Rehearse out loud and perhaps even in front of a mirror what it is you are going to say, keeping in mind the need to use mostly "I" statements. "I feel . . . " "I wish . . . " "I hope . . . " Plan to include compliments wherever possible.

d) Be prepared to stop the session if anger appears, or if you cannot remain on the subject. Leave the door open by ending the failed negotiation session with an assertive statement like, "Well, we can talk about this again. This issue is very important to me and I really want to find some common ground," etc. etc.

e) Don't be surprised or hurt when you encounter resistance which will probably appear in the form of a single, or a series of defense mechanisms. We must now explain and demonstrate what a defense mechanism really is.

Defense Mechanisms

The early objections and plaintive excuses offered by people explaining why they will not, or can not, agree in any way to a proposed negotiation or request are called defense mechanisms.

People use these various ploys or excuses to keep from having to do something, go somewhere, or sometimes just to escape some facet of reality which they dislike.

Sigmund Freud thought up the concept of defense mechanisms about a hundred years ago. Your knowing about and being able to recognize various defense mechanisms when they appear is going to be a tremendous advantage for you, because once a defense mechanism is recognized and identified, the solution to a problem, or at least the possibility of an end-run is within your grasp.

In counseling training the student therapist is taught to expect and cope with defense mechanisms as they are presented. In therapy, the process of stripping away defense mechanisms is called "peeling the onion." The connotation being that the therapist simply does not accept the initial excuses (defense mechanisms) as offered or presented for anything more than they are: the outer layers of an "onion" of consciousness, and by peeling away the phony husks (excuses), they will eventually get to the heart of the problem.

On your own, you can probably expect to "peel the onion" and have to wade through extensive layers of non-pertinent and sometimes even silly objections and excuses, in order to get to the core, to the real deep-down reason for a person's objection or reluctance to go along with the suggested change(s).

Here's a little bad news: Many times the defense mechanisms presented are true, but they are not the real or total underlying reason for the action, or inaction. For example, you ask your spouse to do some task, and find out he needs to go get a haircut. Can't talk about it now. Maybe he does need a haircut, but that's not the reason he won't do what you want done, only the presented reason he won't talk about it.

Tip: Do NOT get caught up discussing the presented defense mechanism(s) even if they happen to be true. If you do, you have fallen into the "trap of irrelevance," and will spend the entire session talking about issues or complaints that are completely beside the point. Just simply ignore the defense mechanisms and move on with your own subject matter as best you can.

Defense mechanisms really do exist, and here is a list of some of the more common ones you might encounter when attempting to bring about a negotiation process:

REPRESSION: The person's simply refusing to talk about the subject. "I don't want to talk about that now," would be a firm indication of a repression-type defense mechanism. "Stuffing it," in other words. Rather than force the issue which might be an error, one possible approach would be to respond with, "Well, okay, but we have to talk about it sometime because this is very important to me, so when would be a good time?" And set a time.

REGRESSION: A variation of the repression mechanism occurs if the anxiety of the other person becomes so great that he reverts back to an earlier behavior in his life which gave him pleasure.

A classic example would be the person who starts sucking his thumb, but other examples could include the marriage partner who, upon refusing to negotiate, runs home to mother every time there is a big argument. Or, the man who goes out and jumps into his car or on a motorcycle and roars off into the countryside when confronted with the need to face the reality of a problem in their relationship. Little boys are inclined to "run for it."

RATIONALIZATION: Overthinking an issue. Analyzing small insignificant details to a great extent, to keep from looking at the big picture. The rationalizer is always able to come up with some often twisted "reasonable" even if screwy excuse for some attitude or behavior. Rationalization as such is frequently adorned with a generous helping of the "victim" syndrome, which holds that the viewpoint or performance of the person is never his own fault, but always the fault of "society" or some other condition or set of circumstances that "made" him behave or think the way he does.

DISPLACEMENT: Transferring feelings from one object or situation to some other object or situation. For example, if one had a bad day at work and then went home and shouted at the kids and wife, his behavior would be an example of the displacement of his anger or frustration at work. Instead of being angry at the job or at himself, he takes it out on someone else. Displacement, as such, seems to be an unfortunate part of all our lives.

PROJECTION: Attributing our own shortcomings or errors to someone else. Again the "victim" syndrome. Everything that happens is always someone else's fault. People who use projection as a defense mechanism fail to accept responsibility for their own shortcomings and failures. When we can't face our own unwanted feelings, we sometimes project them on to others, and in effect, excuse the other person as having and performing the behavior or feelings that we cannot accept personally.

ANGER: Of all the defense mechanisms, this one is perhaps the most commonly used, and is easily identifiable when the person with whom you are trying to negotiate suddenly becomes very angry. People who use their anger to escape, think and hope, often with success, that their display of anger will derail and effectively cancel the attempted negotiation process. The trouble dealing with anger, if you will recall the "Dance of Anger," is, in order to keep from constantly butting your head on his anger as a defense mechanism, you must find a way to "break the step" in the dance. You must let the person using the dance of anger know it won't work any more. He must come to grips with the issue that bothers you and that drives him into a furious funk. You might go back and re-read the "**A**" Stands for 'Anger' chapter.

INTELLECTUAL DISHONESTY: This can be a very exasperating defense mechanism in that the person simply becomes dishonest in his thinking and will try to convince you that black is white, right is wrong, in is out and up is down. There is no way for anyone to know whether a person who is being intellectually dishonest, believes the nonsense he is spouting. One thing you can be sure of, however, is that if you accept intellectual dishonesty in the course of an attempted negotiation, the battle is lost. You must persist with reasonableness and truth, and hope to eventually prevail.

PRESENTMENT: The issue of "presenting" as a method or means of diversion to escape the reality of a situation has been covered earlier, but the concept is of such importance that a quick review is in order.

Presenting occurs when a person offers some lame or almost completely irrelevant excuse for behaving, acting, or thinking as he does. As mentioned just a bit earlier, the excuse presented might actually be true, but it also may not be the real and complete reason for the objection. And, that's what you have to figure out for yourself.

Medical people use "presented" in a fairly similar manner. For example if you went to the doctor with a headache, he will write on the chart that the patient "presented with a headache." This does not mean that he will look at your head, rather he will take your temperature, blood pressure, check your ears and throat and poke fingers and tubes into often delicate parts to see if he can figure out the cause of your headache. He "peels the medical onion." Layer, after layer. They call this the "differential diagnosis" process.

Whenever someone quickly gives what seems to be a lame or glib excuse for some behavior or thought process, think and wonder if what he said might not be a "presented" excuse, which the person hopes against hope you'll accept as the gospel truth. Remember that presented information may be true, but it also might not be the real reason for the refusal or reluctance to go along with your request. That's what you have to figure out.

Other defense mechanisms exist, but this brief list should alert you to the fact that you might run into some off-the-wall excuse which doesn't make a lot of sense, but is nonetheless offered as a justifiable reason for the behavior or attitude. If you let the defense mechanism derail or deflect the conversation, it's your own fault. You lose.

Once you detect the presence of a faulty defense, about all you can do is wade through all the baloney, and see if you can't find out what the REAL reason for the objection might be. One of the hardest things to do when confronted by a lame excuse is to not be deflected, but to stay "on task" and keep focused.

Focus

Earlier in the general codependence section we looked at a symptom of general codependence known as triangulation which occurs when one person habitually gets other people involved in his disputes, rather than face up to the argument alone. In that earlier explanation a triangle was shown, and here's another one, except that this one has to do with our subject of negotiation.

Picture a triangle, again with the two marriage partners at the bottom, but this time the issue which you are trying to negotiate is at the top.

The trick is to focus and talk ONLY about the issue. No other subjects, personalities or behaviors can be allowed in the discussion. All attention and comments are to be directed to each other and to the issue. If a defense mechanism or side-tracking subject is brought up, simply ignore it. However, if you find that you cannot maintain clear focus on the issue or issues, bring the negotiation session to a close saying perhaps, "I see we aren't going to make any progress at this time, and since this is very important to me let's set another date when we can talk about it." And try real hard to set another date for a follow-up session.

But don't feel too badly; here are a couple ground rules:

1) Assume you will fail on the initial negotiation attempt.

2) When preparing for the next session, keep in mind that the way you present your case is of critical importance too. Not only is the setting and time frame of significant importance, but also even your tone of voice and body language. A logical and reasonable presentation of your thoughts on the subject will have all the bearing in the world on the outcome. Be calm, honest, assertive, and above all, reasonable. Keep cool.

Don't lose your temper or get cranky. Your spouse very likely has his own point of view on this issue too. With reference again to Dr. John Gray's book, he points out the almost universal tendency for men and women to approach issues differently. Doctor Gray says that "women are like waves." His thought, and most married men will recognize this trait, is that a woman will bring up the same subject over and over and talk about the same issue until hubby thinks he is going nuts.

Therefore, in any negotiation effort, women have an inherent advantage because of their tenacity and inborn persistence.

Males on the other hand have a "one-shot" mentality. They will; a) typically say their piece, only once. And, b) once a decision is arrived at, that's it. It's over. For males reading this, you really ought to try to give up the "one-shot" approach.

The ability to effectively negotiate issues is nearly priceless. By using good and proven techniques, anyone can come surprisingly close to getting almost anything he wants, whether in their marriage relationship, or career. Without being able to negotiate, one can come surprisingly close to getting nothing more than whatever naturally falls through the cracks of the floor of life.

Never forget this old saying:

"In life we don't get what we deserve, we get what we negotiate."

S

Stands For 'SEX'

At long last we come to our consideration of the final one of those three issues which typically cause the most trouble in marriages. Again, the three main sore spots are: money, sex and relatives.

As a communication procedure, sexual activity goes two ways. On the plus side, good healthy sex is incredibly exquisite and can be a wonderfully bonding activity. On the minus side, trouble with or over sex in a marriage relationship can cause much confusion, anger, disappointment, frustration, misunderstanding and, if allowed to deteriorate to extreme levels, can be a prime factor in the disintegration of a marriage by virtue of a developed state of total incompatibility.

This do-it-yourself, in-home, self-help marriage counseling guide is not in any manner a performance-driven medically diagnostic sex-counseling manual. We are going to deal herewith only with the apparent down-side or troubling aspects of sexual activity as it may enter into anybody's marriage relationship. If anyone wants to improve or enhance his sexual prowess, or progress, he shall have to look elsewhere for such information.

If ever one of the primary rules of logic were to be violated, this might be the case, where it can be said almost without any chance of dispute that every married couple at some time in their marriage have some measure of trouble over sex. Maybe somewhere, somehow, sometime in this wide world there is or was a marriage which has not endured a shred of sexual discomfort and/or stress, but wherever such a relationship exists, so does Camelot.

As a general rule, matters sexual go along pretty well in your typical marital situation, and the sexual activity can and does accomplish wondrous things in the human caring and sharing department, as well as in the intimacy sector. After all, life is sexually transmitted, so maybe that's what it's all about.

Intimacy as an element in a marriage will be discussed quite extensively just a little later as the last I in Relationship. Sexual activity, although intimate, is not intimacy per se, as you will see defined in that later section. We shall get to that explanation in due course.

However, human sexual experience, if properly approached, used and enjoyed, provides an integral and necessary part of the elemental basis of that larger and far more encompassing and hugely complicated relationship, the marriage contract.

The subject of sex as it is considered within the Marriage Relationship concept needs to be approached from several different points of view, and so we begin with:

Sexual Dysfunction

Sexual apparatus in both males and females can fail to work properly, but when the male or female sexual machinery does malfunction, aside from issues of chagrin and desperation, there is often an underlying reason for the misfire. We will have a brief overview of some of the reasons for sexual troubles, and list a possible remedy where there might be one.

Medical articles and books recount some of the problems that can be encountered, and these articles further tell us that there can be real reasons for sexual dysfunction, or difficulty, and these failures or malfunctions of sexual appreciation or ability are almost sure to fall into one of the following categories:

As a Side-effect of Medication

Physical sexual dysfunction can and does occur as a side effect of medication. For example, some high blood-pressure drugs, some anti-depressants, and other drug compounds and combinations of drugs can cause unexpected sexual malfunctions. If one begins treatment for some disorder with a new drug and finds shifts or changes in his sexual abilities or inclinations, the best thing to do would be to immediately contact the prescribing physician and tell him of the changes in your condition (ability) and see what he says.

In these days, pharmacists often know as much, or more, about the side-effects of drugs than the prescribing doctor, so they too can be a good source of information. Almost always now when a new prescription is picked up from the pharmacy, a page is included in the package listing possible side-effects. With the huge number of different drugs on the market nowadays for each illness, a change in medication might be all it would take to be able to control or manage a drug side-effect malfunction.

Without going into an elaborate discussion, a new drug named Viagra has appeared on the market which is intended and, according to reports, does successfully enable an impotent male to temporarily regain his sexual abilities. It takes about an hour for the drug to kick in, and it reminds me of my own experiences in Disneyland, waiting in line the better part of an hour for a two minute event. However danger lurks: A side-effect of this drug can be the demise of the male who took Viagra if he is concurrently on some types of heart medicine. Before taking the drug, it would be more than prudent to ask the prescribing medical practitioner if it is okay for the person to ingest the medication. Otherwise, you win some and you lose some.

Use of Alcohol and "Controlled Substance" Drugs

Heavy use or abuse of alcoholic beverages, and of course psychotropic side-effects from using controlled substances such as prescription painkillers, can cause trouble with sexual capabilities. The obvious answer would be to restrict or eliminate the use of the alcohol, or the drugs. However, to an alcoholic or to someone who is "hooked" on some legal prescription medication, that advice is most certainly easier said than done. In order to restore normal sexual function, whatever that might be, as well as other physical abilities, the addict or abuser might have to go to some sort of rehabilitation center, and/or contact an appropriate support group. See: **A** Stands for 'Addiction.'

Physical States or Conditions

Other physical states or conditions such as an illness or extreme anxiety can cause sexual dysfunction. For example, a disorder such as male impotence can come about as the result of a problem with a male's vascular or nervous system.

The problem with illness or physical disorder causing sexual malfunctions is that the misfire or default might precede the diagnosis of an illness, and turn out to be a precursor or a warning sign. So, to look at the issue in reverse, if there is a change in sexual ability, or interest, maybe that change is a symptom of some other physical problem brewing in the person's body and which is causing the sexual dysfunction. An early visit to your doctor would be appropriate.

If the physical exam proves negative and the conclusion indicates mental origins, rather than ignore the condition perhaps either the drug Viagra, or a quick trip to a sex therapist could be in order. Please recall from our earlier discussion about depression, in the opinion of many the best treatment for many types of mental upset is the combination of an appropriate medication and psychotherapy. More will be said about mental involvement in just a minute.

Individuality

Contrary to popular belief, there exists a wide range of differences between males, and between females, with regard to interest and capability in matters sexual. Some males have a very high and consistent interest in sex, some don't, and the rest fall in the middle. Females can respond in the same manner—high to low interest. It is an error, therefore, for females to categorically think that all men are either sex maniacs, or sexually indifferent. Conversely, males ought not to think that females are all the same. Tepid. You never know. The conclusion is, what you get is what you got, all based on that particular individual's sex-drive.

Mental States

Estimates by most therapists and medical people hold that as high as 90% of sexual dysfunction is the direct result of a mental state or condition, the source of which is lodged directly between the ears of the person with the problem.

Obviously there would be no clear-cut way to statistically measure how many mentally caused sexual malfunctions actually do exist. In fact, not only is the 90% figure suspect, but even worse news is that there really aren't a lot of treatment plans out there to remedy mentally-induced sexual imbalance. Presumably, if a person is really upset about something and the anxiety is hurting the sexual activity, when the cause of the distress is over, the sexual capability ought to return to whatever was the normal level at the beginning of the turmoil. All you have to do, is figure out what is causing the stress.

Some of the more common areas and/or sources of psycho-induced sexual malfunction range from a simple dispute or misunderstanding between the marriage partners, stress, as just mentioned, sorrow, confusion and, God-only-knows how many other mental states a person can get into.

Here's a problem: Sometimes folks go through the wildly exciting courtship days, and then find out one day the honeymoon is over. This always happens. The mental problem then, is to remember that no matter how hot and steamy a relationship is at first, the passion will fade and there had better be something else to take its place.

Developmental Changes

An additional compounding factor is the continual physical development or aging of individuals with regard to sexual outlook, interest and physical capability. Much has been said earlier in this guide concerning lifelong developmental changes, and here is the subject again. Of particular note would be a divergence in interest in sex between marriage partners who have a rather wide spread in their respective ages. For example, some older people know they can get along without sex better than they can without their glasses. But the bottom line in any sexual conflict or disappointment would be that what is really important is for the two marriage partners talk the situation over, and come to some kind of mutual agreement or understanding on the issue of sex as it may, or may not, exist in their marriage relationship.

Reality vs. Fantasy

The noted television personality-psychologist Doctor Barbara DeAngelis authored a pertinent article which appeared in the January 12th, 1993, issue of the *Family Circle* magazine with the headline asking, "Are you sabotaging your sex life?"

The gist of her article, and indeed of the question that needs to be asked is, what is reality, and what isn't?

Doctor DeAngelis cites a personal experience concerning her having gone to a sexy movie with her husband. As she recounts the experience, during the entire film the hero busily kept trying to seduce the heroine in a variety of most innovative and romantic always. Later back home, her husband, who was obviously "inspired" by the film, attempted to initiate his own close encounter of the sexual kind in, as she felt, his own characteristically non- or un-romantic manner. Not at all like the dude in the movie. She reports being totally turned off, which brought his romantic attempt to a screeching halt, with the resulting typical hard feelings, some pain and angry disappointment. Reality vs. fantasy? She thought: why couldn't her husband act like the hero in the movie? Maybe the key word is "act."

Doctor DeAngelis contends that no one deliberately sets out to destroy his or her own sex life, but that many of us have some bad or unfortunate sexual habits which can and do inhibit a possible state of sexual passion. Her point is that a person can become immersed in a fantasy, no matter where it came from, then when the marriage partner fails to live up to that dreamy scenario, even though the spouse has no knowledge at all of the dream-scene, here cometh rejection, stress, trouble and frustration. The obviously reasonable answer to a reality vs. fantasy conflict would be for the marriage partner with the fantasy to tell the other partner about it, stand back, lie down, or whatever, and see what happens. Typically, marriage partners want to please each other, so maybe a simple communication of wishes and desires will suffice to approach the level of intensity that exists, or existed in the fantasy.

With regard to that communication, refer to the "criticism vs. feedback" discussions. How and when someone tells another person what he wishes, is the key to success.

Stress As a Culprit

The issue of stress was mentioned earlier in the "mental states" section, but stress as a culprit in sexual difficulties needs a little closer attention. Most people can only think about one thing at a time, but if the thought or thoughts occupying a marriage partner's total mind is one of great concern it causes a substantial level of stress.

Because of this preoccupation with, or worry over, a problem or difficulty, things sexual might not work out as planned, or as hoped for by the other non-stressed marriage partner.

Situational conditions such as a job loss, a family illness, a death, a birth, just plain old down-cycle burnout, a state of fairly deep depression, and God-only-knows how many other real and perceived stressors or disasters can cause a temporary loss of interest in sex, and maybe even the physical capability for the distressed marriage partner to successfully participate in sexual activity. Hopefully, such high levels of stress do not last for a very long time, and the apparent first course of action for the non-stressed marriage partner is to simply give the mate all the caring, support, and time and space needed to eventually get past the issue.

If the stress doesn't go away on its own in a fairly short time, all hands should look out for depression or the existence of an on-going "major depressive episode." As I mentioned earlier, the combination of psychotherapy and a prescribed medication proves to be the best and quickest way out of a deep and serious depression.

Of course, just talking with and expressing understanding for stressed people with their problem might help them through a difficult period. Unfortunately, if you will recall, as Dr. Gray points out in his book *Men Are From Mars, Women Are From Venus*, most men will simply refuse to talk about a problem until they have come (out of their cave) to some conclusion or resolution of the problem, at which juncture they will then talk. So, it would be rather difficult if not impossible for a woman to try to talk to her husband if he won't even talk about it in his male fashion.

Women, on the other hand, not only will talk about a stressful problem, but they need to talk, not only about that problem but all their other problems as well. What a huge difference and source of great misunderstanding between men and women, but that's the way life is.

Inhibited Sexual Desire (ISD)

Some couples don't have a lot of sexual activity in their marriages for the reason or reasons imbedded in their brains under a rather fancy term, "Inhibited Sexual Desire" (ISD). ISD wears several masks, none of which are particularly easy to remove. On top of that, the longer any one particular ISD mask is worn, the more difficult it is to get any substantial relief. Some of the more common forms of ISD include the following reasons or conditions:

Anger. Deep, imbedded, never-ending anger at the other marriage partner. The reason for the anger is important only if a resolution is possible, and there is always the chance that one marriage partner may not even know, or admit, the reason for the mate's anger. Of course if let go on too long, such deep abiding anger could result in that state of total incompatibility which, please recall, is one of the three reasons to divorce. Anger over matters sexual can come to pass by simply having one of the marriage partners continually disappoint the other partner over a long period of time.

Life's normal body functions. A relatively little known fact is that as long as a human male lives, he continues to produce sperm. The produced sperm are then accumulated in a little reservoir called the epididymus, which is located in his scrotum. When the reservoir is full, it sends an emergency communiqué to the male's brain informing it of this congestion, including a very urgent request that something has to be done, like right away or damn soon at the latest, to somehow evacuate or drain off the way-too-full reservoir of accumulated sperm.

Two considerations enter the picture: One is that not all males produce sperm at the same rate, and the other is that as the male ages, the rate of sperm production diminishes. But, from that physiologic fact comes, to a good extent, the level or frequency of male interestedness in sex, to say the least. Fewer frantic, panicky messages from the epididymus to the brain means less intensity and interest.

Females, on the other hand, can possibly experience heightened sexual interest at that time in the menstrual cycle when the egg is produced and pops out of the ovary into the first section of the fallopian tube, with its instinctive inclination (hope?) to expect to get fertilized, almost as if the egg has its own mind.

Whether or not the egg gets fertilized is another story. But in those few days when the egg is coasting majestically down on the cilia in the fallopian tube, it is reported that the female apparatus (tubes etc.) send if not frantic, at least "now pay attention!" messages to the female's brain inclination center that the time is here and now, and the woman's sexual interest is reported to be increased. Conversely, reports and studies indicate that female interest in matters sexual is diminished in the off-season.

General Codependence

Unfortunately some parents bring their children up to think that sex in any form and at any time in life is evil, bad, dirty, disgusting, and to be avoided. The reason they bring up their children like this is, most likely, that is exactly the way that their parents brought them up when they were children. And so on, and on, and on back into much earlier generations. To say that such sexual inhibitions can be difficult to auto-overcome is probably the understatement of the year, and if carried over into adult life from childhood they could well require the input of a psychologist or psychiatrist who specializes in the treatment of sexual dysfunction. There are such people.

As if being brought up in that atmosphere isn't bad enough, the feelings of wrongdoing and acute self-consciousness will be passed on to the young person so that when normal marital sexual activity does occur, as it should and must, they are extremely uneasy and suffer strong feelings of guilt.

These inclinations for the person to feel bad or evil can cause them to be so on edge that a mouse sneezing two blocks away can bring a sexual encounter to a sudden halt. A door closing, a door opening, a car honking, a dog barking, a leaf falling, or any other minor noise can bring an abrupt end to the sexual activity.

"What happened," he asked.

"I heard a noise," she replied.

Solutions to such feelings of self-insecurity would have to include taking reasonable steps to try to absolutely preclude any interruption by anyone. Locks on the door, music to drown out the distant sneezing of birds and other noises from afar might help. If all else fails, a trip to a distant planet (motel), or perhaps a visit with a friendly psychologist to try to discover, and remedy, the reason for the acute level of sensitivity.

Some Possible Remedies for Sexual Disappointments

It is said to be the rare married person who has not heard the words, "Not tonight, dear." Unfortunately these words, when uttered, are typically pronounced at probably the worst time: One of the marriage partner's need for sexual activity is in the acute stage, and the other's isn't. A Dr. Anthony Petropinto, M.D., along with a woman named Jacqueline Simenauer, authored a book titled *Not Tonight Dear: How To Reawaken Your Sexual Desire,* in which the authors tell of the results of their survey of some of the country's leading sex therapists, who advise the following remedies for cases of sexual dysfunction or dissatisfaction:

1) Think intimacy and togetherness, not sex. The point being that as the marriage partners get to know each other more and more intimately, their sexual relationship will deteriorate. They know each other too well. People who know each other too well tend to lose the excitement of love they had enjoyed in their early days together.

2) Communicate personal feelings. Speak up. A woman wouldn't expect her husband to guess how she would feel about a new and controversial subject, but too many marriage partners expect and even demand that the spouse know intuitively, or by consulting a nearby crystal ball, of their likes and dislikes in lovemaking.

3) Don't be predictable. They tell of the long-married man who found sex more enjoyable when he laid on his right side. He could see the TV that way. New sexual excitement can be found by simply breaking routines and changing the setting or circumstance of a sexual encounter.

4) Be reasonable. Don't try to initiate a sexual episode when the other marriage partner is busy, tired, preoccupied or ill.

5) Keep battles out of the bedroom. This admonition while clearly easier said than done, can be accomplished by simply deciding or establishing a written-in-granite rule that arguments are most definitely not allowed to carry over into the bedroom, or to be begun before, during, or after a sexual encounter. Maybe between sawing badly on his fiddle, and his one-liner's, the late Henny Youngman, who thought he was just being funny, was right on the mark after all when he said: "Never go to bed mad, stay up and fight."

6) Make time for love. Make it a priority to carve out some private moments when you are physically and emotionally together. In these hectic days of two-careers, kids, sick kids, business trips, and too many household chores pulling at both marriage partners, one of the first things to be lost is lovemaking. Postpone the laundry chores if need be, or the housecleaning, or the tennis or golf games. If all else fails, consider hiring a baby sitter to come in and enable your escape to some romantic island. (aka motel—resort—etc).

A famous psychologist, Dr. J. Haley, has an interesting paradoxical method of treatment he uses for couples who come to him for help and therapy regarding problems sexual which he calls "prescribing the symptom," and it works this way: Dr. Haley tells the couple to change their lives to the extent wherein they spend more time together taking walks, having quiet dinners, talking, bathing together, giving each other a massage, but absolutely no sex for 30 or 60 days, or whatever period of time he knows is going to be too long for them to live through. The couple heads out the door with firm intentions to follow his suggestions, and of course, when the couple comes back for the next session at the end of the prescribed time, all that can be reported is, for some reason, they had failed. Too much intimacy and togetherness meant they were unable to keep from having sex.

Indeed it is written: "Familiarity breeds attempt."

Don't feel badly, sexual activity in married couples varies widely. In a book titled *Celibate Wives*, written by Joan Avna and Diana Waltz, published by Lowell House and reviewed in the November 3rd, 1992, issue of *Family Circle* magazine, the authors address the issue of marriage without sex. As ex-therapists, the authors were able to accomplish a study of 100 women across the country ranging in age from 29 to 72 concerning celibacy or the complete absence of sexual activity in their marriages.

The conclusion of the authors from their survey was that celibacy in marriage is a well-concealed fact of life in many bedrooms and marriages in America today. The authors estimate that from 10% to 25% of all married couples are celibate at some time during the life of their marriage. Absence of sexual activity does not necessarily call for the end of the relationship, and some couples, the authors report, after due discussion and consideration, mutually agree to celibacy. However, the authors then set out to provide a positive approach to cure or bring to an end the sexless marriage, and suggest as remedies many of the very courses of action mentioned above.

The thing to keep in mind is that your love life, as well as other crucial life conditions, may and will undergo change. But variation does not mean the end of the world, unless you let it bring about a crisis. If you suffer from sexual dysfunction in your marriage, take heart; you are not alone. However, with a little good will and effort, the prospect of renewing or establishing satisfactory sexual activity in your marriage relationship is excellent.

Anybody can take the helm of a boat in calm water, but in the spirit of "any port in a storm," if problems sexual seem to be too great in your marriage relationship, seek professional help from some qualified psychologist or psychiatrist who holds himself out as a sex therapist.

And start screwing around.

H

Stands for 'HONESTY'

Everybody knows that the word "honest" means being truthful and not telling lies. Also included in any definition of honesty are other considerations such as the concept that the behavior of a person is honest, true, fair, honorable and consistent, with regard to agreed-upon actions, intentions and principles. In other words, honest people keep their promises.

Promises and kids are a lot alike. Both are fun and easy to make, but they can be tough to deliver.

Initially, as a lesser concern in a marriage relationship, I address the issue of speaking the truth, that is, of not telling out-and-out lies to one's marriage partner. There is the old saying which goes, "Nobody tells all the truth all the time," which is true. The tendency to sometimes exaggerate and distort elements of fact and true circumstances lie within all of us. Especially we who are right-brain dominated.

The companion book entitled *Some of the Reasons We Behave the Way We Do*, outlines the right brain/left brain behavioral phenomenon. Briefly, those who are right-brain-dominant people typically have trouble being exactly truthful all the time, in addition to owning a goodly number of other easily identifiable behavioral quirks. Anyone living with a right-brain-dominant person will soon figure out that person simply does not care for accuracy. Right-brain dominant people don't exactly lie, but surely tend to embellish or exaggerate the numbers or the situation, just a bit or quite a lot, according to their style. Needless to say, this tendency can be annoying to a long-suffering spouse who might be a left-brain person. But, that's the way the (us) right-brainers are, and since their (our) brain is irrevocably connected in that manner, really all you can do is learn to live with and expect them (us) to stretch the truth a little, one way or the other. Hey, no big deal.

Another consideration with regard to being honest has to do with the fact we can sometimes avoid hurt feelings and arguments by telling little "white lies," or at least by not telling the entire truth about a matter. Nowhere is it written that anyone must tell all the truth about a matter or issue all the time.

For example, if asked about past relationships, a person does not have to lie, but most certainly any thinking and considerate male or female could downplay or minimize the story and leave out the gory play-by-play details of an earlier entanglement.

Q. Who wrote, "Sticks and stones may break our bones, but words will break our hearts"?
A. Robert Fulghum, in: *All I Really Need To Know I Learned in Kindergarten.*

Similarly, sometimes fibs or lies can be kind. For example, to tell someone that they are as handsome or as beautiful as they ever were, might be a gross exaggeration, but at the same time such an outrageous fib might could be a sincere expression of affection and loyalty for the person. Does anyone have too much loyalty and affection? We all tell "kind" lies, from time to time, to be nice people, to escape the awful truth, or an argument.

It is written that liars are apt to overestimate their own good will, motives and chances of escaping detection. A wife can convince herself that she is lying about something in order to spare her husband, when what she is really trying to do is to avoid his bad mood or anger. A husband might lie to his wife, out of sheer disrespect for her intelligence or status as a human being. Some people lie when they don't need to and thereby take away from their marriage partner the chance to develop understanding, tolerance and generosity.

When tempted to tell a fib or to outright lie one could ask himself two questions; the first would be: "Self, what would happen if instead of lying, you told the truth?" And the second question would be to ask yourself if you might just use some tact rather than lie. The more tact you use, the less retract(ing) you'll have to do.

For example, if a male had been dragged to concerts he hated for years and years, what would be wrong for him to simply say something to the effect, "Honeybun, (etc) I think I've had enough of concerts, so, let me buy the season tickets, and you find a friend to go with you who will enjoy the music more than I do."

Finding honesty with each other and avoiding lies will become easier if you realize that telling the truth does not mean that you have to reveal everything. Sometimes the truth is better swallowed if ladled out slowly over time. Sometimes the whole truth should never be told. However, one has to watch out for falling into the habit or trap of constantly telling what appears to be harmless deception, which might eventually lead one to tell the poisonous lie.

Although the spoken word and the possibility of deception is of great importance in any marriage, the greater concern with regard to the issue of honesty, in our consideration of the 20 elements of a marriage relationship, is the question which asks: Are the marriage partners sexually faithful to each other and to their spoken marriage vows? In other words, is anybody cheating?

In days of not-so-yore the standard marriage vows contained the final vow which stated, " . . . and I plight unto you my troth." Nobody really knew then, or knows now what the word "troth" meant. It means to be "true," faithful and sexually exclusive; a promise to not become sexually involved with anyone else once the couple is married. By and large, the old word "troth" has been deleted from present-day marriage vows, but nonetheless, in order to hold to the importance of sexual faithfulness, these days you'll hear people during the ceremony pledge fidelity to each other with different words. For example, "I promise to be faithful," is a rather common present-day marriage vow. Same thing: a vow to be a sexually exclusive and faithful marriage partner.

Times have changed. In days gone by it was much more socially important to maintain the integrity and honesty of the marriage relationship as well as the family unit. Just look at some of the shifts in public opinion:

Social stigma: In slightly earlier times people who were divorced were more or less outcasts, and said to have less "character" than the married folk. That certainly isn't the case in these modern times when almost the reverse is the rule and it is "in" and "modern" to be divorced.

Birthright: Babies born out of wedlock in the not-too-distant past were considered bastards, which status they never overcame, or could hope to surmount only with great difficulty. Birth announcements seen in today's daily newspapers proudly list births to single females. A very few decades ago, if a young lady became pregnant out of wedlock her family was disgraced, and not infrequently she was sent to a faraway city to have the baby, who was then almost always given up for adoption.

Disease: In the days before the discovery of penicillin and other antibiotics, contraction of a "social disease" was not only a social stigma, and a disgrace, but also possibly fatal. In present times, while diseases such as gonorrhea and syphilis do not seem to be as terrifying as they once did because of antibiotics, the appearance of AIDS and some of the awful sexually transmitted incurable herpes infections ought to be to be a deterrent to our modern-day "free sex" social climate. But such does not seem to be the case.

As I have stated before, within the concept of a Marriage Relationship, there are only three legitimate reasons for anyone to divorce, and for the umpteenth time they are: abuse as defined, total incompatibility, and infidelity that can't be stopped or tolerated. This issue of honesty being defined as being faithful and sexually exclusive to one's mate and to one's marriage vows therefore becomes one of the three most critical components of anyone's marriage relationship, as far as the possibility of divorce is concerned.

What then is the definition of infidelity?

Infidelity is defined as a breach of faith and a violation of the marriage vows which exists when either one of the marriage partners become sexually active with someone else.

Atlanta psychiatrist Dr. Frank Pittman has been in private practice for some 20 years and is generally considered in the psychological community to be the guru of ideas relating to the detrimental effects of infidelity with regard to people's marriage relationships.

Doctor Pittman has written several books, but the one that seems to hit the nail on the head is his book, *Private Lies,* in which he lists and identifies four different types of marital sexual infidelity. Doctor Pittmen also sets out quite clearly all the trouble that a breach of faith, or sexual cheating on one's marriage vows, can and does cause people in marriage relationships.

After all these years of practice in marriage counseling, Frank Pittman firmly holds that "over 90% of all divorces stem from infidelity." Or, said another way, a breakdown in what we are calling honesty, in his opinion, is the root cause of 90% of the present-day divorces—90%! Imagine that!

In his book *Private Lies,* infidelity or sexual cheating on the marriage vows falls into four distinct categories:
a) The philanderer.
b) The marital arrangement.
c) The accidental infidelity.
d) The romantic infidelity.

To consider each circumstance separately, we begin with:

The Philanderer

Philanderers are almost always males who feel that they must have sexual relations with every female they can get their hands on. Throughout their lives, philanderers run from one sexual encounter to the next in reckless fashion, without regard to any consequences of their behavior. This affects not only their own families, but also the females involved, their husbands and children. A perfect example is the behavior of the 44th President of the United States whose irresponsible, totally reprehensible sexual behavior has disgraced not only himself, but his family, the United States, and the office of the Presidency.

To overlay disaster upon disaster, the dishonest, irresponsible and destructive behavior of a philandering parent is seen by the male children in the family as proper role-model behavior to be copied later on in their own lives, and marriage relationships.

According to Doctor Pittman, "philanderers are nuts," and the reason they feel that they must run irresponsibly from one sexual encounter to another, in spite of their marriage vows is, in the case of males, that "their fathers never told them they were a man." Philanderers keep chasing after and trying to prove their manhood by having one sexual encounter after the other. Of course, to no avail.

Female philandering is quite rare, Doctor Pittman says, and when it exists the situation or condition is often confused with the mental disorder known as nymphomania. He further reports, as a practicing psychiatrist, his success rate at attempting to cure someone from being a philanderer, male or female, is poor.

How, you ask, could a gal who's only trying to get married to a guy she "loves" ever figure out before the fact of marriage if he is a philanderer, a chaser? Answer: Simply look at, and inquire about his father. Like father, very likely like son might well be the rule.

Chasers Beget Chasers,
Philandering Engenders Philanderers,
   and
Divorce Breeds Divorce.

Marital Arrangement

What do you do once you find out, as a wife and mother, that our dear hubby is a "chaser," or is having an affair? Or, what if you are the husband of a woman whom you discover is "on-the-town"? What then?

Our present-day society seems to have embraced a double standard status which holds: If a man finds out his wife is being sexually unfaithful, in almost all instances he will divorce her. Not always, but as a general rule. However, male fidelity is not at the top of most women's lists of marriage requirements.

When a woman is faced with her husband's infidelity she will go one of two ways; either lay down the law and insist on his behavioral corrections, with the expressed or implied threat of divorce, or simply look the other way and tolerate his cheating. The later-stated condition is the one that Doctor Pittman calls the marital arrangement.

People, males and females alike, are known to tolerate the infidelity of their spouses for several reasons including: money, social status, prestige, family appearance, family integrity, (holding the family together for the children's sake) or for whatever other reason they can think up.

The degree of incidence of this condition known as the marital arrangement is not known, but probably every reader knows of some couple or couples who live in this manner. The syndicated newspaper columnist L. M. Boyd recently had a squib in his "Love And War" department which said that 65% of the marriage partners whose mates were cheating actually knew their spouses were being unfaithful, but did nothing.

As mentioned earlier, divorce is certainly an option, but evidently marital arrangements do exist, and one can only wonder the if accommodation of an affair by the cheated-upon spouse, known as the cuckold in the case of a male, doesn't earn somewhere, somehow, sometime, a measure of revenge or retribution.

The marital arrangement as such does exist in our badly mixed-up society for whatever set of reasons, and we come to the next type of infidelity defined by Doctor Pittman, which is:

Accidental Infidelity

Picture this: A person is in a setting somewhere like in a business meeting or a convention and things are going along well, too well in fact, with an associate, newly-met friend, or a waitress/waiter, and somehow, some way, in some mysterious off-the-wall manner both persons find themselves in bed with each other, and not exactly taking a nap. This event was not planned, pre-arranged or contemplated, it was simply an occurrence that came to pass as in an "accident."

Grant that convincing the offended, the cheated-upon marriage partner how innocently this "accident" came to pass would be next to impossible. But what if the event really was just an accident and the sexual encounter really only happened that one time? How can this sort of "accidental" behavior cause trouble?

Because far too frequently the idiot marriage partner who had the accidental sexual encounter and cheated on his marriage vows and on his marriage partner, develops overwhelming feelings of guilt, and in an effort to make himself feel better, he confesses all and tells his spouse about the random infidelity.

Imbeciles like this, who feel the need to assuage their own guilt, fail to realize that the cheated-upon marriage partner is an innocent person or victim, and may not be able to handle and live with the revelation. The cheater may feel a whole lot better himself for the confession, but you can bet the poor person who was cheated upon will feel worse.

In a curious twist, Doctor Pittman relates that the really sad thing about the accidental brand of infidelity is that in many instances, when the unfaithful spouses do not tell their mate of their infidelity—get that, do **NOT** tell their mate of their accidental cheating episode—eventually, being unable to live with their own guilt, will file for a divorce on some phony set of mythical "presented" circumstances because they cannot either:

a) live with their own guilt;
b) bring themselves to tell the spouse of the cheating.

The tragic result of such weird behavior is that the persons who were cheated upon will probably never know of the accidental infidelity of their spouses, and worse, may spend the rest of their lives trying to figure out really why their marriage partner got a divorce. Like, "what did I do?"

Myth: We have to tell our mates everything.

Of all the stupid things to think, this insane idea is close to the top rung. Where did anyone get that idea? Another popular modern-day myth or saying is that marriage partners have to be "best friends."

But why? Why do people think they can ease their own guilt by confessing their own gigantic error(s) to an innocent spouse?

The good-looking young student's wife was an absolute knockout and they had a beautiful two-year-old baby boy. In a moment of sheer idiocy and indiscretion he found himself coupled with a very comely fellow lady student on "only a couple of occasions," he said.

At a later date, bearing guilt feelings of the heaviest sort and looking for some way to make himself feel better, this idiot told his lovely wife of his sexual indiscretion. The first thing she did was go to an attorney to initiate divorce proceedings, and then she went to an abortion clinic and killed their second child who was another baby boy, with whom she was seven months pregnant.

Q. How stupid can one male individual be?
A. Nobody has any right to shift his own guilt to someone else.

The obvious solution to avoiding the accidental type of infidelity is for both marriage partners to always be on guard. Do not let your emotions run amuck. Be careful, and keep focused on what is really important in your life, and most of all, if you do screw up and an accidental infidelity occurs, keep thy big mouth shut!

Which brings us to the fourth kind of infidelity; people who can't keep their mouths shut or keep their emotions under control either and find themselves in that state of consummate stupidity which Dr. Pittman calls:

Romantic Infidelity

Romantic infidelity, Dr. Pittman explains, is committed by people who are psychopathic. In plain English, crazy. Nuts. People who immerse themselves, or get caught up in an emotionally out-of-control "romantic" infidelity or affair, are actually dangerous, Doctor Pittman says, because while suffering from their romantic illusions and delusions, they have lost all their sense of social balance, judgement and common sense. They are incapable of basic reasonable thought, and are capable of unreasonable thoughts and actions.

Everyone surely knows of people who have fallen head-over heels "in love" with someone, and as a result have destroyed their entire lives and the lives of their family. Fools afflicted with romantic infidelity can lose their jobs, their property and money, the children and sometimes even their lives, just because they are convinced they are suddenly and oh-so-completely in love with someone else. Oh Brother.

A very well-regarded middle-aged, successful businessman in our community who owned a beautiful home, had a lovely wife and family, had the bad luck to go to a business meeting out of town where he met a young lady some 25 years younger than he, with whom he promptly "fell in love." Madly, deeply, hopelessly, consummately in love. Don't worry about the fact she lived 2000 miles away, or that she was almost young enough to be his granddaughter.

After some steamy phone conversations and a quick rendezvous or two, or six, he went home to wife and family and told them all that he was in love with another woman, so, goodbye all. He packed his stuff and left. He quit his job, and moved the 2000 miles to be with his true love. Of course, you know how this one came out, don't you? These two, who were so much in love, never did get married. Their infatuation lasted about 10 days. Mr. "so-in-love" found himself standing out on the curb with no wife, no job, no toys, no family, no money, no car, no place to stay and no self-esteem. Nobody respected him. The only things he did have were a ton of debt, family anger, frustration, regrets and richly deserved feelings of endless and overwhelming stupidity.

The really bad news concerning romantic love, according to Dr. Pittman, is, an instance of romantic love, if it happens, is almost impossible to head off, because, as previously stated, the person who has fallen victim to and is immersed in this chaotic state is completely out of his mind. He is incapable of rational thought, crazy and potentially dangerous. Newspapers and TV news programs, almost on a daily basis, tell of episodes of murder and mayhem committed by lunatics in a state of "romantic love."

Constructively speaking with regard to the above true story, one could say that there is always the chance that if matters had been a little better in their marriage relationship, and they had worked to ease some of the stress and strain between them, the fool romantic love-episode may never have happened.

If you keep your marriage relationship in as good a shape as possible, you do stand a chance of warding off such lunacy as a case of "romantic" infidelity.

Well before Judith Wallerstein's previously mentioned recent study ever came to pass, Dr. Pittman has been registering how very upset he is about the trauma he sees, and all the damage to the children of broken marriages because of the indiscriminate sexual wanderings of confused and dissolute parents. It's been said before and is worth saying again: The children are the real casualties of every divorce. How very rewarding to hear Dr. Pittman say of infidelity, "It ain't worth it, no way, and an excellent reason to stay together and work things out is for the children!" Should you stay together "for the kids"?

YES! YES! YES! YES! YES!

I have said this before and I will say it again: Nobody said or is saying that you should stay together and be miserable or unhappy beyond the normal range of the ups and downs that exist in everyone's life and everyone's marriage. All I'm saying is that you should work things out the best you can and stay together. It doesn't take a rocket scientist to know that the paradigm in which you presently live is not the only life-plan that is offered, and available. Things can be better.

Hold your own marriage relationship sacred and work as hard as you can to be happy together. Don't pay any attention to the popular "for myself," "just for me," "on my own," liberal attitudes. Remember the old admonition given in schoolrooms with regard to taking tests: Your initial guess is probably the best guess. Your first choice for a marriage partner is probably your best choice, so don't turn your back on your first best-effort marriage relationship as so many people foolishly do.

If you can't seem to get enough agreement or flexibility in your attempts to negotiate disagreements, then, by all means, get some professional help. Help through counseling is available, and if you do decide to seek help, you will have such an advantage over most clients because you have gone through our Marriage Enhancement guide. You already have identified the problem areas. You won't have to spend a lot of time and money wading through all the presenting complaints to get the therapist to that point where they know what issues to work on.

Mark Twain once said:

"The surest deterrent to
temptation is cowardice."

It is wise to be fearful about what might happen should you find yourself on the road to divorce. If something is wrong or ailing in your marriage relationship, fix it, don't blow it! And, be honest, no matter how much of a struggle it is. Those who are honest with themselves, and others, get farther in life. Which brings us to the final, ultimate idea embodied in the concept of honesty, and it is:

Trust

Is defined: unquestioning dependence on another's integrity, honesty, reliability and loyalty.

All relationships are based on mutual trust, and people hold those they trust in high regard. Trust is a two-way street; you trust others, and they trust you. Implicitly. Completely. Unconditionally. Especially in your marriage relationship.

In his recent book former Notre Dame football coach Lou Holtz devotes an entire chapter to the subject of trust. After a lifetime of coaching young athletes, Holtz says the prescription for generating trust is easy: do right, live honorably, avoid wrongdoing and maintain high and dignified standards of behavior.

Coach Holtz says: "Get trapped in a single falsehood, and you can forsake a lifetime reserve of credibility."

But, since we are dealing in this chapter primarily with the subject of being sexually faithful and true, reference to another book written by J. R. Greer M.D., titled, *How Could You Do This To Me? Learning To Trust After Betrayal,* seems appropriate.

Doctor Greer defines trust as an "unspoken assumption of how we will behave toward, as well as be treated, by others." He continues, "Because trust is unspoken, we assume everyone else operates from the same reference point as we do. We expect those WE trust to be faithful, loyal and honest." **Because we are!**

However, as you can see by the very title of his book, the thrust has to do with what people do, or feel, or think when they find out to their great dismay that they have been cheated upon. Their marriage partner, their dear spouse has been unfaithful.

Doctor Greer says that a failure of trust shatters the self-esteem and even destroys the very dignity of the one cheated upon. It is his observation that the victims suddenly don't feel safe, either emotionally, physically, spiritually, and even financially.

He has observed in the wake of a betrayal, the victims discover they can't trust themselves any more either, because evidently their judgement was faulty. They trusted someone who did not deserve their trust, and they feel foolish, thinking they should have known, and stupidly missed what must have been obvious signs of deception.

So, the loss of confidence, loss of faith, plummets the innocent victim into a crisis of self-doubt, and forces them to come to a painful reality they did not choose, or ignored, and they must now make some decisions. Which takes us back up into the foregoing text in this chapter; how in the world does one get out of a mess of infidelity?

Another question: How can anyone be so stupid as to get into a cesspool of cheating, and jeopardize his family?

Once again: You are the captain of your ship. You must make your own decisions and live with them. You are responsible for yourself. If you choose to make a mockery of your life, family and marriage by being a cheater, then, lots of luck. If you are the victim, what do you do? Do you forevermore have to be ever on alert and suspicious? Should you be angry and vindictive and get even? What do you tell the children, and relatives, if anything? How do you structure, or maybe better said, restructure your life to go forward?

Infidelity that can't be stopped or tolerated is one of the three reasons to divorce.

Don't screw your life up.

I

Stands for 'INTIMACY'

In the definitions section under the last I, intimacy is defined as the transmission or communication of feeling or feelings, from one person to another person.

Within the framework of the human species, females know all about, need and in fact crave intimacy, while males, generally speaking, don't have a clue about what intimacy is. Even if they did know a smidge about intimacy, they would not be inclined to participate in any personal type conversations because that wouldn't be "manly."

Males are brought up as little boys to know that "big boys don't cry," or share and talk about their feelings. (See "G"—general codependence.) On top of that, if you asked 1000 males for a definition of intimacy, a huge majority, if not all, would say intimacy was making whoopee. Granted that sexual activity, aka "making whoopee," is intimate, to say the least, but that's not what we are talking about, with regard to this communication process called intimacy.

Once again we refer to Dr. John Gray's book, *Men Are From Mars, Women Are From Venus,* where author Gray clearly points out that on the planet Venus from whence he facetiously contends that all human females emanate, women know all about intimacy, how to be intimate with each other, and they constantly practice and enjoy sharing each other's thoughts and lives. On Mars, however, where males come from, men are steadfastly taught not to be intimate with each other, and any attempt to engage in a sharing of confidence and feelings is to be avoided at all costs.

Hence the core of the problem: Females know all about and need intimacy while males don't know anything about and are scared to death of it, and think that they should not participate in any manner, ever, in such a practice.

The task then: How do you explain to males what intimacy is? Could they ever learn how to be able to share, even a little, their close personal feelings and thoughts with their wife? Once that is done, all you have to do is explain to females that males don't have a naturally intimate bone in their body, so, don't expect too much from them.

If a female has ever been able to get her man to be a little intimate, savor the experience. Tell him how much you appreciate his sharing feelings or thoughts with you, and continue with your efforts to get him to be even more open with you.

The truth is, no matter what Martian males think, all humans need some measure of intimacy in their lives. The trouble is, if you can picture this, the day a couple gets married, she goes into the relationship with high hopes and a firm intention to train her man into the behavioral frame in which she wants him, so that he can be like her. He, on the other hand, being blissfully unaware of her plans, has his own agenda which includes continuing his life in the newly married state much the same as it was when he was single. Darn, here comes conflict between the newly married partners because both will find out that they will be unable to live their dreams: She will not be overly successful in changing him, and he, also, will find that for the most part, it will not be possible for him to continue his life in a manner to which he had become accustomed.

Complications further arise because of the general codependence of each of the marriage partners. Everybody has his own load of special and sometimes weird carry-over behaviors and attitudes which he brought to the marriage feast from his original family structure. Unfortunately, it can happen that when confronted with the new more intense atmosphere of closeness and affection, aka love and marriage, a defensive reaction with regard to each person's "boundaries" can appear. This is because each individual carries into marriage an assortment of his original-family codependent behavioral patterns.

A fascinating exercise in the practice of psychology is the old "string test," which has to do with the boundaries people feel exist, or will allow, around them. Boundaries, per se, are defined as perimeters or parameters of closeness and safety.

Here's the way it works: The therapist has both clients sit on the floor facing each other and gives each one a piece of string about four feet long, with instructions that they should place the string about them where they feel their own boundaries might be. How close they allow, or will permit people get to them.

Some people who are more inclined to be able to be intimate with others will place the string quite close to their bodies. Others will put the sting out as far as their arms can reach, indicating that their personal boundaries (for intimacy) are a long way off, and saying, in effect, "Stay away from me." Sometimes, when this symptom is pointed out, they will try to move the string to what they think might be a more acceptable distance, but too late. Anyone, especially the therapist, can see how close each of them may come to being intimate with the other. Then the poor therapist has to go to work on that problem or defect.

In their splendid and easy-to-read book, *Centering and the Art of Intimacy*, listed in the bibliography, authors Gay and Kathlyn Hendricks, both Ph.D.'s, list several of the possible adverse behavioral symptoms of the conflict which can arise when one of the members of the marriage relationship gets "too close" to the other partner, and one (or both) of the partners feel the need to retreat back into his own shell by using one or several various defense mechanisms.

Defense mechanisms were covered at length earlier, but with regard to the Hendricks' work, here are a few of those; listed again:

- Resorting to old previously-seen parental defensive maneuvers, as are listed in the section on general codependence.
- Blaming the partner. Retreating. Sulking.
- Changing the subject.
- Detachment. Going numb, letting the mind drift. No response. (A favorite male escape word is, "whatever.")
- Changing the focus to a power-struggle conflict.
- Display of anger or righteousness.
- One of the partners becoming "ill."

With reference to the anger or "illness" of a spouse, there comes to mind an old semi-humorous set of guidelines governing the behavior of many people known as "Rule #1,":

Rule #1. The person knows everything and is always right.
Rule #2. If the person doesn't know everything, or is wrong, refer to Rule # 1.
Rule #2a. If that won't work get mad.
Rule #2b. If getting mad won't work, get sick.
Rule #2c. When you get through with 2a, and 2b, return to Rule #2, which says refer to Rule #1. (Like, what is your problem?)

While considering the positive side of this thing called intimacy, one must also consider the other side of the coin and give some consideration to one of the most difficult aspects of a marriage, and that is the everlasting struggle of the marriage partners to each somehow maintain their own identity and autonomy, while subjecting their own personalities and characters to the demands of their marriage. People need their own space and time occasionally, and sometimes they (we all) need to share intimacy and closeness. Belonging. Thus is the age-old conflict in marriage. A roaring dichotomy.

The Doctors Hendricks include in their fine book an extensive consideration of a type of marriage they call an "entanglement" vs. a real marriage relationship. In their definition, an entanglement is a lopsided relationship which occurs when one of the marriage partners has many personal needs, feels very wanting and incomplete; a basic state of inequality exists between the partners. In their view, in a relationship, the two marriage partners see each other as equals, as opposed to the one/down-one/up relative status in an entanglement.

Symptoms of an entanglement according to the Hendricks include:

1) One of the marriage partners is trying to get something from the other marriage partner which they failed to receive in a prior relationship. For example, a woman who was married to a typical non-intimate male would try to find real male intimacy in a second marriage. Another example: a child who was rejected by a parent seeks a parent-like relationship with the new marriage partner in order to replace the missing Mommy or Daddy.

2) The need for one marriage partner to get (force) the other person to meet certain expectations, hoping and praying that the new marriage partner will compensate for his own self-perceived shortfalls. This, once again, is the old "opposites attract" disaster syndrome.

3) The difficulty that marriage partners have in letting their spouse be themselves emotionally. Along with this unfair restriction, that person also would not be at all interested in listening to, or care about, what is bothering the other marriage partner, and why he is being so emotional anyhow? Some people are simply more emotionally driven than others.

4) One marriage partner exercising almost complete control over the spouse.

5) Inability to handle conflicts. Arguments end up with one person always being the loser and wrong, while the other one is always right. One of the marriage partners ends up feeling and being the victim, while the other one becomes or plays the role of the perpetrator (aka the "bad guy").

Those are some of the identifiers and symptoms of a failure of intimacy in a marriage relationship. So how then to begin to try to achieve a better level of personal closeness in your own marriage?

Psychologists write volumes upon volumes of advice and suggestions on how to achieve more closeness, and some of these hoped-to-be-helpful tips include:

- Share your own feelings, but don't overwhelm the partner. Some things do not need to be, or should not be shared.

- If you do share a feeling or thought and the marriage partner doesn't respond, don't get discouraged and tell yourself that "he doesn't care," because it might just be that he has some other deep concerns on his mind or, he just wasn't paying enough attention to what you were saying. Maybe he might not be ready to share his own feelings just yet, so his response is silence. Don't forget: No response is a response. The worst news you could have is that he is the not-intimate type.

- Respect your partner's privacy. When he needs time to be by himself, leave him alone. In like manner you have your own right to be left alone when you feel the need.

- Be readily available. If your partner begins to open up to you, it is important that you be a considerate, attentive and reliable source of support to and for him.

Males: Keep in mind that when women talk about a problem or all their problems, they are searching in their minds for their own solutions, and they are not requesting that Mr. Fix-it (you) come up with a solution. All they want you to do is listen!

So KEEP YOUR BIG MOUTH SHUT!

Females: Keep in mind that when a man talks about a problem he has already come to his conclusion and has made whatever decision he felt was needed, and now is simply looking for support and trust from his woman. Unless of course he says, "Honey, what do you think?" Then tell him, but very kindly.

Listen intelligently. When the marriage partner is telling you about something that is important to him, listen to both the words and the feelings that lie behind them, and closely watch his body language. Refer to the companion book, *Some of the Reasons We Behave the Way We Do,* or peruse the books of Julius Fast or Dr. Pease listed in the bibliography to find out more about body language.

In the meantime, here are a few body language movements which could be indications feelings of either aggression or defensiveness:

Aggression	Defensiveness
puffs out chest	seems to shrink
bobs head in a rhythmic manner	interrupts frequently
pelvis pushed forward	pelvis back
waves arms and hands	blinks eyes
talks loudly	face is flushed
walks about	fidgets

- Keep in mind your partner's upbringing. Always try to remember that spouses, when under pressure, will strongly tend to duplicate the behavior they observed their parents use when they were children (general codependence again).

- Be trustworthy! Never, never reveal a confidence given by your marriage partner, and never, never use a given confidence as a weapon to be used in conflict between you! Never!

- Ladies, acknowledge with gratitude any confidence or feeling shared by your male partner. Tell him that whatever he is feeling is okay with you (hopefully) and reassure him that he has the right to feel the way he does, even if you don't understand why he feels that way. Especially, do NOT challenge his feelings at the time of disclosure, for if you do, forget about his sharing any future feelings or attitudes.

- Don't be afraid to ask your partner if he wants to talk about what he feels, or ask what you can do or say that will make him feel emotionally safe with you. If he says, "no thanks," or wobbles away, let it go. Maybe next time.

Women need what is known as "validation," which simply means that women need to know that their feelings and thoughts, and therefore themselves, are of value.

Males need to know that what they feel is okay and that they are trustworthy. Both of these considerations are of prime importance to males.

- Don't press your partner to talk about some issue if he doesn't want to. Sometimes males will not have arrived at a decision-point in their deliberations about a problem or feeling, and will not want to talk about what they have decided until they have made up their mind, (and come "out of their cave").

- If women are from Venus and know all about intimacy, and Men are from Mars and don't know a whit about intimacy, then it is important for females to know that on Mars males display intimacy in an "instrumental" manner. Instrumental intimacy can be best explained by pointing out that instead of actually saying the words, "I love you," or, "I care for you," or, "I like you and you sure make me feel good," or, "I appreciate you and what you do," a male will go out and wash her car, or mow the lawn, or take out the garbage, or trim a tree, or turn off a light, or open a door, or any of another 1000 subjective deeds that a male might do to keep from having to actually articulate out loud the words, "I love you."

When asked if he ever told his wife that he loved her, he replied, "Why would I have to tell her that?" Or, "She knows I love her." Or, "I told her that once."

Q: "When was it you told her you loved her?"

A: "Oh, 25 years ago or so."

Once in a while one can see a couple who have gotten the intimacy thing down pat because you can see them exchange glances or looks, or maybe hold hands for just an instant, or brush up against one another. Sightings of these couples seem to be few and far between.

Intimacy is a learned behavior both for males and females, and the way it works is either of two ways; one learns about intimacy as a child in the original family setting, or learns the skills of intimacy in a more challenging way . . . through experience. The first task would be to accept and relish the concept as it exists, and then learn how to display and receive intimacy.

The practice of Intimacy is a learned behavior.

Any behavior that is not learned, can be learned.

And vice versa.

P

Stands for 'PRIORITIES'

How unfortunate that one of the most important factors, if indeed not the most important factor in anyone's marriage relationship, or in his life, too, for that matter, finds itself back here at the tail-end of the discourse, under the letter **P** which stands for 'Priorities.'

A priority is defined in the dictionary as a listing, usually in rank of relative importance. In this case the listing would be of those things in life that are important to an individual, and because of this assigned importance, any item listed achieves a priority status in that person's life and/or in their marriage.

But, wait a minute. "What about values?" she asked.

Precious little is written about the subject of values, even though the psychology books do mention what they like to call "value systems" once in a while.

A value system is loosely defined as the listing of those personal traits or beliefs that are important to a person. For example, one person's value system (hierarchy) might place a very high level of importance on honesty, while someone else might not attribute a whole lot of significance to that trait. The range of values that can be included in a system could be as long as the person wants it to be. If you are married to someone with a substantially different range of values than you, all you can do is try to negotiate some level of equanimity or balance between you. Whether or not values can be negotiated remains to be seen.

But, to get back to the issue of priorities, let us grant how extremely serious it is for people to have at least some general idea or general sense of what direction it is they personally want to pursue in their life. True, a lot of us seem inclined to drift along seemingly quite willing and agreeable to accept whatever happens to us, although we have been known to register a post-occurrence protest. However, for a marriage relationship to endure successfully through the years it is quite critical for the priorities of the two partners to come pretty close to coinciding.

I did not say that your own personal and your spouse's life-priorities must be exactly the same. Even from a basic male/female point of view, the life-goals of each of the marriage partners will vary, simply because of sexual orientation. Add to that, the life-direction they were given by their parents when children.

For example, sometimes one can hear of the breakup of a marriage only to learn at a later date that the reason for the failure of the marriage was that the priorities of the partners were not close enough. Occasionally the dissolution of a marriage comes about wherein the basic complaint is that one of the couple wants to have children and the other says, "Absolutely not; you never said anything about having kids!"

Q. How can this happen?
A. It happens because either a) people don't sit down and talk about the really important things and what it is they each want and hope for in their life and marriage relationship, or, b) maybe they actually did talk about their respective life-scripts, found out that they did not coincide very closely, but one of the individuals foolishly thought that when marriage ceremony was over, he would be able to bulldoze his way to success and force, or perhaps wheedle a change in the partner's attitude or ideas.

"Guess what, honey," she said, "I'm pregnant."
Crash!!!
Thus I suggest, in the gravest of terms, that every married couple should sit down, and each person write down on a piece of paper what their own individual life-priorities might be for the selected periods, as they see them at the present time. Then, on the right side of that same page, each person should list what he hopes for and sees as his own priorities for the marriage relationship. Again, as seen at the present time! You will end up with two priority lists on each page of paper; the one on the left side is your personal list, and on the right side is designed for your relationship.

A form has been provided for your use at the end of this chapter.

I have previously made the point that we change as we grow older. We change physically, we change mentally, and we also change developmentally in a predictable manner. So obviously, the effect of time will influence the scope of our personal hopes, desires and capabilities. For example, not too many 75-year-old males are searching for a new business career. A wife or a new girlfriend maybe, perhaps a new fishing hole, but not a career.

So it is logical, too, that everyone's personal and marriage relationship priorities will inevitably change as the years go by.

For example, as younger people, the early-life priorities for females might include desired goals or achievements such as getting married, having children, advancing personal career goals, home purchase, family initiation and structure, and homemaking.

Males, on the other hand, in addition to their family and occupational goals, might be interested in other personal activities such as fishing, hunting, sports, cars, airplanes and who knows what else. The "different strokes for different folks" rule is in full force and effect, and, in case you hadn't noticed, girls are a good bit different from boys.

Another facet concerning the lists is that each partner's personal and marriage priorities must be reviewed and discussed on a regular basis in a calm and intelligent manner. The obvious reason for review is to provide the opportunity for addition or deletions of any listed priorities.

A less critical issue is the time between the periodic reviews and adjustments of each person's life and marriage priorities. A thumb rule, a process which might result in the beginning of a new family ritual, would be for the two of you to sit down on New Year's day (between or before the football games,) or maybe New Year's eve, the 4th of July, on a birthday, or at any regular notable time period, and take a few minutes to go over the listing of each partner's priorities. You could both take a look at the lists as they stood for the past year, and see what if any changes need to be made. If adjustments appear to be necessary, then take the time to discuss the new ideas and see if they really deserve to modify the two listings for the coming time span.

Six months is probably too soon to make adjustments; however, if that short time period works, then go for it. Someone else might say two years would be a goodly time span for review but that seems like a rather long time, especially for the short-term term priorities. Anything longer than two years between a revision of priorities would be far too long. Too much can happen over that length of time which can change individual thinking and selective preferences.

Another big advantage of listing and periodically reviewing priorities is the mutual sharing and comprehension each person will gain by being acquainted with his partner's priorities. A touchy situation can develop in this seemingly advantageous discourse and exchange of ideas if a partner runs into a priority of his spouse's which he does not like very much; and then tries to dissuade or change the other partner's idea or goal to suit his own personal needs or preconception of what he feels his partner should think. If such a conflict does come up, simply return to the *Negotiation* section and come to some understanding of the variance.

Debate exists in the psychological community regarding the time spans applicable in the ranges of human development. This discussion means that the periods which are applicable for an examination of life priorities are also up for grabs. Freud, Jung, Adler, Erikson and even the very popular and prolific author Gail Sheehy, (*Passages*) seem to hit on somewhat different ranges of spans for life changes. But, for the sake of simplicity, let's agree, for the time being, on the following breakdown of possible periodic revisions of new or renewed listings of life and marriage relationship priorities:

Short term: From today to 1 year.
Intermediate term: From 1 year to 10 years.
Long term: From 10 years onward.

Short-Term Priorities

As the very name suggests, this list of five or so personal and marriage relationship priorities deals only with the next few months or year. As you should expect on any such inventory, some goals will be met within the designated time span and drop off of the list, while others will or can pop up and need to be added.

For example, let's say that one of a person's personal priorities is to accomplish a certain educational course, or to finish a household task such as build a deck or some other similar effort. Obviously, once the goal or project is completed, that priority is no longer operative and would fall off the list. Other short-term priorities would continue through several list-revisions until they too would be completed or become simply inapplicable. Then new priorities would be added.

The question is asked: How many priorities should a person have in each of the categories for each time period? Of course, there cannot be a fixed number. The five mentioned here is not a magical number. Any person, or set of marriage partners, might have more or less than five personal and marriage relationship priorities. Some folks are very highly goal-driven and could be inclined to have a longer list of personal needs and targets than their marriage partner, while other people live much simpler lives and do not bother themselves with a large assortments of wants, wishes, or requirements.

Males especially are inclined to adhere to the old axiom, "If it ain't broke, don't fix it." Females on the other hand, being from Venus, as author John Gray points out, typically think: "If it ain't broke, swell, but let me help you make it work even better." And such is the stuff of conflict.

Of prime importance for marriage partners is the idea that people cannot expect their mates to have the exact same list of either personal or marriage relationship priorities as they do. Furthermore, the short-term list will very likely change in order of importance from time to time. A priority which is further down the list may become of more concern to a person and move up at a later time, and of course the reverse also can come to pass. Such is life. The critical concept to retain is that everyone needs to establish and recognize some listing of short-term priorities in his personal life, and in his own marriage relationship as well.

Intermediate-Term Priorities

This category of priorities, ranging in time from one year to ten years, deals with those items of personal and marital concern which have a longer life-term expectancy.

Obviously, as the time spans increase, it becomes more difficult to list what a person dreams and hopes he can accomplish. Some of the priorities may eventually occur, while others are doomed from the day they were first written down. But, it's okay for a person to hope and dream, isn't it? As I mentioned earlier, if you can dream it, you can do it. If you are afraid to dream, nada.

Long-Term Priorities

When it comes to long-term priorities, the concept of dreaming really enters the picture because who knows how long they will live? Nonetheless, as with the intermediate-term variety, it doesn't hurt to list what you hope for in life's later years. Sometimes a dream or hoped-for goal can become a dream or goal realized simply because the person got a good head start on the idea. An obvious example of the value of pre-planning would be the fact that it would be foolish to wait until age 60 to begin saving for retirement.

A previously mentioned, danger lurks in the long term for marriage partners with children, because it is at the later years in the marriage when the last child leaves home and the nest is empty for the first time in many years. If you will recall from the earlier discussion, this situation or condition is known as the "Empty Nest Syndrome" (ENS). Unfortunately, the empty nest syndrome is alive and well, and when it shows up, can bring about the end of a marriage.

A positive priority in the long-term list could then be to remain aware of ENS, and promise yourselves that if and when that event happens, you will both work very hard to become re-acquainted with each other, and pledge to work diligently towards happily continuing your marriage contract to its conclusion.

Of prime importance is the critical need for personal honesty in the listing of priorities, and, conversely, the need to recognize and honor your marriage partner's right to think and desire whatever he wants. If differences exist and misunderstanding does occur, then work together and negotiate mutual agreement and accommodation. (See **N** for Negotiation.)

Marriage partners must strive always to be honest, not only with themselves but also especially with each other, and try not to influence the other partner's lists, or capitulate and deny their own priorities under pressure by saying "Whatever you want honey." etc., ad balonium infinitum.

In conclusion, a brief admonition concerning the difference between the concept of priorities vs. goals:

Priorities are listings of those life-conditions or dreams that a person hopes for, sometimes placed in an order of importance, and which he will try to bring to fruition in his lifetime. Whatever is important to a person is important, and thus can be a priority for that person. A priority may or may not be a goal.

Goals, on the other hand, are specific aims, purposes or conclusions which are sought by a person.

For example, a priority might be to have a family, and the goal would be to get pregnant. Another example: A priority for a person might be to strive to do as well as he can in his occupation. A goal might be to get an advancement or a raise in pay.

One final suggestion: When you sit down to complete your priority list, exact items might not immediately pop into your mind. How can you think of all these weighty things at one time? Not to be concerned, for such is a normal human condition. As I mentioned earlier, my suggestion is to pencil in the priorities as they occur to you so they can be erased and removed from the list if those thoughts lose their importance, or they can be moved up or down to a different level. Add new priorities as they appear.

On the following page is a sample form which you might use to list your priorities. If you wish, make copies of this page too so the original page will stand the test of time and erasing. They say, that when the eraser runs out before the lead in the pencil does, you are in some trouble.

And so we have come to the conclusion of the "solutions" section. I will finalize this do-it-yourself marriage counseling guide with this advice; hold on to that wondrous thing called hope, and persevere with all determination keep your marriage relationship intact and precious until the end of your marriage contract: the death of one of you. Nobody ever won the game by quitting, and your marriage relationship is the most important contest of your life. So, whatever you do, don't quit on it. The final chapter deals with the critical need for you both to retain and always hold hope in and for your marriage.

PRIORITIES

For_____ On_____ 20___

Personal   Marriage Relationship

SHORT TERM

Personal	Marriage Relationship
1._____	1._____
2._____	2._____
3._____	3._____
4._____	4._____
5._____	5._____

INTERMEDIATE TERM

Personal	Marriage Relationship
1._____	1._____
2._____	2._____
3._____	3._____
4._____	4._____
5._____	5._____

LONG TERM

Personal	Marriage Relationship
1._____	1._____
2._____	2._____
3._____	3._____
4._____	4._____
5._____	5._____

CONCLUSION

The Elusive Elixir of Hope

Such is the title of an outstanding journal article written by psychologist Larry Hof, which appeared in the first volume of the 1993 series of *Family Journals*. As Dr. Hof points out, too little is written about this wondrous mental attitude called hope, which is defined in the dictionaries as, "a desire accompanied by expectation, anticipation and confidence."

Doctor Hof defines healthy, well-functioning couples as those who have a positive view of their potential, a strong sense of trust in each other and confidence in their marriage relationship. They look forward to living their lives together as an exciting adventure. Furthermore, these well-directed folks know and plan that they, as a couple, will be able to withstand the unfortunate downturns that will surely occur in their lives.

How, you ask, did they attain these attitudes? They got that way by having a wealth of optimism, along with sincere commitment, intention and HOPE to succeed in their marriage, no matter what difficulties they may encounter.

On the other hand, Dr. Hof identifies a dysfunctional divorce-bound couple as two people who have negative outlooks, who are distrustful of each other and are filled with pessimism, despair and hopelessness. Doctor Hof points out that too often it is these unfortunate folks who climb aboard the marriage counseling merry-go-round as the course of last resort after a long history of relationship disasters and failed interactions. These couples are filled with blame, feelings of powerlessness, anger and frustration. They are grasping for a miracle long after they should have sought out effective marriage therapy, as is offered in this book.

Marriage therapists know too well that the best time for any hope for success from professional marriage counseling is when the couple finds for the first time that they cannot solve a serious early conflict on their own. Marriage counselors know from their experiences that married folks need to develop more effective communication and negotiation skills, and they desperately must learn how to get to know each other better.

Since most couples wait far too long to

seek help, it is no wonder that the field of marriage counseling has such a mediocre-to-poor track record.

Some of the more specific causes of divorce according to Dr. Hof, and as cited earlier in this text, include the following:

- Too many couples enter marriage filled with romantic ideas, and incorrect and even dysfunctional expectations of what their new marriage relationship will be like. Once married, they collide almost immediately with the realities of life. This subject can be reviewed earlier in the **E** Stands for Expectations section.

- A mental condition known as the "myth of naturalism" which holds incorrectly that "love" is all it takes to make a marriage relationship live and work. Reference has been made earlier to the book *Love is never enough*, written by famed psychologist Dr. Aaron Beck. This book is listed in the bibliography and is well worth your reading. And no, love is NEVER enough.

- The couple who feels they can't change because of the earlier failures in their marriage, and have given up all hope of ever getting their marriage partner to behave as they want them to. To make matters worse, these folks find themselves locked into faulty and dysfunctional patterns of relating and communicating with each other, traits and patterns brought to their new marriage from their original families. As they saw their parents behave, so will they. See **G** Stands for General Codependence.

How does one maintain or regain hope that their marriage relationship is sound and will last? Doctor Hof suggests the following courses of action and planning:

1) Realize that the stress and strain of "going along" and enduring the times of strife and conflict in their marriage is normal. Every married couple goes through the same agony. You will win some and you will lose some, but never, ever give up hope that you can make your marriage relationship better. If you have hope, you will succeed.

2) Realize that in order to make your life and marriage better you are going to have to make some personal changes. Please read that sentence carefully: YOU are going to have to make some changes. You will need to take the risk of facing these adjustments in your own behaviors and attitudes on your own—and once these small modifications in yourself are made, you will discover that the sacrifice, and the cost of making those changes is cheap compared with the benefits derived from a much happier relationship.

3) Realize that in order to make the necessary changes in your lives you will need support, lots of support. Support from each other, support from friends and relatives, and, where possible, support from a self-help, church or religious group. The absence of effective support might well mean that any attempted changes in behavior eventually will fail, and where gains and advances were once visible, without

support, your marriage relationship again will deteriorate to its original state of disarray. Don't be afraid to ask for help, but be wary of what we call outsiders. If need be, go back and re-read that section.

4) Realize that the benefits of change will yield an increase in self-esteem for both of you; your interpersonal relationships with others will be better; your personal satisfaction and pride in your marriage relationship will greatly increase. Realize too that change, as it occurs, does so slowly, and in stages.

Doctor Hof concludes his article with the admonition that, "hope is the genuine elixir [for marriage relationships] and with it couples feel nourished, somewhat healed, and are able to continue to learn and change. Without hope, your (marriage) relationship is dead."

Another splendid source of hopeful inspiration is a book written by Dr. Robert Veninga while at the University of Minnesota School of Public Health. The exact title of the book is: *A Gift of Hope: How We Survive Our Tragedies*, listed in the bibliography, and well worth your reading to help you through a period of adversity and disappointment.

While Dr. Veninga's book is, as the title suggests, aimed primarily in the arena of recovering from grief and disaster (crisis) reconstruction, his ideas are applicable to the Marriage Relationship concept.

For one thing, Dr. Veninga holds that "crisis changes people, and you can survive (any crisis) if you want to." This admonition could well apply to trouble which erupted in any one or an assortment of the 20 components of the Marriage Relationship format.

"Heartbreak" is the word he applies the deep reaction to a disaster or setback, and isn't that appropriate? His suggestion to overcoming the heartbreak of disappointment engendered by a crisis in a category of concern is to:

- Understand what the crisis does to us - recognize how we think.
- Learn from the crisis and plan how you are going to think when the next crisis appears.

We went through that second step in the earlier explanations of Stress Inoculation (Dr. Donald Meichenbaum) and the "A-B-C" steps in cognitive thinking (Dr. Albert Ellis).

Doctor Veninga shares with us some very important ideas concerning adversity:

"The bigger the crisis the greater the possibility we think there is no hope for the relationship to be saved."

"If you see options, (for a solution) YOU SEE HOPE !

"If you see hope, you (your relationship) will live.

The Finishing Touches

By the time you have progressed to this point in the book you should have a grasp on the following truisms:

ALL MARRIAGE RELATIONSHIPS have some difficulties.

ALL DIFFICULTIES are negotiable.

DIVORCE is not a solution to a troubled marriage, but is an action which produces additional gigantic problems.

And,

THE REAL LOSERS IN A DIVORCE SITUATION ARE THE OFFSPRING no matter what age they be when the divorce occurs.

Hopefully someday the fabric of our sick and shattered society will find repair by virtue of better general understanding of the importance of marriage. We need to educate young people at an early age about the make-up and complexities of a marriage relationship. Our society must bring about individual awareness of the need for personal flexibility, as well as great patience and forbearance in the marriage setting.

Today's authors and columnists spend too much time telling people how to get themselves and their children through a divorce. Better they should tell and advise people how not to get divorced. A parallel would be articles in abundance which tell the reader how to recover from a self-inflicted gunshot wound to the foot. Instead, why don't they tell people how to avoid shooting themselves in the foot or anywhere else.

Have hope, perseverance, patience, understanding and love, and, Good Luck!

BIBLIOGRAPHY

A

Agras, S. W. (1972). *Behavior Modification: Principles and Clinical Applications.* Massachusetts: Little Brown & Co.

American Psychiatric Association (1997). *Diagnostic & Statistical Manual Of Mental Disorders* (4th Ed.). District of Columbia: The American Psychiatric Association.

Anastasi, A. (1988). *Psychological Testing.* (6th Ed.) New York: Macmillan.

Atkinson, D. R., Morten, G, & Sue, D. W., (1989). *Counseling American Minorities: A Cross Cultural Perspective.* (3rd Ed.). Iowa: Brown.

Avna, J. & Waltz, D. (1992). *Celibate Wives.* California: Lowell House.

B

Beck, A.R. (1978). *Love Is Never Enough.* New York: Harper Row.

Bigner, J. J. (1983). *Human Development: A Life-Span Approach.* New York: Macmillan.

Bograd, R. & Spilka, B. (1996). "Self-Disclosure and Marital Satisfaction in Mid-life and Late-Life Remarriages." *The International Journal on Aging and Human Developement* 42,(3) 161-172.

Borcherdt, B. (1989). *Think Straight! Feel Great! 21 Guides to Emotional Self-Control.* Florida: Professional Resource Exchange Inc.

Brandon, N. (1994). *The Six Pillars of Self-Esteem.* New York: Bantam.

Broder, M. S. (1993). *The Art Of Staying Together: A Couples' Guide To Intimacy And Respect.* New York: Hyperion.

C

Calahan, C. A. (1996). *Correlations of Scores on the Kansas Marital Satisfaction Scale and the Quality Marriage Index.* Psychological Reports. 78, 530.

Carlson, C. (1990). *Perspectives on the Family: History, Class and Feminism.* California: Wadsworth.

Cohen, H. (1980). *You Can Negotiate Anything.* New Jersy: Stewart.

Copi, I. (1978). *Introduction to Logic.* (5th Ed.). New York: Macmillan.

Corey, G. (1991). *Theory and Practice of Counseling and Psychotherapy* (4th Ed.). California: Brooks/Cole.

Corey, G. (1990). *Theory and Practice of Group Counseling* (3rd Ed.). California: Wadsworth.

Corey, G. & Corey, M. (1989). *Becoming a Helper* (3. (3rd Ed.). California: Brooks/Cole Publishing Company.

Cutter, R. (1994). *When Opposites Attract.* New York: Penguin.

D

DeAngelis, B. (1992). *Are You the One For Me? Knowing Who's Right and Avoiding Who's Wrong.* New York: Delacorte Press.®

Dinkmeyer, D & Carlson, J. (1984). *Time For a Better Marriage.* Minnesota: American Guidance Service.

Donovan, D. & Marlatt, G. (1988). *Assessment Of Addictive Behaviors.* New York: Guilford Press.

Dyer, W. (1976). *Your Erroneous Zones.* New York: Funk & Wagnalls.

E

Erickson, S. & Erickson M. (1988). *Family Mediation Casebook: Theory and Process.* New York: Brunner/Mazel Inc.

Eysenck, H. J. & Kelly, B. N. (1985). *"I DO"; How To Choose Your Mate and Have a Happy Marriage.* New York: World Almanac.

F

Fast, J. (1970). *Body Language.* New York: Evans Inc.

Feagin, J. R., (1984). *Racial and Ethnic Relations* (2nd Ed.). New Jersey: Prentice Hall Inc.

Fenell, D. L. & Weinhold, B. K. (1989). *Counseling Families: An Introduction to Marriage and Family Therapy.* Colorado: Love.

Figley, C. R. (1989). *Treating Stress In Families.* New York: Brunner/Mazel, Publishers.

Fincham, F. & Bradbury, T. (1993). "Marital Satisfaction, Depression, and Attributions: A Longitudinal Study." *Journal of Personality and Social Psychology.* 64,(3) 442-452.

Fintushel, N. D. & Bradbury, T. N. (1993). "Marital Satisfaction, Depression, and Attributions: A Longitudinal Analysis." *Journal of Personality and Social Psychology.* Vol. 64, No. 3,

Fintushel, N. & Williard, (1997). "Everyday Rituals." *Parents*. Vol. 72, Number 8.

Fishman, B. & Ashner, L. (1994). *Resonance: The New Chemistry of Love*. New York: Harper Collins Publishers.

Frankl, V. (1992). *Man's Search For Meaning* (4th Ed.). Massachusetts: Beacon Press.

G

Giblin, P. (1994). "Anger in Marriage and The Family." *The Family Journal: Counseling and Therapy for Couples and Families* 2,(3). 241-245.

Giblin, P. & Chan, J. (1995). "Predicting Divorce." *The Family Journal: Counseling and Therapy for Couples and Families*. Vol. 3,(2) 134-138.

Gilliland, R. W. & James, R. K. (1988). *Crisis Intervention Strategies*. California: Wadsworth.

Goldenberg, E. & Goldenberg, H. (1991). *Family Therapy: An Overview*. (3rd Ed.). California: Brooks/Cole.

Gottman, J. & Silver, N. (1994). *Why Marriages Succeed Or Fail, And How You Can Make Yours Last*. New York: Simon and Schuster.

Graham, J. R. (1990). *MMPI-2: Assessing Personality & Psychopathology*. New York: Oxford University Press.

Gray, J. (1992). *Men Are From Mars, Women Are From Venus*. New York: HarperCollins Inc.

Gray, J. (1993). *Men, Women And Relationships* (2nd Ed.). Oregon: Beyond Words Publishing, Inc.

Greer, J. (1997). *How Could You Do This to Me: Learning To Trust After Betrayal*. New York: Doubleday.

Greteman, J. (1981). *Coping with Divorce*. Indiana: Ave Maria Press.

H

Hendricks, G. & Hendricks K. (1985). *Centering & The Art Of Intimacy*. New York: Prentice Hall.

Herlihy, B. & Golden, L. B. (1990). *AACD Ethical Standards Casebook* (4th Ed.). Virginia: American Association for Counseling & Development.

Hilgard, E.R., Atkinson, R. C. & Atkinson, R. L. (1975). *Introduction To Psychology*. (6th Ed.). New York: Harcourt Brace Jovanovich.

Hof, L. (1993). "The Elusive Elixir of Hope." *The Family Journal: Counseling and Therapy for Couples and Families*. 1,(3). 220-227.

Holtz, L. (1998). *Winning Everyday*. New York: HarperCollins Inc.

Hothersall, D. (1985). *Psychology*. Ohio: Merrill.

I

Ivey, A. E. (1988). *Intentional Interviewing & Counseling: Facilitating Client Development* (2nd Ed.). California: Brooks/Cole.

K

Karney, B.R., Bradbury, T. N., Fincham, F. D., Sullivan, K. T. (1994). "The Role Of Negative Affectivity in the Association Between Attributions and Marital Satisfaction." *Journal of Personality and Social Psychology.* 66,(2), 413-424.

Kleinman, A. (1988). *Rethinking Psychiatry: From Cultural Category To Personal Experience.* New York: Macmillan.

Kubler-Ross, E. (1969) *On Death and Dying.* New York: Macmillan.

L

Landorph, J. (1982). *Irregular People.* Texas: Word Books.

Lazerus, A. (1985). *Marital Myths.* California: Impact Publishers.

Lehman, R. S. (1991). *Statistics and Research Design in the Behavioral Sciences.* California: Wadsworth.

Leman, K. (1985). *The Birth Order Book.* New Jersy: Revell.

Lerner, H. G. (1985). *The Dance of Anger.* New York: Harper/Row.

Levinger, R. & Moles, O. C. (1979). *Divorce & Separation: Context, Causes and Consequences.* New York: Basic Books Inc.

Lewis, J. A. (1994). *The Codependence Concept and the Status Quo.*

The Family Journal: Counseling And Therapy For Couples And Families. 2(3), 238-240.

M

MacEwen, K. & Barling, J. (1993). "Type A Behavior and Marital Satisfaction: Differential Effects of Achievement/Striving and Impatience/Irritability." *Journal of Marriage and the Family* 55,(2) 1001-1010.

Martin, D. G. (1989). *Counseling & Therapy Skills.* Illinois: Waveland.

Masters, J. C., Burish, T. G., Hollon, S. D. & Rimm, D. C. (1987). *Behavior Therapy: Techinques & Empirical Findings* (3rd Ed.). New York: Harcourt Brace Jovanovich.

Millon, T, & Everly, G. S. (1985). *Personality and Its Disorders: A Biosocial Learning Approach.* New York: John Wiley & Sons.

Moramarco, F. & Zolynas, A. (1992). *Men Of Our Time: An Anthology of Male Poetry in Contemporary America.* Georgia: University of Georgia Press.

Morokoff, P. J., Gilliland, R. (1993). "Stress, Sexual Functioning, and Marital Satisfaction." *The Journal of Sex Research*, 30,(1) 43-53.

Mullan, H. & Rosenbaum, M. (1978). *Group Psychotherapy: Theory and Practice* (2nd Ed.). New York: Macmillan.

O

Osherson, S. (1992). *Wrestling With Love: How Men Struggle with Intimacy, with Women, Children, Parents and Each Other.* New York: Random House.

P

Pease, A. (1997). *Body Language: How To Read Other's Thoughts by Their Gestures* (3rd Ed.). London, England: Sheldon Press.

Pease, J. (1990). *Ladies, Women and Wenches.* North Carolina: The University of North Carolina Press.

Peck, M.S. (1978). *The Road Less Traveled.* New York: Simon & Schuster.

Pietropinto, A. & Simenauer, J. (1990). *Not Tonight Dear: How To Awaken Your Sexual Desire.* New York: Doubleday.

Plutchik, R. & Kellerman, H. (1989). *Emotions: Theory, Research And Experience.* Psychopathology and Psychotherapy. California: Academic Press.

Pittman, F. (1989). *Private Lies.* New York: W.W. Norton & Company.

Prata, G. (1990). *A Systemic Harpoon into Family Games: Preventive Interventions in Therapy.* New York: Brunner/Mazel Publishers.

R

Risman, B. J. & Schwartz, P. (1989). *Gender In Intimate Relationships: A Microstructural Approach.* California: Wadsworth.

Romney, R. & Harrison, B. (1983). *Giving Time a Chance: The Secret of a Lasting Marriage.* New York: M. Evans Co.

Rowan, D. G., Compton, W. C. & Rust, J. O. (1995). "Self Actualization And Empathy As Predictors Of Marital Satisfaction." *Psychological Reports*, 77, 1011-1016.

S

Sachs-Wise, P. (1989). *The Use of Assessment Techniques By Applied Psychologists.* California: Wadsworth Publishing Co.

Santrock: J. W. (1986). *Human Development: The Science of Mind And Behavior* (2nd Ed.) Iowa: Brown.

Sarason, I. G. & Sarason, B. R. (1987). *Abnormal Psychology: The Problem of Maladaptive Behavior.* (5th Ed.). New Jersy, Prentice Hall, Inc.

Schiamberg, L. B. (1985). *Human Development* (2nd Ed.). New York: Macmillan.

Schuller, R. (1993). *Power Thoughts*. New York: Harper/Collins.

Sheehy, G. (1972). *Passages: The Predictable Crises of Adult Life*. New York: Dutton.

Sullivan, B. F. & Schwebel, A. I. (1995). "Relationship Beliefs and Expectations of Satisfaction in Marital Relationships: Implications for Family Practitioners." *The Family Journal: Counseling and Therapy for Couples and Families*. October.

T

Tannen, D. (1990). *You Just Don't Understand: Men and Women in Conversation*. New York: William Morrow & Co.

Turner, J. S. & Helms, D. B. (1987). *Lifespan Development* (3rd Ed). Florida: Holt, Rinehart & Winston.

V

Vaillant, C. & Vaillant, G. (1993). "Is the U-curve of Marital Satisfaction an Illusion? A 40-Year Study." *Journal of Marriage and the Family*. 55, 230-239.

Veninga, R. L. (1985). *A Gift of Hope. How We Survive Our Tragedies*. Massachusetts: Little, Brown and Company.

W

Wallerstein, J. S. & Blakeslee, S. (1995). *The Good Marriage. How and Why Love Lasts*. New York: Houghton, Mifflin.

Walsh, W.M. (1992). "Twenty Major Issues in Remarriage Families." *Journal of Counseling and Development*. July/August 1992, Vol 70. 709-715.

Watzlawick, P. (1983). *The Situation Is Hopeless, But Not Serious.*

———.*The Pursuit of Unhappiness*. New York/London: W. W. Norton Co.

Willerman, L. & Cohen, D. B. (1990). *Psychopathology*. New York: McGraw Hill.

Wise, P. S. (1989). *The Use of Assessment Techniques by Applied Psychologists*. California: Wadsworth.

Wolinsky, M. A. (1990). *A Heart Of Wisdom: Marital Counseling with Older and Elderly Couples*. New York: Brunner/Mazel Publishers.

Wood, G. (1986). *The Myth of Neurosis*. New York: Harper & Row.

Z

Zunker, V. G. (1990). *Career Counseling: Applied Concepts of Life Planning*. California: Brooks/Cole.

Zvonkovic, A. M., Schmiege, C. J., & Hall, L. D. (1993). "Influence Strategies Used When Couples Make Work-Family Decisions and Their Importance for Marital Satisfaction." *The Journal of Family Relations.* 43, 182-188.

INDEX

A

Abuse, 38, 119
Accidental infidelity, 247
Addiction, 42, 179
Addiction, treatment of, 185
Addictive codependence, 190
Addictive evaluation, 184
Addictive intervention, 184
Addictive self-admission, 183
Adult children of alcoholics (ACOA), 191
Affectivity, 2
Al-anon, 190
Alcoholics Anonymous (AA), 183
Anger, 36, 83, 88, 230
Assertiveness training, 168
Assessment of addictive behaviors, 179
Assumed power, 224
Attorneys (as outsiders), 214
Attributions, 2
Authoritative power, 224
Avoidant Marriage Relationship, 7

B

Barling, Julian, 3
Beck, Aaron, 56
Bograd, Ruth, 4
Bradbury, Thomas, 2

C

Centering & the Art of Intimacy, 254
Chan, Judy, 10
Client control, 214
Cohen, Herb, 223
Coldness, 2, 239
Communication problems, 127
    Verbal, 127
        Non-verbal, 130
Consensus power, 225
Consumer credit counseling, 81
Contempt, 7
Counselors (as outsiders), 211
Covert training, 170
Criticism, 7, 221

D

Dance of anger, 85
DeAngelis, Barbara, 236
Defense mechanisms, 88, 228
Defensiveness, 7
Delegated power, 224
Depression, 2, 175
Diagnosis of addiction, 180
Differential diagnosis process, 230
Differentiation, 9
Displacement, 229

Divorce, valid reasons for, 59
Do as I say and not as I do, 136
Donovan, D., 179
Don't enjoy yourself, 136
Don't rock the boat, 138

E

Effect of divorce on children, 17
Effect of divorce on older siblings, 19
Ellis, Albert, 101
Emotional design, 83
Emotional disability, 131
Empty nest syndrome (ENS), 199, 263
Enabling, 191
Energy, 40, 143
Entanglement in marriage, 255
Everly, George, 140
Existentialism, 106
Expectations, 41, 135, 159
Exterior respect, 151

F

Family budget form, 80
Family expenses, 68
Fast, Julius, 257
Fee-ability (legal), 215
Feedback, 222
Fincham, Frank, 2
Fixed expenses, 68
Four horsemen of divorce, 7
Four meanings in life, 107
Four stages to divorce, 9
Frankl, Viktor, 105
Freud, Sigmund, 228
Friends, (as outsiders), 211

G

General codependence, 15, 39, 125
Giblin, Paul, 10
Gilliland, Ruth, 3
Giving time a chance, 201

Goals, 263
Gottman, John, 5
Gray, John, 57, 132, 210, 226, 253
Greer, J. R., 251
Group therapy, 169

H

Halfway house, 189
Harrison, Beppie, 201
Health concerns, 170
Hendricks, G. & K., 254
Hiring a counselor, 213
Hof, Larry, 265
Holtz, Lou, 251
Honesty, 44, 243
Hope, 265
Housework, 9

I

Inability to talk about problems, 132
Information in negotiation process, 227
informed consent, 188, 213
Inhibited sexual desire (ISD), 238
Instrumental behavior, 131
Integrity, 37, 111
Intellectual dishonesty, 230
Interior respect, 153
Intermediate-term priorities, 262
Intimacy, 44, 253
Intrusions, 203
Irregular people, 100

K

Karney, Benjamin, 2
Kilgariff, 11
Kitchen lawyers, 209
Kowit, Steve, 148
Kubler-Ross, Elizabeth, 108
Kurdek, L., 10

L

Landorph, Joyce, 100

Lazerus, Arnold, 133
Legal influence, 15
Lerner, Harriet, 85
Likert-style quiz, 55
Living, 41, 164, 171
Logotherapy, 106
Long-term priorities, 262
Love, 56

M

MacEwen, Karyl, 3
Man's search for meaning, 106
Marital arrangement, 247
Marital Myths, 133
Marital satisfaction, 1
Media influence, 14
Mediation, 217
Meetings (in AA), 186
Meichenbaum, Donald, 173
Megan's Law, 120
Mental abuse, 38, 120
Men Are From Mars, Women Are From Venus, 57
Millon, Theodore, 140
Money, 35, 65
Money management—allocation, 74
Money management—how, 72
Money management—sample %, 78
Money management—who, 71
Monthly expenditure schedule, 70
Moreno, James, 168
Morokoff, Patricia, 3
Murphy's law, 54

N

Negative reinforcement, 166
Negative thinking, 2
Negotiation, 43, 221, 227
Now! (do it-), 200

O

On death and dying, 108

Opposites attract, 138
Outsiders, 43, 209
Over-functioners, 86

P

Passive suicide, 181
Pease, A., 257
Peeling the onion, 228
Peer pressure, 15
Personality and its disorders, 140
Personality Type A & B, 3
Philanderer, 246
Physical abuse, 38, 119
Pittman, Frank, 245
Plutchik, Robert, 83-84
Positive reinforcement, 166
Power in negotiation, 223
Predicting divorce, 10
Presentment—presenting, 230
Priorities, 44, 259
Private lies (Pittman), 246
Projection, 229
Pro-se divorce, 216
Punishment, 166

Q

Quality time, 193
Quantity time, 196
Quiz (The), 49

R

Rational Emotive Therapy (RET), 101
Rationalization, 229
Regression, 229
Relatives, 37, 93
Religious factors in divorce, 11
Remarriage concerns, 20
Repression, 229
Respect, 40, 151
Reversals, 37, 103
Rituals, 147
Romantic infidelity, 249

Romney, Ronna, 201
"Rose, The" (poem), 149

S

Schuller, Robert, 155
Self-confidence, 153
Self-disclosure, 4
Self esteem, 2
Selfish—unselfish, 135
Serenity prayer, 54
Sex, 3, 43, 233
Sex and general codependence, 238
Sexual abuse, 38
Sexual dysfunction, 234
Short-term priorities, 261
Spilka, Bernard, 4
Sponsor (in AA), 186
Stress, 3, 237
Stress inoculation (ABC), 107, 173
String test, 254
Suicide, 176
Sullivan, Keran, 2
Symptoms of divorce, 10

T

Tests, 2, 182
The elusive elixir of hope, 265
Time, 42, 193
Time in negotiation process, 225
Toman, Walter, 10
Trap of irrelevance, 229
Treatment centers (AA), 188
Triangulation, 134
Trust, 250
"Twelve Steps" (AA), 187

U

Under-functioners, 87

V

Vaillant, C. & G., 5
Validating marriage relationship, 6
Validation (in females), 133
Values, 259
Variable expenses, 68
Voirst, Judith, 113
Volatile marriage relationship, 6

W

Wallerstein, Judith M., 25, 218
Walsh, William M., 20
Wingett, Wesley, 16
Withdrawal, 7

The Center for Marriage Enhancement

ORDER FORM

Postal orders to: Box 214
Sioux City, Iowa 51102

Telephone orders: 877-684-4545 (Free call)

Fax orders to: (480) 947-5134

Ordered by: _____

Street address: _____

City _____ State _____ Zip _____

If the book(s) are to be shipped to a different address

Ship to: (name) _____

Street address: _____

City _____ State _____ Zip _____

Please send _____ copies of the *Marriage Enhancement Guide;
a Do-It-Yourself Marriage Counseling Manual.*

1 book	each book	$39.95
2 - 10 books	each book	$30.95
Over 10 books:	*call for special pricing*	
Plus Shipping & Handling	1st book	$4.55
	each add'l book	$2.00
	Total $	_____

(Please add 7% for books shipped into Iowa)

Payment by ❏ Check   Credit Card: ❏ Visa

❏ Money Order   ❏ Master Card

Card Number: _____ Exp. date _____

Name on card: _____

Signature: _____

**Box 214 • 520 Buckwalter Drive • Sioux City, Iowa 51104
Phone (712) 224-2318**